TWO FIRSTS

A FEMINIST HISTORY SOCIETY BOOK

TWO FIRSTS

Bertha Wilson and Claire L'Heureux-Dubé at the Supreme Court of Canada

CONSTANCE BACKHOUSE

Second Story Press

Library and Archives Canada Cataloguing in Publication

Backhouse, Constance, 1952–, author
Two firsts : Bertha Wilson and Claire L'Heureux-Dubé
at the Supreme Court of Canada / Constance Backhouse.

(A feminist history society book)

Includes index.

ISBN 978-1-77260-093-3 (softcover)

1. Wilson, Bertha, 1923-2007. 2. L'Heureux-Dubé, Claire. 3. Canada.
Supreme Court. 4. Judges–Canada–Biography. 5. Women judges–Canada–
Biography. I. Title. II. Series: Feminist History Society book

KE8246.B33 2019   347.71'03534   C2018-905195-7

KF345.Z9.A1B33 2019

Editor: Andrea Knight
Managing Editor: Kathryn Cole
Cover: Isabelle Cardinal
Book design: Melissa Kaita

Every effort has been made to secure permission and provide appropriate
credit for photographic material. The publisher deeply regrets any omission
and pledges to correct errors called to its attention in subsequent editions.

Printed and bound in Canada

*Second Story Press gratefully acknowledges the support of the
Ontario Arts Council and the Canada Council for the Arts for our
publishing program. We acknowledge the financial support of the
Government of Canada through the Canada Book Fund.*

Published by
Second Story Press
20 Maud Street, Suite 401
Toronto, ON M5V 2M5
www.secondstorypress.ca

To founders of the Feminist History Society, Beth Atcheson,
Lorraine Greaves, Diana Majury, and Beth Symes.

CONTENTS

Acknowledgements

I would like to thank the many people who assisted me in the conceptualization of *Two Firsts*: Beth Atcheson, Nancy Backhouse, Olga Backhouse, Natasha Bakht, Marina Ball, Kim Brooks, Tomiko Brown-Nagin, Suzanne Bouclin, Mordecai Bubis, Rosemary Cairns Way, Angela Cameron, Janice Carment, Nathalie Chalifour, Sharon Cook, Andrea Davidson, Jane De Hart, Nathalie Des Rosiers, Adam Dodek, Chloe Georas, Philip Girard, Charlotte Gray, Lorraine Greaves, Shirley Greenberg, Vanessa Gruben, Sally Kenney, Ian Kerr, Pnina Lahev, Paul Leatherdale, Maureen Lennon, Vanessa MacDonnell, Diana Majury, Carissima Mathen, Michel Morin, Peter Oliver, Maureen O'Neil, Sanja Petrovic, Jim Phillips, Douglas W. Phillips, Wendy Rickey, Teresa Scassa, Elizabeth Sheehy, Catherine Strosberg, Harvey Strosberg, Beth Symes, Martin Teplitsky, David Wexler, Leandra Zarnow, and Ellen Zweibel.

Talented research assistants Mark Bourrie, Vanessa Carment, Desirée Hayward, and Mayoori Malankov also provided invaluable assistance. Veronique Larose provided stellar technical and administrative support.

I greatly appreciate the expertise and assistance of the many women who came together to help produce this book at Second

Story Press: Allyson Aritcheta, Natasha Bozorgi, Kathryn Cole, Melissa Kaita, Andrea Knight, Emma Rodgers, Ellie Sipila, and Margie Wolfe.

Constance Backhouse
Ottawa, Spring 2018

Chronology

1923   Bertha Wernham is born in Kirkcaldy, Scotland on September 18 to Archibald and Christina Wernham.

1926   Bertha Wernham and her family move to Aberdeen, Scotland.

1927   Claire L'Heureux is born in Quebec City, Canada on September 7 to Paul and Marguerite L'Heureux.

1935   Claire L'Heureux and her family move to Rimouski, Quebec.

1939   Bertha Wernham meets John Wilson for the first time.

1941   Bertha Wernham graduates from high school, Aberdeen Central Secondary School.

1943   Claire L'Heureux graduates from le Monastère des Ursulines de Rimouski, completing the matriculation course at age fifteen.

1944   Bertha Wernham graduates from the University of Aberdeen with a master of arts degree.

1945   Bertha Wernham obtains a teaching parchment
        from the Aberdeen Training College for Teachers

        Bertha Wernham, age twenty-two, marries John
        Wilson, age twenty-five, on December 14, 1945.

1946   Claire L'Heureux graduates from Collège de Bellevue,
        obtaining a *baccalauréat-ès-arts magna cum laude* at
        age eighteen.

1948   Claire L'Heureux, age twenty-one, enters
        Laval Faculty of Law.

1949   Bertha and John Wilson immigrate to Canada.

1951   Claire L'Heureux graduates with an LL.L. from
        l'Université Laval at age twenty-three.

1952   Claire L'Heureux is called to the Quebec bar and
        becomes a lawyer with Sam Bard's law firm in
        Quebec City.

1954   Bertha Wilson, age thirty-one, enters
        Dalhousie Law School.

1957   Bertha Wilson graduates with LL.B. from
        Dalhousie Law School at age thirty-three.

        Claire L'Heureux, age thirty-one, marries Arthur
        Dubé, age thirty-eight, on November 30, 1957.

1958   Bertha Wilson is called to the Nova Scotia Bar,
        after completing articles with Frederick W.
        Bissett QC.

        The Wilsons move to Toronto, and Bertha Wilson joins
        Osler, Hoskin & Harcourt as an articling student,
        age thirty-five.

1959   Bertha Wilson is called to the Ontario Bar, and
        becomes the first woman lawyer at the Osler firm.

1960   Claire L'Heureux-Dubé's first child, Louise,
        is born in Quebec City.

1964 Claire L'Heureux-Dubé's second child, Pierre, is born in Quebec City.

1973 Claire L'Heureux-Dubé, age forty-five, is appointed to the Quebec Superior Court, February 9.

   Bora Laskin becomes Chief Justice of the Supreme Court of Canada, December 27.

1976 Bertha Wilson, age fifty-two, is appointed to the Ontario Court of Appeal, January 2.

1978 Arthur Dubé commits suicide, July 11.

1979 Claire L'Heureux-Dubé, age forty-nine, is appointed to the Quebec Court of Appeal, October 16.

1980 Antonio Lamer is appointed to the Supreme Court of Canada, March 28.

1982 Bertha Wilson, age fifty-eight, is appointed to the Supreme Court of Canada, March 4.

1982 *Canadian Charter of Rights and Freedoms* comes into effect, April 18.

1984 Brian Dickson becomes Chief Justice of the Supreme Court of Canada, April 18.

1985 Section 15 of the *Canadian Charter of Rights and Freedoms* comes into effect, April 17.

1987 Claire L'Heureux-Dubé, age fifty-nine, is appointed to the Supreme Court of Canada, April 5.

   The *Pelech* trilogy: See *Pelech v. Pelech*, [1987] 1 SCR 801.

1988 *R. v. Morgentaler*, [1988] 1 SCR 30.

1989 Beverley McLachlin is appointed to the Supreme Court of Canada, March 3.

1990   *R. v. Lavallee*, [1990] 1 SCR 852.

[Prostitution] Reference re ss.193 and 195.1(c) of the Criminal Code (Man.) [1990] 1 SCR 1123.

"Will women judges really make a difference?" Bertha Wilson's speech at Osgoode Hall Law School, Toronto, February 8.

Antonio Lamer becomes Chief Justice of the Supreme Court of Canada, July 1.

1991   Bertha Wilson, age sixty-seven, retires from the Supreme Court of Canada, January 4.

Bertha Wilson becomes chair of the Canadian Bar Association's Task Force on Gender Equality in the Legal Profession.

Bertha Wilson is appointed to the Royal Commission on Aboriginal Peoples.

R. v. Seaboyer, [1991] 2 SCR 577.

1992   *Moge v. Moge*, [1992] 3 SCR 813.

1993   *Canada (Attorney-General) v. Mossop*, [1993] 1 SCR 554.

1994   Pierre Dubé, Claire L'Heureux-Dubé's son, dies, age thirty, March 17.

1999   *R. v. Ewanchuk*, [1999] 1 SCR 330.

2000   Beverley McLachlin becomes Chief Justice of the Supreme Court of Canada, January 7.

2002   Claire L'Heureux-Dubé, age seventy-four, retires from the Supreme Court of Canada, July 1.

2007   Bertha Wilson dies, age eighty-three, April 28.

2008   John Wilson dies, June 25.

Introduction

wo women sat quietly together around a side table in a sparsely furnished office in the Supreme Court of Canada. The sombre wood-panelled judge's chambers belonged to Bertha Wilson. The room contained nothing fancy: a desk, and several chairs, no carpet, the plainest of décor.[1] The women sitting there were sharing a singular conversation. Wilson had been appointed to the Supreme Court in 1982, the first woman out of fifty-eight judges in the Ottawa court's 107-year history. Claire L'Heureux-Dubé was appointed the second woman in 1987. The two were reflecting upon what it meant to set toe in the sacrosanct circle restricted for generations to men.[2]

The conversation was not without levity. A friend of L'Heureux-Dubé's had sent her a framed cartoon, a caricature of her with tousled hair and a broad grin sporting the French caption: "*Yahoo! J'arrive Bertha!*"[3] But the dominant tone in Wilson's office that afternoon was not celebratory. Recalling her own reception, Wilson explained to her new colleague that she had felt forced to "prove herself" to a group of men who were skeptical about whether she had won the position on her merits.[4] Wilson cautioned L'Heureux-Dubé that she too would have to prove herself all over again.[5] "We have to prove ourselves every

"Yahoo! J'arrive Bertha!" Photo taken in L'Heureux-Dubé's Supreme Court Chambers, left to right, Secretary Lisette Gammon, Claire L'Heureux-Dubé, Law Clerk Teresa Scassa, in front of caricature portrait.

time," L'Heureux-Dubé remembered Wilson saying, "even here at this court."[6] It was not a false warning, as time would soon tell.

The unspoken question was what it meant for women to "prove" themselves as they ascended the path to the Supreme Court, and what it meant once they arrived there.

The term *merit,* which loomed so persistently through both women's careers, was rarely defined or dissected. In fact, most people would be hard-pressed to articulate a *definitive* set of qualifications for law or the judiciary. These occupations are sufficiently complex that one cannot reliably rank-order candidates with a simple checking of boxes. And it usually went unsaid that maleness had topped the list of necessary attributes for centuries. (Whiteness and non-Indigeneity also topped the list, with consequences that will be explored in more detail below.)[7] At least one senior judge made the gender bias painstakingly explicit. When Wilson was appointed, he flatly told his colleagues, "No woman can do my job."[8]

Today, when this type of sentiment is mostly unexpressed, it can be difficult to understand what underpinned such a conclusion. Possible explanations may be rooted in the ideology of "separate spheres," which characterized men and women as physically and intellectually distinct, whether as a result of biology, socialization, or both. Its expression fit seamlessly within the patriarchal legal order that enveloped Canada in earlier decades, barring women from participation as voters, legislators, lawyers, judges, and jurors. For centuries, women had been at the mercy of man-made laws that regulated their sexuality, enforced their subservience within the family, and restricted their occupational and economic opportunities.[9]

Clara Brett Martin pierced the all-male stronghold when she was called to the bar as Canada's first female lawyer in 1897.[10] Helen Alice Kinnear achieved distinction as the first female judge of a county court in 1943, and Réjane Laberge-Colas as the first woman on a superior court in 1969.[11] Wilson took the title as the first female judge on the Ontario Court of Appeal

CANADIAN COURTS

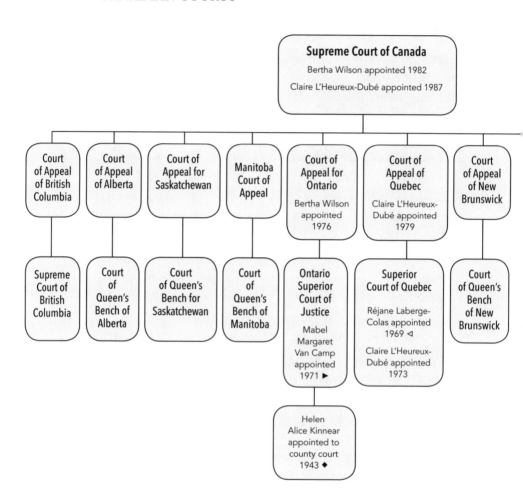

Notes:

This chart represents the majority of the federally appointed courts within the Canadian judicial system. It excludes both administrative and specialized tribunals, military and municipal courts, provincial courts, and the following federally appointed courts: the Federal Court, the Federal Court of Appeal, and the tax courts.[12]

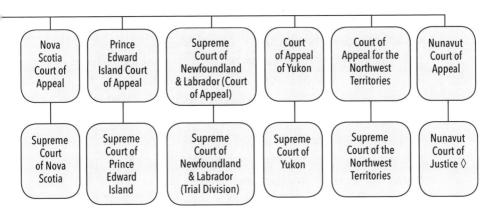

Nova Scotia Court of Appeal	Prince Edward Island Court of Appeal	Supreme Court of Newfoundland & Labrador (Court of Appeal)	Court of Appeal of Yukon	Court of Appeal for the Northwest Territories	Nunavut Court of Appeal
Supreme Court of Nova Scotia	Supreme Court of Prince Edward Island	Supreme Court of Newfoundland & Labrador (Trial Division)	Supreme Court of Yukon	Supreme Court of the Northwest Territories	Nunavut Court of Justice ◊

◊ The Nunavut Court of Justice is established as both the Superior Court and Territorial Court of Nunavut.[13]

▶ At the time of Mabel Margaret Van Camp's appointment, the official name of the court was the Supreme Court of Ontario.

◆ Helen Alice Kinnear was the first woman to be appointed to a county court in 1943. Ontario county courts operated at a level between Superior and Provincial Courts until 1984.[14] In 1985, the *Courts of Justice Act* was passed which combined county, district and Court of General Sessions into the District Court of Ontario.[15] In 1989, under the *Courts of Justice Amendment Act, 1989*, the Ontario High Court of Justice, District Court and Surrogate Court were then merged into the Ontario Court (General Division).[16] The *Courts Improvement Act 1996*, then changed the name from the Ontario Court (General Division) to the Ontario Superior Court of Justice in April 1999.[17] (See also section 1(1) *Ontario Courts of Justice Act* for references of former names of courts).[18]

◁ Réjane Laberge-Colas was the first woman appointed to the Quebec Superior Court, Montreal Division. The Quebec Superior Courts are divided into two divisions: Montreal and Quebec.[19]

in 1976, and L'Heureux-Dubé the first on the Quebec Court of Appeal in 1979. The final hurdle, appointment to the Supreme Court of Canada, came eighty-five years after women's entry to the profession. It was not a speedy process.

While Wilson was the first to the top rung, L'Heureux-Dubé was the first woman from Quebec to reach the Supreme Court of Canada, a "first" that created its own particular challenges. Indeed, there were many female "firsts," all of whom shouldered different burdens along with the curiosity, criticism, and finger pointing that greeted any individual perceived to be a rank outsider. The list could go on and on: the first woman to imagine a legal career for herself; the first woman turned down when she applied to law school; the first female lawyer to seek employment with a law firm; the first female lawyer rejected by a client because of her gender; the first female lawyer to campaign to dismantle sexist laws; the first female lawyer denied firm

Three "Firsts": Bertha Wilson, Jeanne D'Arc Lemay-Warren (one of the early Quebec female judges), Claire L'Heureux-Dubé.

partnership due to sexist presumptions; the first female lawyer to be sexually harassed on the job. The title "first" is attached to both Wilson and L'Heureux-Dubé in particularly notorious ways, but shared by many others. All of the early women faced troubling resistance and backlash as they strode and stumbled through their daunting lives and careers, stigmatized as interlopers in a male world.

This is why it is so important to inquire into what lay behind the assertion of that senior male judge and the chorus of other naysayers who supported his view that "no woman" could do their jobs. Why did they feel so strongly that females were miscast as judges? Perhaps they believed that women were required for housework, childbirth, and childrearing, while men needed to take charge of worldly affairs. Perhaps their definition of masculinity required all-male spaces in which men could hone their competitive skills. Did they fear that even one or two women might contaminate the terrain? Perhaps there was something about women's appearance, demeanour, or emotional makeup that their detractors felt unfit them for "men's" jobs. Or did they wonder whether women might outperform them? They may even have worried that women judges would set about transforming law in their own image.

Was this a reflection of confusion, chivalry, or misogyny? Did it betray anxiety over the precariousness of the gender hierarchy? Did it demonstrate concern that women judges might throw the dyad of masculinity and femininity into disarray? Bertha Wilson and Claire L'Heureux-Dubé's experiences in law may help answer some of these questions.

TWO FIRSTS, TWO OPPOSITES, PARALLEL OBSTACLES

Many judicial biographies follow a typical narrative. The individuals emerge from blissful childhoods inside nurturing middle-class families. They achieve early distinction as stellar pupils. They make their mark as charismatic leaders in law school and achieve fame and fortune in traditional legal practices. They benefit from home lives where their supportive spouses and well-behaved children thrive and add lustre to the family reputation. They obtain court appointment with the avid support of their fellow lawyers and senior judges, and then deliver wise decisions that attract acclaim from bench and bar. The lives of Wilson and L'Heureux-Dubé rarely conform to this pattern.

Full biographies of both women have now been published and their judicial rulings subjected to detailed jurisprudential analysis.[20] This book will not try to duplicate that work. Instead, it will attempt to compare the multiple ways that gender shaped the lives of both women. As "firsts," they had no role models to study, no ground rules to follow. They were women ahead of their time.

They were also two women who were opposites in character and behaviour. Although they took pride in each other's contributions and accomplishments, they were anything but soulmates on the court.[21] Their Ontario judicial colleague, Frank Iacobucci, explained that Wilson was a "stoic Scot," who primarily "stuck to the work."[22] L'Heureux-Dubé was a Québécoise with a reputation as a *femme fatale*, whose flamboyance dominated every room she entered. Their Quebec judicial colleague, Charles Gonthier, described the two women as at "almost opposite ends of the spectrum." Wilson, he characterized as "much more reserved," and L'Heureux-Dubé as "very much of the Latin temperament."[23] One Supreme Court law clerk also linked the differences to ethnic heritage, describing Wilson, the Scot, as "a very low volume person," and L'Heureux-Dubé, the francophone, as "very high."[24]

Bertha Wilson and Claire L'Heureux-Dubé in the Supreme Court of Canada dining room.

Opposites in demeanour and personality, Wilson and L'Heureux-Dubé conquered virtually identical barriers on the way to the top. They experienced parallel obstacles in education, law practice, judicial appointments, and careers on the bench. Starkly different women, they often dealt with the discrimination in different ways. Yet they achieved success in equal measure. There was no one cookie-cutter approach to the top.

The sober conversation in Wilson's chambers that day presaged the hurdles that would continue to confront Canada's first two female Supreme Court judges. If they were forced to "prove" themselves over and over again, what did it take to succeed? What challenges met them and how did they navigate those complicated shoals? Did their careers change them? Did they change the institutions they joined? Did their entry constitute a complete victory for equality? Did the anti-female sentiments vanish, hang on persistently, or take new forms? What can we learn from the strategies these two women adopted, the responses of their supporters and adversaries, and the trails they blazed? To explore the lives and careers of these two path-breaking women is to venture into a world of legal sexism from a past era. The question for the future will be how much has been relegated to the bins of history.

The author interviewing Claire L'Heureux-Dubé at a public lecture, at the University of Ottawa.

CHAPTER 1

Childhood and early schooling:
Scotland and Quebec

Explanatory note: I have referred to Bertha Wilson and Claire L'Heureux-Dubé by their first names and birth surnames when describing their youthful years. After Bertha's marriage in 1945, I switch to "Bertha Wilson." After Claire's marriage in 1957, I switch to her married name, "Claire L'Heureux-Dubé."

Bertha Wernham was born on September 18, 1923, in Kirkcaldy, an industrial town on the east coast of Scotland.[1] Claire L'Heureux was born on September 7, 1927, in Quebec City, an outpost of empire and the centre of French habitation in Canada.[2] Kirkcaldy traced its old-world longevity to a church settlement in the eleventh century, while Quebec City claimed its new-world heritage as the seventeenth-century site of North America's first hospital.[3] Although distanced geographically and culturally, both women could claim deep roots into imperial European nationhood.

Bertha was born into a lower-middle-class Scottish family. Her father, Archibald Wernham, was an affable, modest, and meticulous man. Descended from a wealthy family of commercial stationers, he had been buffeted by financial hardship, requiring him to work as a travelling salesman who struggled to make ends meet. His devoted daughter regarded her father as a

Exterior and interior of St. Machar's Cathedral, Aberdeen, Scotland, established circa 1370.

"gentle and kindly soul who would do anything for anybody."[4] Bertha's mother, Christina (Noble) Wernham, came from a working-class fishing family. A no-nonsense, socially isolated woman, Christina ruled her home with fierce determination and considered life a "pretty grim task."[5] The Wernhams worshipped at the Church of Scotland, where Archibald's sustained faith was a striking contrast to Christina's studied rejection of her strict evangelical childhood. Bertha inclined to her father's religious views, attending St. Machar's Cathedral regularly, participating in the Student Christian Movement, and then marrying a Presbyterian minister.[6]

Claire L'Heureux was born into a lower-middle-class franco-phone family. She had a tumultuous relationship with her father, Paul L'Heureux, who worked as a customs inspector and served as a lieutenant-colonel during World War II. A socially gregarious "ladies' man" who "loved to dance," within the confines of his own home he was a rigid disciplinarian obsessed with military precision, a man of few words and fewer compliments.[7] Claire's mother, Marguerite (Dion) L'Heureux, came from wealthy seigneurial roots but unwise mining investments had catapulted her family into straitened circumstances. Multiple sclerosis struck Marguerite as a young mother, leaving her paralyzed but intensifying her fascination with languages, literature, and intellectual pursuits. Claire revered her mother, whom she described as the greatest single influence on her life. Marguerite's illness strengthened her religious inclinations, while Paul's aloofness toward Sunday sermons marked his deliberate distancing from the Roman Catholic Church. Although Claire herself toyed with the idea of becoming a nun, she became increasingly skeptical of the church during her adolescence and would ultimately disavow all religion, claiming atheism as an adult.[8]

Their religious perspectives may have differed, but the educational paths that would take Bertha and Claire into law were similar. Both soared well beyond their parents in higher education. Bertha's parents had no formal learning to speak of: her father left school at age eleven and her mother at twelve.[9] Claire's father's dreams of a degree from the Seminary of Quebec were foiled by a shortage of money; her mother's desire to study was cut short by the stranglehold of the Catholic Church, which restricted Quebec girls from higher education of any type.[10]

Bertha and Claire might both have been thwarted educationally but for their mothers' tenacity. Bertha's mother was zealous about her children's opportunities, adamant that they receive the schooling she had been denied.[11] She insisted that her daughter enrol in university, when Bertha would have been "just as happy to leave high school and get a job working in a sweet shop."[12] Claire's mother defied her husband to insist that her daughter should have the finest education available, and emptied her own household savings to further the cause.[13] Their mothers' dictates mattered deeply to Bertha and Claire, both of whom were emboldened to live out the older women's aspirations.

THE WERNHAM FAMILY:
GROWING UP IN ABERDEEN, SCOTLAND

Bertha was the only daughter and the youngest of three Wernham children, following her two brothers, Archie and Jim. The eldest brother, Archie, was the apple of his mother's eye, marked from boyhood as intellectually gifted. Christina Wernham was convinced that the Kirkcaldy schools were inferior to her brilliant son's needs, and so the family moved to the more populous city of Aberdeen when Bertha was three. Known as the Granite City after its local quarries, Aberdeen was a shipbuilding, fishing, paper-making, and textile centre stretched along a sandy coastline. Despite its marine climate, its winters qualified it as the coldest city in the United Kingdom. It was there that Bertha developed her broad accent, the Doric dialect of the North-East Scots.[14] She also came to love Aberdeen's rolling sand dunes and the landscapes of yellow Scotch broom and purple heather.[15]

Most important for the Wernhams, however, Aberdeen was also the educational capital of northeast Scotland, home to the University of Aberdeen as well as Robert Gordon's College, where the eldest son, Archie, was enrolled at the age of eight.[16]

Bertha Wilson as a young child.

Bertha Wilson with her parents and siblings in Scotland.

The whole parlour of the family's small bungalow was set aside for Archie to study. His accomplishments would take him to the University of Aberdeen on scholarship, to Balliol College at Oxford, back to the University of Aberdeen as a professor of classics and moral philosophy, and, ultimately, to elevation as dean of its Faculty of Arts. But the cost of Archie's private schooling left the family with no money for Jim or Bertha. The two younger children were relegated to the neighbourhood primary school and Aberdeen Central Secondary School. Despite the less felicitous start, Jim followed his brother to university and eventually became a philosophy professor at the University of Toronto and Carleton University in Ottawa.[17]

Bertha's youthful years evidenced the least intellectual acuity of all three siblings. Her early school years were eclipsed by her prodigy brother, who later described Bertha as "quite an ordinary little girl."[18] Her chief childhood recollection was being ordered by her mother to go outside to shush the neighbourhood children because their noise was disrupting Archie's studies. When she graduated from high school in 1941, the headmaster

Bertha Wilson, Scottish student.

discouraged Bertha from university, insisting that she did not "cut the grade." She was, as she admitted, "a late bloomer" as a student.[19]

It would have been easy for the family to use Bertha's lacklustre performance as a reason to dismiss her educational future. Yet her mother believed that girls deserved schooling. Without her mother's perseverance, Bertha probably would not have sat the entrance examinations. It was a bold step, for few of her classmates graduated from high school, and even fewer lower-middle-class families sent their children to university.[20] Bertha's mother took in summer boarders to pay the tuition and Bertha followed her brothers to the University of Aberdeen, a venerable four-centuries-old institution renowned for its theological scholarship and its intellectual leadership of the Scottish Enlightenment.[21]

Bertha's university years there were greatly affected by the devastation caused by the German bombing during World War II. She volunteered as a "home observer" and "fire watcher," and was deeply sobered when classmates failed to show up the

Bertha Wilson and her mother in Aberdeen.

morning after coastal raids. "I majored in history and philosophy," she later recalled, "but the study of British history or Plato's ideal took on a special meaning, and against the backdrop of the war the discussion of political ideals and social values was far more than an academic exercise. [It made] a profound impression on one's outlook and thinking."[22]

It made less of an impression on her grades. She passed through the university's halls with a master's degree in history and English in 1944, without honours or distinctions.[23] As many young women then did, she enrolled in teachers' college, and obtained her teaching parchment from the Aberdeen Training College for Teachers in 1945.[24] Student teaching expunged any desire to pursue that career, but instilled in her a sense of strict deportment and a pronounced deference toward those in positions of seniority.[25] Bertha Wernham emerged from her pre-law training with a deeply ingrained Protestant work ethic, a self-effacing modesty, and a staunchly hierarchical under-standing of authority.

THE L'HEUREUX FAMILY:
GROWING UP IN RIMOUSKI

Claire L'Heureux's childhood was quite different. Unlike Bertha's position as the youngest and only daughter, Claire was the first-born of four girls: she and her siblings, Louise, Lucie, and Nicole, were each born two years apart. When Claire was six, the family moved farther east after her father was promoted to collector of customs and excise in Rimouski, Quebec. Rimouski was a tranquil forestry and port town on the Lower St. Lawrence, where the massive river swelled to sixty kilometres in width, already salty with tides from the Atlantic Ocean.[26] Bitterly cold humid winds blew continuously from the north, winter temperatures dipped to minus 35 degrees Celsius, and the dense fog banks tinted the entire landscape grey-blue. Claire

Claire as a baby in Quebec City.

Louise and Claire
L'Heureux sitting on a
cannon on the Plains
of Abraham, Quebec.

The four
L'Heureux sisters
on the river front,
with Claire in
front.

revelled in the rugged climate. "We had to fight nature," she explained. "We built up confidence living in that small place."[27] The homogeneous population of Rimouski was 98 per cent of French descent, and her mother taught Claire to treasure the ancestral culture.[28]

As the eldest, Claire became the undisputed leader, always in charge of the sibling activities. She clashed with her father's strict regimen, repeatedly defying his orders and then absorbing more than her share of the harsh physical punishments he meted out. Her wide-eyed sisters characterized her as a "rebel from the time she was born."[29] Well-to-do Quebec families often educated their sons in seminaries and their daughters in convents, and although the private fees were a stretch, her parents paid for the four girls to become boarders in a local convent run by Ursuline nuns. This was motivated by Marguerite's physical incapacity to look after her girls and by a hope that the nuns could temper the eldest daughter's unruliness.[30] In 1937, ten-year-old Claire entered the cloistered Monastère des Ursulines de L'Immaculée Conception in Rimouski, where with the exception of brief family holidays, she would live and study under the twenty-four-hour care of the nuns until 1943.[31]

Claire learned to thrive in this intensely female world. She had no brothers, no male teachers, and no male classmates to tell

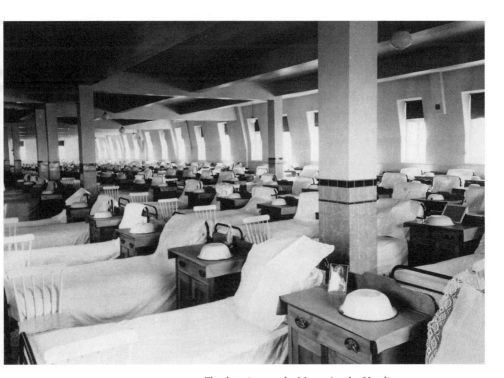

The dormitory at the Monastère des Ursulines.

Prayer in the chapel of the Monastère des Ursulines.

her what girls could or could not do. Despite surprisingly little effort, she amazed the nuns with her top grades, but her impetuousness often disrupted the rule-bound convent. Defying the mealtime protocol of strict silence broken only by nuns reading aloud from the Bible, Claire organized secret card games under the table. She put glue on the chairs. She disrupted the nighttime dormitory by blowing into a paper bag and smashing it in the dark. She ran away herself and helped another girl run away. Threats of punishment for misbehaviour held little sway. Deprivation of parental visits meant little to Claire; her mother was too sick to visit, and her father never came. Even the prospect of expulsion was illusory since the nuns had no desire to lose their star pupil.[32]

At the time, most Quebec girls left school by the end of their ninth year.[33] But the church was starting to loosen its prohibition on secondary education for female students and Claire enrolled in some of the first university prerequisite courses that the convents offered. With the enthusiastic backing of her mother, she transferred to the Collège Notre Dame de Bellevue, an elite convent boarding school in Quebec City. Even though her disruptive antics caused ongoing consternation for the nuns, her determination to succeed intellectually stood her in good stead. Neither her boisterous behaviour nor her aggressive competitive streak harmed her reputation with her peers, who delighted in her escapades and pranks.[34] Her family had long insisted upon the importance of bilingualism and Claire took pains to ensure that her English skills were well polished.[35] In 1946, she completed her twelfth year of secondary school, graduated *magna cum laude*, and carried off the Lieutenant Governor's medal.[36]

Claire's formative years in the confined quarters of convent boarding schools marked out her early path as a confident young woman who was also a risk-taker with a mischievous disposition. She prided herself on achieving scholastic pre-eminence without becoming a slave to her studies. An intellectual leader who was also a sociable and popular young woman, she was already developing the charismatic personality that would become her trademark characteristic.[37]

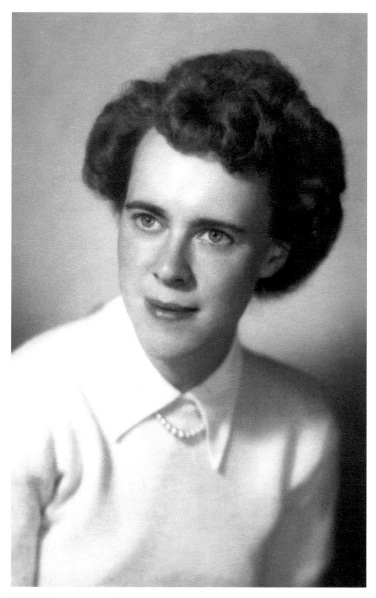

Claire L'Heureux, age sixteen.

CHAPTER 2

Bertha Wilson, the minister's wife

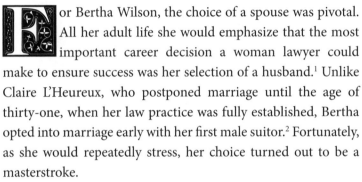or Bertha Wilson, the choice of a spouse was pivotal. All her adult life she would emphasize that the most important career decision a woman lawyer could make to ensure success was her selection of a husband.[1] Unlike Claire L'Heureux, who postponed marriage until the age of thirty-one, when her law practice was fully established, Bertha opted into marriage early with her first male suitor.[2] Fortunately, as she would repeatedly stress, her choice turned out to be a masterstroke.

Romance blossomed in the fall of 1939, when Bertha's older brother Jim brought home a university classmate named John Wilson. Sixteen-year-old Bertha was covered in green paint, a dishevelled spectre midway through the chore of repainting the kitchen walls. Nevertheless, "we sort of hit it off," she recalled.[3] Nineteen-year-old John Wilson, who had grown up on a farm near the Scottish fishing village of Macduff, had excelled in philosophy alongside Bertha's brothers. He would complete his master's degree in arts in 1942, and then obtain a theology degree, carrying off the most prestigious prize in divinity at the University of Aberdeen in 1945. His goal was to be ordained a Church of Scotland minister.[4]

Bertha Wernham, age sixteen.

John Wilson was a deeply spiritual man, who was described at the time as "exceptionally strait-laced."[5] Some wondered what Bertha saw in him. Bertha's classmates considered divinity students, whom they nicknamed "the Divines," to be a "stuffy lot" and John's unfashionable clothes did little to increase their regard. Bertha was short in stature, but John was even shorter, with a hairline that already showed signs of severe thinning. Bertha's mother made no secret of her reservations. As Bertha recalled, "[M]y mother did not view this burgeoning relationship with any great enthusiasm. She had other ideas. She didn't like the idea that I might end up as a minister's wife."[6]

Yet John Wilson's austere exterior masked a more complicated inner character. An intellectually curious, sensitive, politically progressive man, he also had a jovial personality and unflagging good humour. He could perform an energetic Scottish country dance and delight audiences with his recitations at Robbie Burns suppers, delivering the punchline in his broadest burr: "Get oot amon' my neeps ye toon's daert—it's nae fit ye eat, it's fit ye connach an' blad."[7] He would also prove to be a steadfast, egalitarian partner, precisely the sort of spouse that Bertha would later champion as the ideal for professional career women.

Although he could ill afford it, John purchased an expensive diamond and gold engagement ring, and proposed directly after he completed his university studies. The couple was married at King's College Chapel at the University of Aberdeen on December 14, 1945, just months after the cessation of World War II hostilities. Bertha's mother's anxiety over the match had not abated, and she attended the ceremony grudgingly.[8] But the festivities bore no evidence of her misgivings, with the young couple happily attended by two bridesmaids (John's stepsister and Jim's fiancé) and two groomsmen (Archie and Jim). Bertha's wedding outfit was a vivid contrast to her usual attire of tidy tweeds, plain white blouses with Peter Pan collars, and sensible Oxford shoes. She was described as "elegant in a classic satin draped bodice and diaphanous veil with a pearl tiara in her hair."[9]

The wedding picture of Bertha and John Wilson, 1945.

Interior photo of King's College.

Exterior of King's College Chapel, University of Aberdeen, where Bertha and John Wilson were married.

The Wilsons' first posting commenced directly after the wedding. John was ordained and called to become pastor in Macduff, the village of his youth. Constructed in 1805, the church dominated the coastline facing the Central North Sea from the top of the Hill of Doune, where it served as the town's religious and social hub. "Married into the cloth at the tender age of twenty-one years," as she described it, Bertha presided over the drafty, unfurnished manse, a rambling Victorian structure without electricity, stove, or proper heating.[10] She would later credit her Macduff years as a crash course in the "drama" of "daily lives": the tragedies of sailors lost at sea, the loneliness of proud people, the dependencies of the elderly, the unethical practices of shopkeepers. She threw herself into the activities of the Women's Guild, Girl Guides, Sunday school, a nursing clinic, and several youth clubs. She was the epitome of a proper minister's wife.[11]

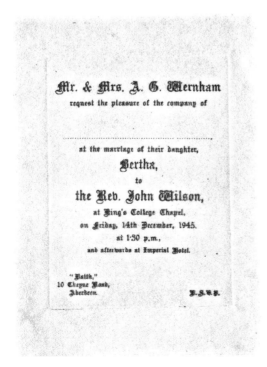

Bertha Wernham and John Wilson's wedding invitation.

Yet Bertha's brother Jim was beckoning from Toronto, urging the young couple to uproot and seek their fortunes in Canada. It was a difficult decision, but John and Bertha were drawn by Canada's stronger post-war economy and its reputation as a country that was less rigidly class-bound than Scotland. In 1949, John secured a new ministerial posting at Renfrew Presbyterian Church in eastern Ontario. Bertha listed herself as a "housewife"—a proper "separate spheres" designation—on the embarkation register of the Cunard Shipping Line, and the Wilsons sailed on the RMS *Aquitania* to Halifax. Then they travelled by train to their new home in the Ottawa Valley.[12] If they had hoped to find family at the ready to ease their transition, they were out of luck. Brother Jim was busy with his philosophy posting at the University of Toronto and his own family responsibilities, and the Wilsons discovered what Europeans often first notice about Canada, that the long distances between cities made travel laborious.[13]

Bertha Wilson leading a Girl Guide camp.

In other ways, however, it was a soft-landing for immigrants from Scotland. The town had been named after Renfrew, Scotland, a shipbuilding town near Glasgow. The members of the church were all second- and third-generation Scottish immigrants, most of them in thrall to their old-world ancestry. Scottish fur traders, merchants, physicians, and ministers had paved the way for them in Canada. Even the first prime minister, Sir John A. Macdonald, had been a Scot. Bertha captured the depth of her adopted country's emotional ties to Scotland when she described their first Robbie Burns supper in January 1950: "Dr. Max MacOdrum, then president of Carleton University in Ottawa, proposed the toast to the immortal memory of Robbie Burns quoting poignantly from his love songs, the tears pouring unrestrained down his cheeks. We had haggis and bagpipes and all that! And I felt the country to which I had come was more Scottish than the one I had left behind."[14] Although she and John rarely travelled home again, they remained attached to the country of their birth. Decades later, when the nationalist movement surged in Scotland, the Wilsons would become strong supporters of its goal of independence.[15]

Bertha was well aware that her immigrant background was only discernible because of her Aberdeen burr, an accent that singled her out as preferred stock in Canada. As she put it, her adopted country seemed to have a "magnetic attraction for the Scot," and she speculated that there may even have been a "mysterious element of Scottishness in the Canadian psyche itself."[16] She was partly, but perhaps not fully, conscious of the privilege that Scottish heritage bestowed in Canada, a position distinct from visibly racialized immigrants and those with less favoured accents, whose outsider status was of a different order. However, Bertha felt that her "audible minority immigrant" status still relegated her to an uncertain footing. Speaking decades later, she described her feelings by saying that "An immigrant is someone who lives always on the boundary between two worlds. She has, in a manner of speaking, been

Name of Ship "AQUITANIA"
Steamship Line CUNARD WHITE STAR LIMITED.
NAMES AND DESCRIPTIONS OF **BRITISH** PASSENGERS EMBARKED AT THE PORT OF

P.M. 21.
Date of Departure 24TH AUGUST 194 9
Where Bound HALIFAX N.S.
SOUTHAMPTON.

(1) Contract Ticket Number	(2) Port at which Passengers have contracted to land. HALIFAX N.S.	(3) NAMES OF PASSENGERS.	(4) CLASS TOURIST	(5) AGES OF PASSENGERS.			(6) Last Address in the United Kingdom.	(7) Profession, Occupation, or Calling of Passengers.	(8) Country of last Permanent Residence.	(9) Country of Intended Future Permanent Residence.
244792		WILSON JOHN					DOUNE MANSE, BANFF SCOTLAND.	MINISTER	1	CANADA
DO.		DO. BERTHA		25			DO.	H'WIFE	1	CANADA
194687		WILLIAMS EDWARD		30			ROSE MOUNT, OLD LONDON RD. FLINT.WALES.	MINER	1	CANADA
DO.		DO. DORIS		25			DO.	H'WIFE	1	CANADA
DO.		DO. DORIS			2		DO.	CHILD	1	CANADA
DO.		DO. EDWIN		80			DO.	NONE	1	CANADA
178664		WINFIELD Keith		16			WIN-MILL ENXIME OXFORD.	FARM WORKER.	1	ENGLAND
243725		WHITE PETER		35			5 GLANVILLE PLACE. EDINBURGH.	TR.DRIVER	1	CANADA
DO.		DO. THERESA		34			DO.	H'WIFE	1	CANADA
DO.		DO. GLORIA			10		DO.	SCHOLAR	1	CANADA
DO.		DO. VALERIE			5		DO.	CHILD	1	CANADA
DO.		DO. ALLAN			5		DO.	CHILD	1	CANADA
DO.		DO. IAN			12		DO.	INFANT	1	CANADA
232319		WARDLAW — STET					C/O C.A.L.E. LONDON.			CANADA
232318		WOODWOCK G					DO.			CANADA
244498		WALEAU RAYMOND		28			52 RAGLAN COURT. WEMBLEY PK.MIDDX.	CATERER	1	CANADA
DO.		DO. BETTY		29			DO.	H'WIFE	1	CANADA
DO.		DO. KATHLEEN			7		DO.	SCHOLAR	1	CANADA
196572		WITTHAMES FLORA		63			42 STATION ROAD. LETCHWORTH.HERTS.	H'WIFE	1	CANADA
DO.		DO. BEATRICE		30			DO.	STOREKEEPER	1	CANADA
207847		WILLIAMS ARCHIE		44			15 VARDHE RD.CLY-DACH.SWANSEA.GLAM.	TRANSPORT DRIVER.	1	CANADA
DO.		DO. OLWEN		40			DO.	H'WIFE	1	CANADA
DO.		DO. VERNON		21			DO.	SALESMAN	1	CANADA
DO.		DO. NEVILLE			11		DO.	SCHOLAR	1	CANADA
DO.		DO. MELVIN			7		DO.	SCHOLAR	1	CANADA
DO.		DO. HANNAH		72			DO.	H'WIFE	1	CANADA
T.W.95092		WIGSTON. BERYL		30			7 BOSTON GARDENS, HANWELL.LONDON.W.7.	HOUSEWIFE	1	CANADA
DO		WIGSTON. ANDREW			3		DO	CHILD	1	CANADA
DO		WIGSTON. JOAN			1		DO	CHILD	1	CANADA
T.W.686		WILKINSON. DAISY		59			26 NEVISL STREET, CURRIE.CHESHIRE.	HOUSEWIFE	1	CANADA

*By Permanent Residence is to be understood residence for a year or more. Northern Ireland and Eire are to be regarded as separate countries.

The embarkation record of the RMS *Aquitania*, Cunard Shipping Line, listing Bertha Wilson as "housewife."

born twice; and this personal duality colours and shapes all her thoughts and actions."[17]

The Renfrew ministry turned out to be short-lived. In 1951, John signed on with the military as a Presbyterian naval chaplain. This took him overseas in 1952, ministering to sailors fighting the Korean War.[18] Bertha moved to a rental duplex in a working-class district of Ottawa, sixty miles east of Renfrew, where she carved out an independent existence for the first time in her life. She learned to drive. She learned to type and took a job as a dental receptionist, where she made appointments, developed X-rays and kept the books.[19] She volunteered with the Knox Presbyterian Church and practised her French at a nearby Catholic Church. Reflecting on this much later, she said, "I was often very lonely, but in a strange way it felt good to be doing something by myself.... I was my own centre of reference now.... I know that this first experience on my own was a necessary prelude to my career in law."[20]

When John's naval chaplaincy posted him back on shore in Halifax, Bertha moved again. By now they were accustomed to making do with substandard rentals, and they settled into a

Bertha Wilson, as a young minister's wife in Renfrew, Ontario.

low-ceilinged Halifax basement apartment at 82 Oxford Street. They dug trenches around the doorway to forestall the regular flooding in rainstorms, and they hung their clothes to dry on the exposed ceiling pipes. John's work took him away much of the time, on rotation to three different naval bases. Bertha secured another job as a medical receptionist.[21]

By 1954, Bertha had decided to return to university. A modest lifestyle and frugal parsimony had allowed her to save the tuition. Dalhousie University in Halifax was the obvious institution. John thought she would enrol in philosophy courses or study fine art. Bertha had other ideas.[22]

CHAPTER 3

The decision to study law

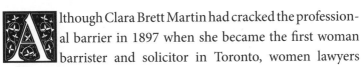lthough Clara Brett Martin had cracked the professional barrier in 1897 when she became the first woman barrister and solicitor in Toronto, women lawyers remained scarce for the next seventy years. Male lawyers, judges, politicians, and journalists opposed their entry. Drawing upon traditional "separate spheres" arguments, opponents claimed that women were biologically and intellectually unfit, that their only proper role was that of wives and mothers, and that their presence would disrupt and demean the practice of law.[1]

Physicians furnished medical support for these theories, warning that women's mental exertion would "weaken their developing wombs," promote sterility, inhibit lactation in nursing mothers, cause serious mental disturbance, and produce pelvic distortion.[2] They asserted that men's heavier brains facilitated "volition" and "cognition," while female brains were relegated to "sensory functions."[3] Male lawyers agreed, insisting that the male species reasoned with logic, whereas women were captive to emotion and instinct.[4] They worried that women lawyers would fail to comport themselves within the constraints of feminine decorum, and conversely, that their femininity would "disgrace the profession."[5] "To refuse to allow them to embark upon the rough and troubled sea of actual legal practice," insisted the

Clara Brett Martin, Canada's first female lawyer

editors of the *Canada Law Journal,* was "being cruel only to be kind."[6] Chivalry would reign.

Nova Scotia legislators delayed opening the doors to women lawyers until 1917. Quebec, the last holdout in Canada, barred the way until 1941.[7] Things were no better back in Scotland. The British Parliament forestalled legislation permitting women to become lawyers until 1919. The first woman admitted to the Scottish bar in 1923 practised as the lone female until 1948.[8]

It was an uninviting landscape in which to dream of becoming a woman lawyer.

CLAIRE L'HEUREUX: "THE ONLY GIRL FROM RIMOUSKI WHO TOOK LAWYERS' LESSONS"

Claire L'Heureux preceded Bertha Wilson into law school, but it was not a straight path there. At the time of her graduation from the Bellevue convent in 1946, female lawyers represented

1.6 per cent of the Canadian profession.[9] Only eleven women had been called to the bar in Quebec.[10] Years later, Claire would state that, "This was the time when society, especially Quebec society, allowed women neither the choice of their destiny nor the possibility of making a free choice. Their life was traced in indelible ink: on the one hand, marriage, maternity, and the role of a faceless partner, and on the other hand, the life of a spinster, teacher, or secretary. [trans.]"[11] And still Claire confided in her Bellevue classmates that she aspired to become a lawyer. None wished to join her, but they presented her with a special graduation gift: a miniature Quebec Civil Code.[12]

What caused Claire L'Heureux to select law? First, she was inspired by another Bellevue graduate, Jeanne D'Arc Lemay, who had joined the first Laval University law class that included women in 1942. While still a law student, Lemay had returned to speak at Bellevue and she encouraged Claire to believe she could succeed in law. "I remember clearly, after that, I thought—hey, if she can do it, I can do it," explained Claire. "You had to be motivated by someone, otherwise why would you go into a man's field?"[13] Secondly, Claire identified growing up with four sisters as important. She claimed that she had never been forced to share the limelight with boys and never developed a "feeling of inferiority toward men."[14] Thirdly, there were her parents. Claire's mother took top billing. "She would have loved to go on, to be independent, and to become a lawyer," recalled Claire. "Justice was very important to her. She had talent galore, but she couldn't get to her full potential. She couldn't do it, but her children would."[15]

Claire's father was equally influential, in reverse. "He didn't want her to be a lawyer. He was against it," remembered Claire's sister Louise.[16] Her sister Nicole agreed that "[h]e would have liked us just to go to high school and be a clerk at the Kresge store. My mother said, 'They have the potential to do better than that.' It's amazing, because he himself would have liked to go to university. But for us, he didn't think women needed an

Marguerite and Paul L'Heureux,
Claire L'Heureux-Dubé's parents.

education."[17] Claire, the rebel, refused to knuckle under. "My father thought it was silly that I went into law. He thought I would marry, [that it was] not worth it. Marriage was the profession for women.... [But] I never thought in terms of marriage. [It was] not my goal. I wanted to learn."[18] Claire's choice of law was as much a challenge to her father's sexism as it was a desire to fulfill her mother's ambitions. She soundly rejected a vision of women as fit only for a life of domesticity.

But first, there was a two-year hiatus. Claire's father put a halt to her plans when he insisted that law was financially beyond the family's reach. Insisting that she become self-supporting, he bought her a typewriter and demanded she teach herself stenography. Trying to remain positive, Claire decided that secretarial skills could be useful. "I never believed I could succeed in getting a job as a lawyer," she reflected. "[I] always thought I would earn my living as a secretary."[19]

In the fall of 1946, Claire started her first secretarial job. Since such positions were usually obtained through patronage, her father used his customs office connections to find her an opening as a typist for the federal government in Rimouski. A childhood friend in the typing pool who helped Claire master the job recalled that "[Claire] was ambitious. She was funny. When she didn't know how to do something, she tried, she tried, and she did it. She never said she couldn't do it. She was typing with two fingers and then she got the whole method."[20] When a woman with more connections bumped Claire from the post, her father found her another one at the Canadian Cod Liver Oil Research Institute. It involved working mostly in English with American chemists who travelled to the Gaspésie region to test cod tongues. Claire's bilingualism progressed.[21]

Claire's stint as a Rimouski secretary hit a full stop in 1948, after she lost all patience with taking orders from a male boss who was less educated than she was. He dictated a letter. She

Claire as young woman with a bicycle.

corrected his mistakes. He called her into the office shouting, "I didn't say that," and threw her revised letter into the garbage. Claire retorted that she had had enough, that he "should be on her side of the desk" and she "should be on his."[22] When Claire's mother heard the tale, she decided that admission to law school had become urgent.

Together, mother and daughter came up with a plan. Twenty-one-year-old Claire would move to Quebec City and enrol at Laval University's Faculty of Law that fall. The financial challenges could be resolved if Claire could secure secretarial work alongside her legal studies. Laval classes ran from 8 a.m. to 10 a.m., and from 4 p.m. to 6 p.m. to accommodate the professors who also practised in busy downtown law offices. If Claire could work as a secretary between the hours of 10 a.m. and 4 p.m., she could pay for law school. Claire's mother called in the support of Rimouski's most prominent businessman, whose wife was a good friend of hers. He found Claire a position in a trust company office next to the law school.[23] Claire arranged to board with her Quebec City aunt and uncle, and her mother paid the $150 registration fee from her housekeeping money. In the words of one childhood friend, Claire was on the way to becoming "the only girl from Rimouski who took lawyers' lessons."[24]

The receipt for law school fees paid, 1948.

BERTHA WILSON: "QUITE SURPRISED" WHEN SHE JOINED THE LAW SCHOOL

Bertha Wilson took the decision to study law without personal role models to follow, with no Jeanne D'Arc Lemay several years ahead of her to serve as a shining example. If Bertha's two older, philosophically inclined brothers had predisposed her toward law, she never admitted as much. Her brother Jim had his own thoughts on the matter. Speaking to the *Toronto Star* on the occasion of his sister's appointment to the top court, he chalked it up to an automobile accident Bertha had in Renfrew. It was a relatively minor crash, and when she represented herself in court, the judge had complimented her on her advocacy. Jim mused, "I think that was the first time she thought of being a lawyer."[25]

Were Bertha's parents a factor? Her mother had championed higher education for all her children, including her only daughter, and had insisted that Bertha study at the University of Aberdeen. She had urged Bertha to become credentialed as a teacher. She had been against Bertha's early marriage to a minister because she saw this as curtailing her daughter's opportunities. But Bertha had been living on another continent with her husband, John, for five years. By this point, John outweighed earlier parental influences. And ironically, it was his *absence* that was a motivating force. "[I]t seemed as if my husband was contemplating at least some years in the navy, and there was no role for a chaplain's wife," explained Bertha. "I decided that it made good sense for me to go back to school and pick up my education where I had left off when I married into the cloth."[26] This was no rejection of the "housewife" role she had selected to describe her status on the voyage from Scotland. Only now there was a vacancy in the post of "minister's wife" that she had signed up for. Not one to sit back idle, Bertha opted to fill it with something useful.

Although John Wilson knew that his wife wanted to

Bertha and John Wilson meeting in the wardroom of HMCS *Nootka* during John's naval chaplaincy.

continue her studies, he never imagined that she would enrol in law. He remembered being "quite surprised" when Bertha told him she had "joined the law school."[27] He chalked it up to a moment when the two found themselves across the street from Dalhousie University Law School precisely when Bertha was pondering what to study. The location of the building, the route they were walking, and the timing of Bertha's moment of decision, it seems it was sheer happenstance that the first female judge on Canada's top court opted for law. The selection that day, as John Wilson later explained, proved just "how fortuitous things were."[28]

John Wilson's serendipitous description modestly discounted his own role. He may not have known that his wife would pick law, and he may not have urged her to do so. But he was a man who was leagues ahead of the stereotypical 1950s husbands of the *Father Knows Best* generation. He was not committed to establishing a family with a patriarchal breadwinner and a stay-at-home wife. He had no misgivings about Bertha's desire for a professional education. In fact, he would delight in her success as a law student.

At thirty-one years of age, Bertha was a decade older than Claire when she began her first year at Dalhousie Law School in Halifax. Her studies had been interrupted by a ten-year hiatus. While the two women each had several years of secretarial work in common, Bertha's law career had also been delayed by her marriage, her responsibilities as a minister's wife, and her immigration to Canada.[29] When Bertha arrived at law school in 1954, she was marked as a "mature" student, isolated not only by age and marital status, but also by gender. In this final salient factor, Bertha and Claire ventured into masculinist law schools aligned in full.

CHAPTER 4

Claire L'Heureux and
Laval University Law School

In the fall of 1948, Claire presented herself at the Laval law school, an imposing five-storey stone building in the heart of old Quebec City. She was sent to the registration office, where an overbearing male official told her that the legal profession was "only for men."[1] When a university administrator told her to go into social work instead, Claire asked if there were any laws barring her admission. He conceded there were none. He filed the paperwork. She was less successful with the law professor who handled scholarships. Guy Hudon told her bluntly that these were reserved for men. Claire chose not to challenge anything further. She may have been "a rebel who fought to get into the law school," but by this point she admitted that she had "had enough."[2]

The first day of the semester, Claire found herself surrounded by more than fifty male classmates. Many were the offspring of Quebec legal dynasties with a few of more modest beginnings from farms and rural villages. All were neatly attired in suits and neckties.[3] Many would become future leaders at the bar, government officials, law professors, politicians, diplomats, cabinet members, senators, even one lieutenant governor.[4] Twenty per cent of them would be appointed judges.[5] One would reach the Supreme Court of Canada eight years before Claire.[6] Another

Laval Faculty of Law, late 1940s.

would be forced to resign from the judiciary due to misogynist and anti-Semitic comments he delivered from the bench.[7] None could have imagined that a woman student would stand a chance at glory.

There was one other female student in the class: Judith Gamache. The two young women found they shared an irreverent sense of humour and became inseparable.[8] Only a handful of women had passed through Laval law since Jeanne D'Arc Lemay's first admission in 1942. Eight preceded Judith and Claire's arrival, and nine more would enrol before their graduation in 1951.[9] In the end, Claire's career would outdistance all of the women in her cohort, and all of the men as well.

The female law students met with some resentment. Like the lawyers who had protested the entry of women into the profession, the law professors and students felt that allowing women into the school devalued their masculine domain. Jeanne D'Arc Lemay believed it necessary to defend her career choice in the Laval student newspaper, where she argued that although women might wish to become spouses and mothers,

Women law students relaxing at Lac Sept-Îles, Quebec. Left to right: Calin Morin (who enrolled the year after Claire), Claire L'Heureux, and Judith Gamache.

they should not have to renounce other occupations.[10] "We would come to the school, and they would close the door in our face," remembered Claire. "It was kind of an expression of 'You don't belong here.'"[11] It was almost as if the men feared their male privilege was a house of cards that could be toppled by even a few token women.

Some of the male students recalled that Claire and Judith "stayed always together in the classroom," probably for "joint support."[12] One of the young men who socialized with his two female classmates recognized that the young women had "to fight a lot" to be accepted. He remembered Claire as a woman who "wanted to be first," and characterized her as "competitive" and "very intense," an individual with "a steel will."[13]

Laval Law Library, 1933.

THE LAVAL CIVIL LAW PROGRAM:
"VERY LITTLE FOR THE MIND"

Laval Faculty of Law, almost a century old, was designed to create a professional and social elite rather than to serve as a centre for intellectual inquiry.[14] The faculty formed "a veritable Family Compact," with professors selected for their prominence at the bar, a quarter of them sitting judges, interlinked through career and family ties. The lectures incorporated a static vision of law and its conservative role in society.[15] The teaching style was "expository and didactic." Readings were confined to the *Civil Code* and the *Criminal Code of Canada*, along with a few French and Quebec treatises.[16]

Guy Hudon, the professor who had refused Claire a scholarship, would place his hand on his forehead and "recite in a deep voice for one and a half hours," speaking in prolonged sentences for upwards of ten minutes using perfect grammar and syntax.[17] Louis-Philippe Pigeon, appointed to the Supreme Court of Canada in 1967, ruled his classes with a strict old-school manner and terrified generations of students with his probing oral exams. The effect was magnified by Pigeon's falsetto sing-song voice and his peculiar mannerism of twisting his face while rubbing his nose.[18]

Marie-Louis Beaulieu was something of a maverick: he was one of the only professors to profess any interest in the connections between law and society. A short man with an unusually large bald head and a reputation as a gambler, Beaulieu was tagged with the unfortunate nickname "*la tête à deux jaunes*"—the "head with two yolks" or "egghead."[19] Law students reported ruefully that one of the other professors reread verbatim the lectures *his* father had devised when he taught a generation earlier.[20] The formalistic legal education did little to prepare students for the complex legal world that they would inhabit over the succeeding decades. As one of her classmates summed it up, there was "very little for the mind."[21] It would be a slow process and it would

A cartoon in the Laval student journal *Le Carabin* depicting from left to right:
Henri Turgeon, Guy Hudon, Marie-Louis Beaulieu, and the laboratory attendant
(l'Appariteur).

take many years before Claire would be prepared to shake off the legacy of a formalized, black-letter approach to the law.

There were also gender-based challenges. Criminal law professor Gérard Lacroix left a special impression because he asked Claire and Judith to leave the classroom when he lectured about sexual offences.[22] It was a Laval tradition that continued for years.[23] Claire said it never entered their minds to refuse to leave. "They would have locked the door! Anyway, we loved the break. We were not interested in criminal law."[24] Sexual harassment presented additional problems. Reluctant to name the offending professor even decades later, Claire explained that, "He would invite [me or Judith to his office] on one pretext or another. He would get up and put his hands on our behinds. We had names for him—*le cochon* [the pig]—but we never thought of reporting it. We were shy about it. Judith and I would exchange but we wouldn't mention it to anybody else. We felt it was something we shouldn't talk about."[25]

Despite the sexism, Claire breezed through her studies. Judith admired her friend's capacity to negotiate law school so effortlessly, noting that "Claire was not panicky ever. [S]he laughed all the time."[26] In the end, there were two students who led the class: Claire L'Heureux and Julien Chouinard, both eventually named Supreme Court judges.

Julien Chouinard, an incisive leader, was regarded by his classmates as straight-laced, conservative, quiet, and abstemious.[27] Her classmates regarded Claire as the complete opposite: a young woman who was "obviously bright as a light," but all for "going out" and "having fun."[28] It was Julien who obtained first prize in civil law. Claire carried off the labour law prize and finished second in civil law.[29] Both Claire and Julien expressed interest in a Rhodes scholarship that would fund a year of legal education at Oxford in England. Claire was advised that women were ineligible. Julien carried off the Rhodes unopposed.[30]

Claire's graduation day, when she was awarded a bachelor of laws (LL.L.) *cum laude* in 1951, passed without celebration.

Claire L'Heureux's call to the bar, 1952.

Despite her elevated standing, the twenty-three-year-old retained little memory of the occasion: "I think there was a ceremony. They gave us our diploma. My mother couldn't come, and my father didn't."[31]

That year the Quebec Bar imposed a fourth year of practical training. Over time this would morph into a one-year articling *stage* (clerkship) at a law firm, but initially, the task was assigned to the law schools, and Claire's class was required to pursue courses at Laval for one more year.[32] Claire again excelled and she passed the bar examination *cum laude*. She was called to the bar in the fall of 1952. Across the province, only twenty-six women had preceded her.[33]

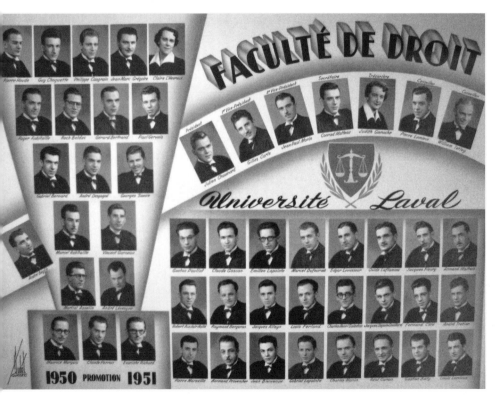

Laval law graduating class, 1951; Claire L'Heureux is in the top row, fifth from the left, and Judith Gamache is in the top curved row, third from the right.

In contrast to Bertha Wilson, Claire did not marry her first suitor. The reputation as a *femme fatale* that commenced in her youth lasted a lifetime. From her earliest years, her friends remarked on her interest in boys and her popularity with the opposite sex. According to one, "Boys would turn their heads, and she would turn too."[34] Another recalled that "although she never said bad things about the other girls, every girl was afraid to leave their boyfriend with Claire. She had a way to talk to boys. She was friendly, joking easily, talking about everything. She was never with any boy for long."[35] At law school, Claire was regarded as more modern than most, an "audacious" young woman who "liked men" and was not afraid to show it.[36] A brief engagement to Gabriel Gagnon, an engineer almost ten years older than she, ended during law school when Claire decided she would rather play the field.[37]

Yet events on the home front were sobering. Her mother's multiple sclerosis worsened to the point where she struggled to cope with the simplest daily tasks. Claire's parents' marriage was fraying at the seams, with her father increasingly chafing over familial responsibilities. Then, completely unexpectedly, the third-born of the four L'Heureux sisters, Lucie, fell desperately ill. Lucie died at home of heart failure at age twenty, on July 1, 1952, one week after Claire's final bar exam. Her sister's tragic death devastated Claire, who spoke through tears about it years later: "I think of her very often. Our deaths don't leave us, especially as we grow older."[38] It was just the first in a searing pattern of heartbreaking deaths that would haunt her family in the coming decades.

CHAPTER 5

Bertha Wilson and Dalhousie Law School

ertha Wilson started law school in 1954, six years after Claire L'Heureux.[1] Dalhousie had enrolled its first female student in 1915, more than a quarter of a century before Laval.[2] Dalhousie's Constance Glube, who entered two years ahead of Wilson, would be appointed the first female chief justice of a Canadian superior court in 1982.[3] Wilson's class contained six women out of seventy, the largest female cohort ever admitted to Dalhousie and triple the number in L'Heureux's class.[4] But sexism continued to lurk in the corners. Applicants had to complete an interview with Dean Horace E. Read, famous as a leader who ruled by the "Divine Right of Deans."[5] His conversation with Wilson would become "indelibly printed" on her mind.[6]

Like the Laval administrators who tried to convince L'Heureux to study social work, Dean Read did his best to dissuade Wilson. "Have you any appreciation of how tough a course the law is? This is not something you can do in your spare time," he admonished. "We have no room here for dilettantes. Why don't you just go home and take up crocheting?"[7] It was another appropriation of "separate spheres," banishing women to the decorative arts. Although Wilson replied politely that needlework might be a "pleasant way" to spend the leisure

Horace E. Read, Dean of Dalhousie Law School.

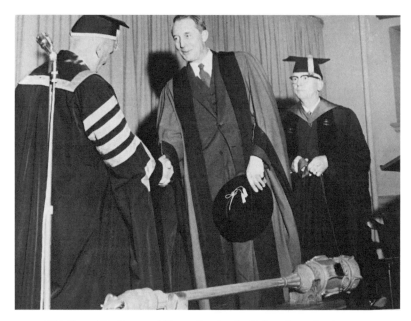

C.D. Howe, F.R. Scott, and Horace Read at the Dalhousie graduation.

hours, Read's dismissal of her intellectual interests rankled. "It was hard for me to persuade him that I was a serious student," she recalled, and that crocheting "could not be the be-all and end-all of one's most productive years."[8]

The crochet reproach may have been a perfunctory warning that Dean Read delivered to every female applicant. But as many victims of discrimination do, Wilson feared that the comment might be directed to her personally. She worried that her status as a married woman had aroused suspicion, reflecting a presumption that wifely duties would take precedence over law books.[9] Like L'Heureux, she did not hold much hope of a future legal career and she wondered if she had provoked the rebuke by expressing interest in law as furthering a liberal arts education. At age thirty-one, Wilson was a decade older than most of her classmates, and she felt anxiety on that score as well. Her gender, marital status, and age added to the already significant challenges facing law students, many of whom failed out of first-year classes.[10] Yet like L'Heureux, she swallowed her chagrin and her anxieties, and stayed the course.

Six female law grads. Bertha Wilson is second from the right. Others are (uncertain order) Lilias Toward, Enid Land, Patricia Fownes, Justine O'Brien, Yvonne Walters.

A LAW SCHOOL "WITH A LIBERAL
AS WELL AS A PROFESSIONAL ORIENTATION"

Dalhousie Law School, although considerably younger than Quebec's civil law faculties, was the oldest university law school in the rest of the country. Established in 1883, it aspired to something more than the formalist legal education at Laval, modelling itself on Harvard Law School and endorsing a "liberal" as well as a "professional orientation."[11] Yet for decades the curriculum remained mired in "nuts and bolts" practice-oriented courses like evidence, procedure, and maritime shipping, taught by a part-time faculty of local judges and downtown practitioners. When Horace Read assumed the deanship in 1950, he was determined to reshape the curriculum to reflect changing social and economic influences.[12]

Read had graduated from Dalhousie Law School in 1924 and joined a "very long line of Dalhousie men" to obtain a master's degree in law at Harvard, where he studied the ultra-modern "Legislation" course under the famed Roscoe

Dalhousie Law Library.

Pound. Returning to Dalhousie to teach in 1925, he served as its dean from 1950 to 1964. By the time Wilson enrolled, Read had significantly reduced reliance upon "downtowners" and increased the full-time faculty to seven, all men. Read was a dean who took a great interest in his students and drove himself "beyond endurance."[13] His broad conception of legal education should have inclined him to embrace Wilson, whose interest was piqued by the theoretical underpinnings of law. His gender assumptions made this impossible.

BERTHA WILSON'S IMMERSION IN LEGAL EDUCATION: "THE LAW WAS MY THING"

Wilson's first day of law school had much in common with L'Heureux's at Laval. She peered into the Dalhousie classroom and saw "the air blue with smoke" and "the place filled with young men." On the verge of turning heel, she noticed another female and "slipped into the front row" beside her. Lilias Toward, one of the only other mature students, would become her faithful friend.[14]

Dalhousie students were as homogenous as their Laval counterparts. They were mostly from financially secure families with deep roots in Atlantic Canada. Many had grandfathers, fathers, and uncles who practised law. They were "aiming for Barrington Street, not Bay Street," counting upon "jobs close to home in family firms." Academic excellence mattered less than social standing, and the atmosphere was accentuated by a "goodly number of stags or smokers." One student, whose father was a well-known lawyer, achieved notoriety for failing first year three times before he passed.[15]

Did the "club-like" male environment make life difficult for the women? Others said so. Canada's first female lawyer, Clara Brett Martin, had endured ostracism and hissing at Osgoode Hall in the late nineteenth century.[16] In the mid-twentieth, women law students across the country described "gentle lechery" and "baiting" from colleagues who accused them of "status-seeking" and "over-ambition."[17] The Dalhousie basement common room remained the preserve of male law students, but Wilson made no complaint of sex discrimination apart from her interactions with Dean Read.[18]

Unlike L'Heureux, who was notorious for socializing, Wilson immersed herself in lectures and texts. "One term there was enough to tell me that I had found my proper niche," she remembered. "I knew the law was my thing. I took to it like a duck takes to water." Her husband, John, marvelled that by Christmas, "the bug had bitten her," adding, "[T]hat mysterious thing in law, whatever it was, just was the spark that ignited the brain."[19] Wilson's favourite perch was the reading table in the law library, a chapel-like room inside the handsome ivy-covered stone building. Although she was known to share her notes generously, she eschewed the Friday afternoon beer sessions. Instead, she organized a Friday-night study group.[20]

The study group initiated by Wilson and Lilias Toward soon became notorious. Its invitation-only members met weekly, dissecting the readings, debating difficult cases, formulating comprehensive study notes, and preparing lists of questions to put to the professors in class. Several male students were invited to attend, including Ron Pugsley, who would later distinguish himself as a judge of the Nova Scotia Court of Appeal.[21] John Charters, a mature student who left the navy to study law, would outrival them all as the group's most intense member. His aggressiveness brought out Wilson's competitive instincts, although she never abandoned her low-key, gracious manner. As Pugsley observed, Wilson "had a wonderful capacity for analysis, tempered with kindness."[22] Despite her best efforts to beat him, Charters captured the gold medal.[23]

Graham Murray, who taught property law, was one of Wilson's favourite professors, revered for his focus on the subtleties of property concepts and his rapport with students.

Lorne Clarke, who taught corporate law from a "formidably thick syllabus," would go on to become a distinguished Chief Justice of Nova Scotia. Vincent Pottier, a Nova Scotia judge who had graduated from Dalhousie almost forty years earlier, taught Wilson criminal law using a "hard-nosed practitioner" approach.[24] Like L'Heureux before her, Wilson found criminal law uninteresting, but at least she was not barred from the classroom during lectures on sexual offences.

The professor who most influenced her was William R. Lederman, who taught Wilson torts, jurisprudence, and constitutional law. A Rhodes scholar from Oxford, he taught first at the University of Saskatchewan and then at Dalhousie until 1958, when he left to become the dean of law at Queen's University. Lederman rejected notions of doctrinal rigidity and emphasized that "cultural, social, and economic realities" should inform humane theories of justice.[25] One of the most intellectually sophisticated law professors of his era, it was Lederman whose ideas would later frame Wilson's judicial perspectives. One inspirational teacher and one willing student: Lederman's influence may explain why Wilson was prepared to display creativity so early in her career as a judge.

A MASTER'S DEGREE IN LAW: "NOT IN YOUR TIME"

Wilson graduated with her LL.B. (bachelor of law) degree in 1957, proud that she and Lilias Toward were both named prize-winners. Even Dean Read admitted that Wilson's performance in his contracts class had been superb, and that the women had done "extremely well."[26] He would have had to concede that intellectual achievement was not a gendered attribute, but this did nothing to dislodge his bias.

Dalhousie had become a pipeline for students who wished to pursue graduate legal studies. Five students in the year ahead of Wilson had received graduate scholarships to elite American

Bertha Wilson's Dalhousie Law School graduation photograph, 1957.

and English law schools. Wilson wanted to study at Harvard, a law school that had only begun to admit women in 1950.[27] When she learned that Harvard would offer her a scholarship, she made the mistake of seeking Dean Read's advice.[28] His reaction was appalling.

As she laid out her hopes to study property and nuisance law, Read assumed that Wilson desired a teaching position, and exclaimed, "Oh my dear! A woman on faculty! Not in *your* time!"[29] This was an era when deans lamented the dearth of qualified law teachers in Canada.[30] And Read had done extensive hiring at Dalhousie, filling every faculty post with men.[31] In fact, Read was also incorrect. In 1961, the University of Montreal law school would hire Alice Desjardins, who graduated from law the same year as Wilson, to become the first female tenure-stream law professor in Canada.[32] Surrounded by more enlightened advisors, Wilson would have stood an excellent chance of becoming Canada's first female law professor.

ARTICLING IN HALIFAX AND
LICENSURE IN NOVA SCOTIA

Wilson decided instead to qualify for the Nova Scotia bar. Her receipt of the Smith Shield Moot Court award for oral advocacy had overcome her earlier fear that law would furnish no career prospects.[33] But here too, gender inequalities loomed large. Women who wished to complete the requisite one-year term of clerkship in a law office faced a "terrific problem" of getting articles.[34] Ultimately, her corporate law professor prevailed upon Fred W. Bissett to hire Wilson as his first female articling student. "I don't know what Professor Lorne Clarke had to do to get me in there," Wilson later exclaimed.[35]

An eccentric solo practitioner, Bissett worked out of a dingy Halifax office servicing impoverished criminal and family clients, while hoisting his feet on the desk and clicking his false

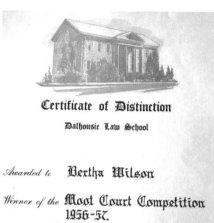

Smith Shield Moot Court certificate.

LAW SCHOOL DEBATERS — Named to compete for Dalhousie University Law School's highest extra-curricular award, the Smith Shield, are the four graduating law students shown above. They are left to right, David Bryson, Halifax, Merlin Nunn, Sydney, Mrs. Bertha Wilson, Halifax and John Charters, Halifax.

Newspaper clipping showing debaters at the Smith Shield Moot Court.

teeth. When courthouse observers saw Bissett and Wilson together, they could not help but make comparisons between the dishevelled, hunched, chain-smoking, talkative male lawyer and his new sidekick, the prim and proper minister's wife, as they stood to speak for prostitutes, drunks, and assorted criminals.[36] If she had complaints, Wilson never voiced them. She described Bissett as "a bit of a character and not the most efficient practitioner, but very experienced and very knowledgeable about the law." In sum, she said, "I enjoyed it very much."[37]

Wilson passed the bar examinations and received her call to the Nova Scotia bar in 1958. She had navigated discriminatory hurdles by adopting a quiet strategy of ignoring differential treatment, ever tactful, ever respectful of authority.

LAUDS WINNERS — Mr. Justice L. D. Currie, of the Supreme Court, congratulates John Cartres, left, and Mrs. Bertha Wilson, right, upon winning the Smith Shield competition of Dalhousie Law School.

Senior Law Students Capture Smith Shield

Mrs. Bertha Wilson and John Charters, two senior Halifax law students at Dalhousie University, are the new winners of the Smith Shield competition, top award in the law school for legal argument.

The award, an extra-curricular activity, was donated by Dr. Sidney E. Smith, a former dean of the law school, now president of the University of Toronto. The students are chosen for their argument and presentation of an appeal case.

The case, a hypothetical contract case, was argued before three judges, Mr. Justice L. D. Currie, A. G. Cooper, Q. C., president of the Nova Scotia Bar Society and R. A. Ritchie, Q. C., of Halifax.

Appellants in the case were Mrs. Bertha Wilson and Dave Bryson, both of Halifax, and respondents were John Charters and Merlin Nunn, Sidney.

The four students in the running for the award were chosen by a selected student committee of the Dalhousie Law Society on the basis of their presentation and argument of moot court cases held the previous year.

Newspaper clipping showing debaters at the Smith Shield Moot Court.

13 Law Graduates Admi

CEREMONY AT COURT HOUSE—One of the largest groups of law graduates in years was admitted to the Bar of Nova Scotia Friday. At left, above, are Gordon S. Cowan, QC, president of the Nova Scotia Barristers' Society, who made the motion for admission; Bredu Pabi, Ghana, West Africa;

:ted To Nova Scotia Bar

Mrs. Bertha Wilson, Halifax, and David Scott Fraser, also of Halifax. In the photo at right are William Bertram White, Halifax; Michael Donald MacDonald, Halifax; David Ward York, Ottawa,- and Ronald Newton Pugsley, Halifax. (Norwood photos).

A newspaper clipping of Bertha Wilson at her call to the Nova Scotia bar.

CHAPTER 6

L'Heureux-Dubé's practice in Quebec City and marriage

dmission to the bar was one challenge facing the early women lawyers. The bigger obstacle was a job offer. Rampant discrimination within law firms blocked most options. Many female Laval grads thought it so hopeless that they refused to apply.[1] Only one had previously entered private practice in Quebec City, briefly opening a solo office and then abandoning law for social work.[2] For Claire L'Heureux, who had no capital to open her own office, and no lawyerly or judicial connections, it was luck that turned the tide.

THE ALL-IMPORTANT FIRST LAW JOB

The unexpected opening sprang from the trouble L'Heureux had with her secretarial job in her last year at Laval. The position at Sun Trust, ideal at first, became untenable when her manager came to work drunk, made sexual overtures, and physically manhandled her. Although the manager's transgressions were common knowledge in the office, no one intervened to stop him; it was understood to be just part of life. L'Heureux quit in disgust and placed an ad in the *Quebec Chronicle-Telegraph* for another position. The man who hired her as a secretary for his two-man law firm was Samuel Schwartz Bard.

Sam Bard was one of two Jewish lawyers in the city's over-whelmingly francophone Roman Catholic legal community.[3] A thirty-eight-year-old native of Quebec City, fluent in French, English, Hebrew, and Yiddish, Bard had graduated in law from Laval as the only Jewish student in 1936. Contemporaries described him as "humane," "courteous," and "dignified."[4] His office on 771 St. Joseph Street East served a predominantly Jewish business clientele.[5]

An outsider himself, Bard upgraded L'Heureux's status to that of a full-time practising lawyer once she was called to the bar. In doing so, he joined a longstanding tradition of Jewish lawyers who hired female and racialized applicants across Canada.[6] Given the anti-Semitism in the province, some of L'Heureux's classmates were shocked when she joined Bard's firm.[7] As one said, that she was "obliged to indenture herself in a Jewish law office" indicated "the general attitude" toward "women *and* Jews."[8]

L'Heureux had grown up surrounded by an anti-Semitic culture, but she was thankful for Bard's generosity: "He hired me at a time when women lawyers couldn't get a job," she said, and the offer was "like gold."[9] In 1952, she became the only woman to enter private law practice in Quebec City.

THE PERFECT MENTOR IN A
GENERAL BUSINESS PRACTICE

One-on-one support from a senior male lawyer was often what distinguished women who succeeded from those who did not. When the law firm's clients were reluctant to deal with a woman, it was Bard who insisted, "Go see Claire. She'll settle that. She's better than me. She will be faster. I've too much to do here."[10] L'Heureux recalled that Sam Bard "trusted," "pushed," and "sheltered" her.[11] Even when she was reduced to tears, mortified

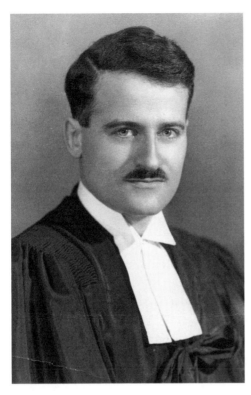

Sam S. Bard "L'Avocat."

over losing an important case, Bard was supportive. Decades later, she still recalled his response: "'Claire, it happens!' Not one word of criticism. I was crying and he would say, 'Count your blessings. Roll with the punches.'"[12] The unflagging mentorship that L'Heureux characterized as a "perfect match" would continue for more than a decade until Bard was appointed the first Jewish judge on the Superior Court in Quebec City in 1969.[13]

Combining solicitor and barrister work, L'Heureux drafted contracts and corporate by-laws, chased after bad debts, handled personal injury cases, dealt with landlord and tenant problems, and resolved employment and bankruptcy disputes. The workday began at 8 a.m., when Bard drove to L'Heureux's parents' home to give her a lift to work. Bard's daughter, who rode to school with them, had a vivid image of L'Heureux hopping into the car. "She was so full of energy, she *filled* the car.

Claire L'Heureux-Dubé practising in her law office.

She would start talking the second she got in, and when I left the conversation hadn't stopped."[14] The office closed around 5 p.m., but both Bard and L'Heureux frequently came back after dinner. No matter how hard Bard worked, L'Heureux worked harder. The janitor expressed concern that she was "always there."[15] The image of a relentless worker epitomized the early successful women lawyers. As one observer put it, the women of that era "had to be tough."[16]

DEVELOPING A DIVORCE LAW SPECIALTY: THE PRACTICE NOBODY WANTED

When L'Heureux was called to the bar, there were no family law lawyers. Divorce was forbidden under the *Civil Code of Quebec*, which stated: "Marriage can only be dissolved by the natural death of one of the parties."[17] In 1968, Minister of Justice Pierre Elliott Trudeau ushered in the federal *Divorce Act,* which provided Quebec spouses with their first opportunity for the judicial dissolution of marriage.[18] L'Heureux was fated to become the pre-eminent specialist in the new field.

Frankly, there was not a lot of competition. Most male lawyers eschewed divorce as odious, describing it as more "social work" than "real law," and expressing reluctance to represent female clients whom they deemed overly emotional.[19] The *bâtonnier*—the elected leader of the Quebec bar—insisted that L'Heureux deliver the first educational sessions on the new *Divorce Act,* because she was the senior woman practising in the city.[20] It was something of a rearguard action to manoeuvre the first female lawyers into the "soft law" of matrimonial relationships and child custody rather than the "hard law" of business and litigation practice inhabited by men. And it seemed cleverly designed to maintain the traditional gender hierarchies.

L'Heureux recognized as much and recalled feeling pressured to take up family law. She added, "People had no confidence in

Claire L'Heureux-Dubé, age 30 in 1957.

women to handle money. But with family law, they were ready to give women their heart if not their wallets." She resolved to make the best of it. "I said ok—now I'll do it right. And then I got interested in it and tried to make changes to the law, to make it into a respectable field of law, which it was not at the outset. I couldn't resist the challenge."[21] The floodgates opened and the firm took on as many as ten new clients a day. It felt to L'Heureux as if she were "divorcing half of Quebec City."[22]

She faced serious challenges with the elderly male Catholic judges, who were brazen in their opposition to the new divorce law. Chief Justice Frédéric Dorion publicly stated that he would never divorce anybody because it was against his religion. And L'Heureux dealt with judges who refused to see proof of cruelty in the bruises of marital violence. "They didn't believe the women," she claimed. "They thought they were exaggerating, that their stories were concocted." She called physicians to testify to the injuries and produced photographs of the bruises. When the judges still dismissed the evidence, she criticized them for thinking that there was "never enough fault."[23]

When the gender biases were impossible to ignore, she registered her frustration dramatically. One day, she got down on all fours exclaiming, "From what I understand, the woman must be on her knees with her husband walking on her, and you would still think it is not enough." She complained about alimony awards denied to poverty-stricken wives. When one judge launched into a tirade about the evils of divorce and accused ex-wives of spending their former husbands' money "with their lovers," she rose and insisted that her female client was "absolutely shocked" at his outburst. She demanded a transfer to another judge. It was granted.[24] Her actions constituted a courageous refusal to condone sexism in law, early evidence that female lawyers might begin to shake up the traditional male justice system.

When the province commenced a major overhaul of the *Civil Code of Quebec*, L'Heureux was appointed to sit on the committee examining family law.[25] Under her leadership, the final report recommended the promulgation of equality between husbands and wives, with both spouses holding "identical rights and obligations in marriage."[26] It was a framework that would see enactment in the revised *Civil Code* years later.[27]

L'Heureux's reputation grew by leaps and bounds during these years. A female lawyer practising in Montreal had high praise: "She was the lead in family law in Quebec—she was the top."[28] "She was not liked by the sexist judges," added one of L'Heureux's male law partners, but "she had influence and a certain radiance. She was brilliant, quick, and she was loved. She gave to the family law its letters of *créance–les lettres de noblesse* [credentials, letters of nobility]."[29]

MATRIMONY AND A FAMILY

In contrast to Bertha Wilson, L'Heureux deliberately delayed matrimony. "If I had married earlier," she explained, "I don't think I would have had time…to make my name. I was free to work twenty-four hours a day, free to do everything I wanted to do."[30] But romance was never far from her mind and among her many suitors, one took on a particular shine.

Arthur Dubé, the brother of a convent classmate, was a brilliant student, a skilled athlete, and a gifted musician, as well as "something of a rebel." A prodigy of the priests at the Rimouski seminary, Arthur had disavowed religion after graduating with a bachelor in science from Laval and a doctorate in engineering from the Carnegie Institute of Technology in Pittsburgh. It was when he took a faculty position at Laval University's new department of mines and metallurgy that he was introduced to Claire.[31] The two met at the Château Frontenac bar, where they began a spirited discussion over the existence of God. Claire, who was captivated by the fiery debater, deemed it "love at first sight."[32]

Arthur Dubé graduating
from Carnegie Institute
of Technology.

The courtship, which did not run smoothly, lasted for eight years. The couple would break up, reunite, and break off again. Claire's mother was particularly uneasy about the relationship, worried that marriage might derail her daughter's career and aghast at Arthur's penchant for gambling and alcohol.[33]

Thirty-one-year-old Claire L'Heureux and thirty-eight-year-old Arthur Dubé finally took their vows during a big snowstorm on November 30, 1957, in the Cathedral-Basilica of Notre-Dame de Québec, in front of fifty family members and friends. White wedding dresses were not the norm in Quebec, and the bride wore a dark, tailored, V-neck suit with a floral corsage and a string of pearls. At the Château Frontenac reception, the guests drank Mumm's champagne, admired the ice sculptures, and dined on salmon.[34]

After her marriage, the bride chose the hyphenated "L'Heureux-Dubé" for her name. "I wanted to keep my name because I had practised law as L'Heureux," she explained. "I didn't even ask Arthur, I just did it, and he didn't mind a bit."[35] Arthur

Claire L'Heureux and Arthur Dubé's wedding reception, 1957.

was supportive of his wife's continuing her law practice, proud of her intelligence and ambition, and mutually committed to independence within marriage. Two children, Louise and Pierre, were born in 1960 and 1964. With a combination of willpower, super-human energy, and a series of nannies, L'Heureux-Dubé hoped to keep both family and law practice afloat.

Claire L'Heureux-Dubé and Arthur Dubé leaving the church.

Claire L'Heureux-Dubé and Arthur Dubé at the Château Frontenac reception.

CHAPTER 7

Bertha Wilson's practice in Toronto

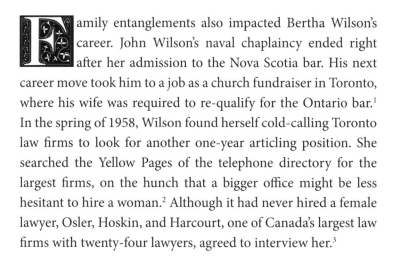amily entanglements also impacted Bertha Wilson's career. John Wilson's naval chaplaincy ended right after her admission to the Nova Scotia bar. His next career move took him to a job as a church fundraiser in Toronto, where his wife was required to re-qualify for the Ontario bar.[1] In the spring of 1958, Wilson found herself cold-calling Toronto law firms to look for another one-year articling position. She searched the Yellow Pages of the telephone directory for the largest firms, on the hunch that a bigger office might be less hesitant to hire a woman.[2] Although it had never hired a female lawyer, Osler, Hoskin, and Harcourt, one of Canada's largest law firms with twenty-four lawyers, agreed to interview her.[3]

"WELL I THINK, MY DEAR, YOU DESERVE A CHANCE"

The Osler lawyers were impressed by Wilson's Dalhousie grades, but even more so by her husband's naval service in Korea. One of the senior partners was "an army man and very service-oriented," explained Wilson. She recalled him as saying, "Well I think, my dear, you deserve a chance."[4] Another Dalhousie graduate who began work at Oslers in 1956, Purdy Crawford, may also have vouched for his female classmate.[5] Wilson remembered being a "little bit irked" that the Osler partners' offer came with a warning that it was for the articling term only, with no prospect for continuing employment.[6] Amused years later by her uncharacteristic bravado, she preserved her own option to exit. "Well," she told the partners, "I think that might be a mutually acceptable arrangement. I might not like it here either." The firm assigned her a makeshift office in a converted supply closet, screened from view by a pebble-glass door.[7]

It did not take long for Wilson to make an impression. The intellectual skill, speed, and meticulous attention to detail that had stood her in such good stead at Dalhousie made it evident that she was a "find." When the articling term ended before she could finish some important research assignments, the lawyers hastily conferred and told her to stay on.[8]

Like L'Heureux-Dubé, Wilson scored a crucial victory in obtaining her first law job, a tribute to talent and luck. Unlike L'Heureux-Dubé, she secured a foothold in one of the largest, most prestigious law firms in the country. Although some of her good fortune was linked to her husband's military service, much hinged on the conviction with which she put her résumé forward to a private firm. L'Heureux-Dubé, more timid in job searching, admitted that she would never have had the courage to apply for a job in practice, and was rescued solely by Sam Bard.[9] Toronto was a different market from Quebec City, a venue in which women had been admitted to practise a half-century earlier, and where a small number of intrepid women had preceded Wilson.[10] In 1959, Wilson became Osler's first female lawyer, an outsider in an insider firm.

A NICHE PRACTICE:
NEW VENUES FOR LEGAL RESEARCH

Osler's nineteenth-century roots as an elite family firm remained on full display in the late 1950s. Five of the eleven partners were family members, and the lawyers were overwhelmingly white, Anglo-Saxon, Protestant Conservatives. They came from upper-crust private boys' schools, many with linkages to the firm's major clients: the Toronto-Dominion Bank, Inco, Eaton's, Molson's, Kodak, and Coca-Cola.[11] The senior partner, Harold Charles Featherston Mockridge, was a descendant of the firm's founders Britton Bath Osler and Featherston Osler. Hal Mockridge's wife often repeated that her husband used to say that "Uncle Britt left him the firm." "Up until the time Mr. Mockridge retired in 1972, every leader of the firm was an

Harold Charles Featherston (Hal) Mockridge.

Osler," recalled one partner. "It was the typical Canadian version of a white-shoe law firm."[12] Yet it was soon clear that the "gentleman's club" was on the verge of transitioning into a diversified corporate-commercial law firm.[13] Wilson would have a pivotal role in the metamorphosis.[14]

As corporate clients multiplied in size and wealth, their legal needs shifted. Simple advice on transactional events was supplanted by ongoing, specialized assistance. The background research memos that the Osler articling students had prepared no longer sufficed, and Wilson's skills fit the changing specifications precisely. Her technically brilliant work, coupled with an extraordinary memory and uncanny speed, elevated her stature beyond what might otherwise have been viewed as mere library skills. What lifted her over the top was her grounded sense of practicality. As one of the firm's top litigators explained, "What she did for us at the law firm was to provide a deeply educated, highly sophisticated approach to the law, without being ignorant at all of the practicalities of the thing. Oddly enough for all the time she spent reading law books, she was a deeply sensible person."[15]

Like L'Heureux-Dubé, Wilson also had an appetite for punishing hours. She met crushing deadlines with remarkable efficiency. A colleague recalled that, "She very seldom drafted and redrafted. She would dictate into a machine and she didn't change it much."[16] Yet when a difficult memo was on her mind, she was not above getting up in the middle of the night and asking her husband John to drive her back to the office to double-check her sources.[17] And she had no trouble holding her own with senior colleagues.[18] One partner elaborated: "She was quietly spoken but she could stand up to people and wasn't about to be pushed off her position simply to accommodate some client's feelings." She had "done her homework" and she "knew she was on pretty good ground."[19]

Wilson was fascinated by technology and among the first to recognize its potential. In the early 1970s, when she learned

Bertha Wilson's passport photo, 1980.

of a pilot program in Ohio involving newfangled typewriters with rudimentary memory capacity, she crossed the border to retrieve the first machines capable of storing legal research. She set up a "huge Rolodex contraption" for capturing, classifying, systematizing, and cross-referencing research, opinions, legislation, and precedents.[20] Under her proficient leadership, Oslers became one of the first law firms in North America to experiment with mechanized data. Other firms scrambled to follow.[21] Had she been born into the digital age, Wilson might have joined the Silicon Valley visionaries.

THE EMERGENCE OF A "LAWYER'S LAWYER"

To many within the firm, it seemed natural that Wilson would forge a separate track at Oslers. Because her colleagues feared that their "old school" clients would not take kindly to being "advised on business matters by a woman," she did her work mostly behind the scenes.[22] She did not pursue litigation, although she later admitted that when she attended court as a research backup, she would think to herself, "I could do that.

The Osler Executive Committee, 1963. Left to right: Stuart Thom, B.M. Osler, George Mossey Huycke, Hal Mockridge, Gordon (Swatty) Wotherspoon.

Why didn't I ever take a crack at it?" As she was the first to admit, however, by then "it was too late."[23] Years later, one of the senior partners recognized that had things been different, she might have become a "first-rate courtroom lawyer."[24]

Nor did Wilson develop into a "rainmaker," networking externally to bring in new clients. She "seldom spoke up" in firm meetings, choosing to raise her points quietly later in private.[25] Her social interaction with colleagues was limited because she did not play squash or tennis, ski, or attend hockey, football, or baseball games.[26] Her outsider status was magnified because she defined herself as a "socialist" and joined the New Democratic Party.[27] It was something that made another partner chuckle as he recalled her criticism of capitalists and the Scottish inflection she would bring to her pronunciation: "cap-*it*-alist."[28]

Yet during her decades at Oslers, Wilson's practice matured into the research heartbeat of the firm. She became recognized as the epitome of a "*lawyer's* lawyer," who "leveraged credibility and social capital from the kind of activity one might associate with the most undesirable aspects of law practice."[29] The Osler lawyers sang her praises as a "superb opinion-giver" and few of them would make final decisions on key matters without checking first with her.[30] Eventually, even some of the clients would inquire, "Have you checked this with Bertha Wilson?"[31] Wilson described her function as "very much a helping role," stressing that she "wasn't going in to be competitive with the male lawyers. Quite the contrary, I was helping them with *their* practice with *their* clients." And, she added, "It was a unique niche, but it was also one that would not have offended their concept of the woman's role. And, of course, I fitted into it very well and it never troubled me to be doing it."[32]

One prominent colleague explained that "she was perhaps the most helpful person" he had "ever encountered" in his "years of advocacy."[33] When the firm took its first steps toward structural reforms, designed to replace the autocratic governance of generations of Oslers with greater internal democracy, Wilson

Prudential Building, housing offices of Osler, Hoskin, and Harcourt
1962–1977.

served as a key change-agent. She was, simply, indispensable.[34] Another colleague summed it up by saying,

> Well, she was both the brains and the heart of the firm while I was there. No serious decision was made without her signing off on it.… She sat in the centre of the firm and her clients were all of the partners. You could hardly get into her office for the people who were lining up to consult with her: Allan Beattie, Purdy Crawford, Ed Saunders, Bill Bryden, Stuart Thom, the Huycke boys…they were all just in love with her.[35]

It was a completely different practice from L'Heureux-Dubé's, in location, size, and field of expertise. The Quebec lawyer built her reputation as a small-firm litigator representing divorcing spouses in court. The Toronto lawyer built her reputation as a big-firm corporate-commercial solicitor in the backrooms of a towering high-rise edifice. Unlike L'Heureux-Dubé, for whom Sam Bard's mentorship had been the *sine qua non,* Wilson turned the tables and mentored her male colleagues, junior and senior alike. In seventeen years of blue-chip practice, and a far cry from the industrious articling student holed up in the supply cupboard, Wilson emerged to become the "brains behind the big names."[36] What would it take to dislodge her from such secure heights?

CHAPTER 8

Practising as a woman

espite the success both women achieved, all was not rosy. When she started, Claire L'Heureux-Dubé was the only woman to take up private practice in Quebec City that year. Bertha Wilson started as the only woman at Oslers. By the mid-1970s, when they left practice, the proportion of female lawyers had yet to top 10 per cent.[1] Both achieved success within a masculine milieu, with no role models to follow and no one to ask for advice. On parallel tracks, they advanced in very different ways.

Each woman embarked upon emerging practices rarely pursued by men. If the profession had to admit women, it was thought more appropriate that they be slotted into compartmentalized corners. L'Heureux-Dubé's success came in divorce law, a newly created practice that would be disproportionately populated with female lawyers. Observers recalled that in the 1960s and 1970s, male lawyers "flicked their wrists" at family law, given the large number of female clients and the low fees anticipated.[2] Bertha Wilson's research practice was another new niche. Her specialty foreshadowed a pattern of directing women to the back offices, recessed from contact with skeptical male clients, to alleviate any concerns that women were competing with men.[3]

Were these career paths freely selected or were the two women nudged, steered, even pushed into them? Family law was not L'Heureux-Dubé's first choice, but in the end, she embraced its professional visibility. Wilson recognized that her research practice was "rather esoteric," but she believed that it was "well-suited" to her "propensities and temperament."[4] Had they been offered more prospects, perhaps both women would have opted for different careers. Yet ensconced in practices that others might have dubbed second best, they surprised even their most supportive allies with their achievements.

They did so by cultivating a ferocious work ethic that was the hallmark of most successful women of the time. L'Heureux-Dubé's late-night hours alarmed the janitor; Wilson's two-in-the-morning forays to the office disrupted her husband's sleep. Charlotte Whitton, who was elected the first female mayor of Ottawa in 1951, became famous for her oft-repeated quip: "Whatever women do, they must do twice as well as men to be thought half as good."[5] L'Heureux-Dubé upped the pace, insisting that it seemed more like working "three times as much and not even being acknowledged as equals [trans.]."[6]

"LA TIGRESSE" AND "RARA AVIS"

The concepts of "femininity" and "masculinity" are socially constructed and variable, but L'Heureux-Dubé and Wilson bumped up against tenacious presumptions as they attempted to chart their way. The *Roget's Thesaurus* of the period synonymized *manhood* and *manliness* with "courage," "fortitude," "valour," "prowess," and "audacity." Words it equated with *womanly* were "little bit of fluff," "softer," and "weaker vessel."[7] The profession prized the so-called male traits of dominance and aggression as tools of the trade, but if women were perceived as masculine, they were disparaged as nasty and mean-spirited. If they leaned too far to the feminine side, it could jeopardize respect from clients, colleagues, and judges. The early arguments that women's feminine demeanour would "unfit" them for the practice of law jumped up to bite them. And every day they faced gendered stereotypical assumptions based on their sexuality, marital, and parental status. L'Heureux-Dubé and Wilson were socialized to be female and perceived as such, but they had to navigate in a man's world. Here, the two women revealed themselves in surprising contrast.

L'Heureux-Dubé's reputation as a *"femme fatale"* commenced long before she became Quebec City's most prominent female lawyer.[8] One observer described her as "extremely desirable and almost sexy," a woman who "almost beguiled" people she met.[9] Colleagues described her as *"une femme charmante,"* whose social acumen was legendary and whose charisma pervaded every room she entered. But no abundance of charm could triumph in law practice without a measure of gristle. L'Heureux-Dubé was respected "because she was a fighter."[10] In the courtroom, as she put it, "I was not a woman. I was the enemy."[11]

Within the profession, some christened L'Heureux-Dubé with the nickname *La Tigresse*. She was not called *Le Tigre*, a title that might have conveyed bravery and heroism—in a man.[12] *La Tigresse* was a female tiger, a feline creature that combined jungle-like ferocity with sensuality. She did not object. She worked to sustain a precarious balance between femininity and the stereotypical masculine qualities of fearlessness and strength. It meant the invention of a new zone, blending femininity and masculinity, and it tipped traditional sex roles off kilter.

Wilson presented differently. Resorting to Latin, she described herself as a *Rara Avis*—a rare bird.[13] The phrase also borrowed from the animal kingdom, but with a gender-neutral image. Unlike L'Heureux-Dubé, she was never depicted as a *femme fatale*. A colleague told her biographer that Wilson was definitively not "a flirt."[14] A minister's wife with a conservative hairstyle, she was routinely attired in "dark V-necked jumpers

Claire L'Heureux-Dubé on holiday with Arosa Line Cruise. The cruise company was one of her clients and offered her a free trip as a business bonus.

with white blouses" or "severe" suits of "steel-grey tweed," low heels, and stockings.[15] One Osler colleague described her as looking "a bit like Margaret Thatcher...erect...well turned out, but probably behind the curve even for the time in fashion."[16] Another observer thought she might even have been "working at being under cover."[17] Her style seemed like a dress code modelled on the conservatism of men's attire, de-emphasizing femininity and meant to convey authority and gravitas to clients and colleagues. It raised the question of whether Wilson would have portrayed herself the same way in a different career, or whether it was an image she deliberately orchestrated to improve her level of comfort at the office.

Bertha Wilson at the office.

Wilson possessed an equal measure of L'Heureux-Dubé's trademark toughness and could turn "steel cold eyes" on people when necessary.[18] "[S]he had a bite to her, you know," explained one lawyer.[19] But her deportment was usually in keeping with notions of the "gentler sex": formal and deferential, her voice soft-spoken with a comforting Scottish burr.[20] Her colleagues described her as reticent, self-effacing, and "not ambitious in the normal sense."[21] She was "a very modest person," said one, careful "not to outshine the lawyers" who were advising clients. "In fact," he added, "she became something of a confidante to her colleagues, always ready to listen and console from the privacy of her office."[22] Still another thought that Wilson saw her job as keeping her colleagues "out of trouble," adding, "In some ways I think she mothered them. This is a woman who had no children. In another sense, she had a whole firm of children."[23] Commenting upon her matronly manner, one observer compared her role to that of a "den mother" or a "great-aunt."[24]

TEMPERED RESPONSES TO SEXISM

Both women were confronted with sexism in their practices. L'Heureux-Dubé faced some inside the courtroom as she tried to advance her clients' cases. She recalled that the judges, some of them "particularly detestable," would belittle the early women lawyers and "try to take advantage of them." As her practice expanded to include male clients, there were judges who embarrassed her in open court with comments such as "How come you represent a man today? You always have women." Some judges were also overly personal with female lawyers. L'Heureux-Dubé recalled, "They would say 'Oui, ma belle'—perhaps meant nicely, but really it was an expression of familiarity or contempt in a way." L'Heureux-Dubé knew that disapproval lurked just below the surface: "The impression was that I should be home caring for my children. I know they were thinking that."[25]

Bertha Wilson at the office in her trademark dark V-necked jumper and white blouse.

Wilson's experiences were largely confined to inside her firm. She was confronted with a male client who told her, "I don't want any bloody woman drafting my will." And she recalled how the faces of other male corporate clients "fell" when she "came through the door."[26] It took her nine years to become Osler's first female partner, several years longer than most of her male peers.[27] Some of her colleagues took to referring to her as "*the skirt*."[28] She was forbidden to travel on firm business with other lawyers, because Hal Mockridge had concluded that it would be unseemly for men and women to travel together. When Wilson questioned the policy, Mockridge insisted that John Wilson and the wives of the male lawyers must grant permission confirming that they were not "troubled by the joint business trips of their spouses."[29]

Like most of the early female lawyers, neither L'Heureux-Dubé nor Wilson spent much time focusing on the sexism they encountered. Dwelling upon unfairness could be paralyzing and counter-productive. Raising objections was seldom career en-hancing. Edra Sanders Ferguson, who practised with her father and two brothers in St. Thomas, Ontario in the 1930s, explained the better approach: "The best way to tackle prejudice is to ignore it. The more women complain about sex prejudice, the more they draw attention to being women, rather than lawyers or doctors or what have you."[30] It was something of an "ostrich syndrome," shared by many who coped with sexism by trying to minimize it.[31] There were simply too few female lawyers to mount any concerted challenge. They were all alone.

L'Heureux-Dubé acknowledged that law was "a gentleman's profession" in a "small community," and insisted that she was "not that kind of a feminist who said, 'I'm a woman, you are discriminating.'" She added, "I was not really conscious of discrimination against women at that time. [W]e accepted it as a fact of life. It was nothing that would spur us to move to the barricades."[32] Although Wilson successfully advocated a maternity leave policy for the female lawyers who came after her, she too responded to gender discrimination with patience and stoicism. She emphasized that she loved her "separate track" in research.[33] Her colleagues described her as a woman who "didn't force things" and had no trouble "blending in," someone who was "not inclined to ruffle feathers," and was "never strident."[34] A historian of the firm added, "She behaved, and believed, in being appropriate. She was willing to accept their ground rules. 'I know you're uncomfortable with a woman lawyer. Let's see what I can get done within that.'"[35]

When they launched their careers in the 1950s, L'Heureux-Dubé and Wilson were well ahead of the rebirth of organized feminism, and neither saw their role as jump-starting a wider movement to press for women's equality. L'Heureux-Dubé explained,

> I never thought of the fact that other women didn't have opportunities. When I was asked to help, I did, but I didn't have women's issues in mind. I treated my secretaries well. I had women clients, but I never had the idea that I was on a feminist mission. It was not in my parameter of views. The feminist movement was not advanced at the time, and I was not one who would have started it first. I had my career, my children. I was occupied twenty-four hours a day.[36]

Yet they were also on the cusp of change. A new generation of women was preparing to follow Wilson and L'Heureux-Dubé. Calling out individual and structural discrimination more directly, the newcomers would demand radical social and cultural change. Buttressed by their growing numbers, these women used collective solidarity to envision a transformed world in which sexism would be totally defeated. When they pressured the authorities to put women on the bench, it was the flamboyant francophone *femme fatale* and the proper Scottish den mother who were ideally positioned. Polar opposites in many respects, they were two talented, tenacious women, perfectly poised for elevation.

CHAPTER 9

First judicial appointments:
"No woman can do my job!"

he Canadian judiciary was a male bastion from its
inception and few saw anything amiss with that. The
brash sentiment voiced by one judge, "No woman
can do my job," said it all.[1] So how did Claire L'Heureux-Dubé
and Bertha Wilson obtain their first judicial appointments? In
1973, L'Heureux-Dubé was named the first woman to sit on
Quebec City's Superior Court. (She followed two other women
previously appointed to superior courts in Montreal and
Toronto.)[2] In 1976, Wilson became the highest-placed female
judge yet, the first named to the Ontario Court of Appeal in
Toronto. The irony was that feminism, a movement to which
neither subscribed, furnished the necessary push.

THE POWER OF ORGANIZED FEMINISM

The women's movement, emerging out of several decades of
relative quiet, surged in the 1960s.[3] Simone de Beauvoir's classic
treatise, *The Second Sex*, circulated throughout Canada and Betty
Friedan's critique of rigid gender roles, *The Feminine Mystique*,
become a national bestseller.[4] Some of the enthusiastic readers
chose to embark upon careers in law. While the number of male

law students in Canada doubled between 1962 and 1980, female law students increased twenty-four times.[5] In 1966, feminist advocates convinced the Canadian government to set up a Royal Commission on the Status of Women.[6] One of their demands was the appointment of women to the judiciary.[7]

The Commission's 1970 report affirmed the call for women on the bench and recommended dramatic changes to law, education, tax, child care, immigration, citizenship, women's prisons, the criminal justice system, the economy, the family, and the role of women in public life.[8] That year, le Front pour la libération des femmes du Québec demonstrated on Mother's Day, calling for abortion on demand while waving placards that read "Queen for a day, Slave for 364 days [trans]."[9] The Toronto Star portrayed the response to the Royal Commission as "more explosive than any terrorist's time bomb."[10] Prime Minister Pierre Elliott Trudeau, who had recently won an election on the promise of a "Just Society," recognized the winds of political change. His Liberal government would name the first women to the superior courts.[11]

Canadian judges are appointed by governments, which makes them, by definition, political appointments. The process could occasionally provoke controversy when the credentials of individuals selected seemed to reflect their political background more than their merits. The debate arose over whether, and to what extent, the government should undertake greater outside consultation. Historically, the process had taken place entirely behind the scenes, where politicians parleyed with lawyers and other judges in private. It usually meant that the judicial pool cloned itself, with powerful elites replicating the status quo. In 1967, Prime Minister Trudeau initiated a more formalized consultation process in which lists of names were sent for review to the Canadian Bar Association (CBA), an organization representing lawyers across Canada.[12] The justice ministers who appointed L'Heureux-Dubé and Wilson (Otto Lang and Ron Basford respectively) also hired a senior official to scout out contenders pre-emptively before compiling the lists.[13]

Edward Ratushny, who filled the new position under both ministers, recalled Lang's complaint that under the old process the minister would "get a nudge and a wink from a colleague in cabinet" and letter-writing campaigns without objective input. Ratushny was tasked with interviewing chief justices, attorneys-general, provincial law society leaders, and lawyers about the reputation of potential judges. His mission was to evaluate the feedback to ensure fairer decisions.[14] The review process had yet to include non-legal informants and no one suggested that there be public vetting of candidates.

For decades, the judicial selection process had adopted restrictive concepts of merit that took little account of diversity. The push was on to cast a (slightly) wider net.[15] Reflecting a new appetite for women in the judiciary, Lang told the Toronto *Globe and Mail*, "If I'm looking at an equal man and woman for an appointment, I'll appoint the woman."[16] It was a sentiment his successor Basford shared.[17] The politicians were in advance of the profession. Recognizing the power of the energized feminist movement and propelled by politically active women, they were willing to contemplate the first steps toward change.

L'Heureux-Dubé and Wilson were moving along twin tracks. They came from different provinces and there were different key players pulling the necessary strings. But there were very few women who had successfully completed the ten years of law practice required by the *Judges Act* for federal judicial appointment.[18] These two amply fit the bill.

JUDICIAL "FIRSTS"

The higher-profile L'Heureux-Dubé went first. She was already on the radar because in 1972, Trudeau had asked her to stand for election in her home riding of Louis-Hébert. It was the first such offer the federal Liberal party had made to a woman in Quebec, and most observers thought she would have made a spectacular

Claire L'Heureux-Dubé at her swearing-in with
judicial robes, sash, white tabs, and roses.

politician. However, L'Heureux-Dubé turned it down.[19] Her rejection of a political career, which made headlines in the Quebec press, only served to highlight her stature as the most senior female lawyer in Quebec City.[20] Honoured in 1969 with the designation of "Queen's Counsel" (QC), she had become widely known for her community work, *Civil Code* reform efforts, and her seat on the governing bar council.[21]

The main instigator of L'Heureux-Dubé's appointment appears to have been the woman who accepted the Liberal nomination for the riding that she declined. Albanie Morin, who sailed to victory in the 1972 election, was a former law client of L'Heureux-Dubé. She later entered law school herself, "inspired by Claire L'Heureux-Dubé's example." She believed that it was long overdue to name a woman to the bench and took her recommendation directly to Otto Lang.[22]

Lang, in turn, consulted Paul-André Crépeau, who was leading the ambitious project to revise the *Civil Code*, and Gordon Henderson, the prominent Ottawa lawyer who chaired the CBA's national committee on the judiciary. Both gave L'Heureux-Dubé a green light. Jean Marchand, the cabinet member who headed the Quebec caucus and had veto power over the Quebec judicial nominations that were forwarded to the prime minister's office, eventually signed on as well.[23] The order in council went into effect on February 9, 1973.

Wilson was less high-profile, but she was Osler's first female partner. She was also the first woman elected to the CBA national council and active with its Ontario branch on wills, trusts, tax, and charities projects.[24] She chaired several United Church committees, including one that had delivered a brief to the Royal Commission on the Status of Women.[25] As the senior woman in a rarefied environment, she had been named a QC in 1974.[26]

There appear to have been several key players in Wilson's appointment. Ratushny, who was searching for promising female candidates, spoke first with Stuart Thom, one of his regular consultants. Thom was the treasurer of the Law Society, a Liberal, and an Osler partner who worked closely with Wilson. Ratushny recalled that Thom "couldn't say enough good about her," describing her as "tough," "strong," and "meticulous in terms of getting things right," with a "lot of depth."[27] Osler partners Edward Saunders and Bill Bryden, and Borden Elliot lawyer William Somerville, who had come to admire Wilson's expertise when he argued a matter against Oslers, also interceded in support.[28]

Bertha Wilson in her judicial gown.

First in Canada

Woman named to Appeal Court

Bertha Wilson of Toronto has been appointed a judge of the Ontario Court of Appeal.

She is the first woman to be named to a provincial court of appeal in Canada.

She will replace Mr. Justice Walter Schroeder who was appointed to the court in 1955 and has reached the mandatory retirement age of 75.

Mrs. Wilson was born in Scotland and came to Canada in 1949. When her husband, a Presbyterian minister, moved to Halifax, she entered Dalhousie Law School and was called to the Nova Scotia bar in 1958.

After her move to Toronto, she was called to the Ontario bar in 1959 and began working for Osler, Hoskin and Harcourt. She is now a partner. A senior partner in the firm is Stuart Thom, treasurer of the Law Society of Upper Canada.

A member of the board of trustees of the Clarke Institute of Psychiatry, Mrs. Wilson has also served on various United Church committees, and was chairman of the church's status of women committee.

In 1970, she became the first woman to be elected to the Canadian Bar Association's national council and she has been active in planning groups with the CBA's Ontario branch.

Mr. Thom said the firm would regret her departure, but he commented that her excellence as a legal researcher and scholar will make her an outstanding judge.

Mrs. Wilson is not the first woman to be named to the Supreme Court of Ontario.

Madame Justice Mabel Van Camp was appointed to its other branch, The High Court of Justice, in November, 1971.

Mrs. Wilson's appointment is effective Jan. 2.

Undated newspaper clipping about Bertha Wilson's appointment to the Ontario Court of Appeal.

Perhaps the most influential was Ontario Court of Appeal judge John Arnup. Before joining the court, Arnup had acted as counsel for an Osler client in the blockbuster case of *Texas Gulf*. Arnup believed that his spectacular success at trial was firmly tied to Wilson's painstaking research and he promoted the nomination.[29] Cabinet minister Donald Macdonald, a Liberal politician highly respected by the Ontario bar, gave the final go-ahead before the name was forwarded to the prime minister's office.[30]

Without litigation experience, it was thought Wilson was better suited to an appellate court dealing with principles of law than a rough-and-ready trial courtroom. Trial courts heard disputes at first instance, listening to conflicting witnesses and their lawyers, assessing contested facts, applying legal principles, and then ruling for one side or the other. Appeal courts heard arguments from those who lost at trial. Their role was to determine whether the trial decision should be overturned because of errors in law. In the end Wilson vaulted even higher than L'Heureux-Dubé, to take a seat on the Court of Appeal on January 2, 1976.[31]

SURPRISE FROM ALL QUARTERS

Both L'Heureux-Dubé and Wilson appear to have been largely unaware that their candidacies were under review. At the time, there was no way to apply and no transparency at any stage of the process. This protocol was defended on the basis that the best people would rarely seek out appointments and would be put off by any public scrutiny of their stature.[32] A requirement for applications might also have forestalled the entrance of women because the early women tended to think a judgeship out of the question. L'Heureux-Dubé explained, "I don't dream about impossible things. [The judges] were all men in black robes. I didn't fit."[33]

L'Heureux-Dubé was taken aback by her appointment and had neglected to return Lang's phone calls for days because, as she told her secretary, she didn't know "any Mr. Lang."[34] Her former Laval classmates admitted that they could never have anticipated such news.[35] Her law partner described the announcement as "a surprise...to everyone."[36] Even her younger sister, Nicole L'Heureux, echoed the sentiment: "Were we surprised when Claire was appointed? She deserved it at the time. But yes, we were surprised!"[37] Wilson was the same, describing her appointment as "completely unexpected," "beyond her wildest imaginings," and "the most surprising thing" that had ever happened to her.[38] Hal Mockridge, the Osler partner who had been so skeptical of Wilson's hiring, was "stunned."[39] Most of her colleagues at Oslers were equally startled.[40]

The Quebec press treated the story of L'Heureux-Dubé's appointment as a novelty. An intimate portrait of the new judge in her Quebec City home, published in *Action Québec*, cast her as an articulate woman, freshly coifed and wearing green eye shadow, who spoke of the honour that surrounded judicial elevation. After scrutinizing her appearance, the reporter also mentioned L'Heureux-Dubé's young son, Pierre, "a sandy-haired devil" who scampered around tapping piano keys, blowing his flute, and complaining that he "hated to go to the shopping centre with his mother [trans.]"[41] It gave L'Heureux-Dubé the opportunity to stress that professional success must not come at the expense of family life. Presumably, it was designed to allay fears that she might be stepping outside the domestic role.

The Ontario press was more business-like. *The Globe and Mail* simply reported that Wilson had been named and recited a brief list of her qualifications.[42] The dining room of Campbell House, where Toronto litigators met for lunch, witnessed more heated exchanges. Osler partners found themselves accosted by lawyers demanding to know "who the hell this Bertha Wilson was."[43] One astonished Toronto lawyer complained, "Quite frankly, I always took her for some kind of high-grade librarian."[44] Another scoffed that the whole idea of a female judge was "nonsense," adding, "I never met a woman who was a good lawyer."[45]

Ratushny admitted that there was "resistance" to the first female appointments from the politicians, the bar, and the judiciary. He described it as a "hangover" feeling that women were "not as good" due to "decades and centuries of social conditioning."[46] One of Wilson's law partners tried to capture the context:

> There were men lawyers who would not have accepted a woman on the Court of Appeal as a sensible appointment no matter who she was, whether she had a halo around her head. Anti-feminine prejudice was very strong.... [Their] view [was] that women couldn't be good lawyers, couldn't be good judges. They were not built mentally to do the job. They were too emotional. A lot of the older lawyers in Toronto...couldn't imagine that a woman had been appointed. [They] just couldn't imagine it.[47]

One Osler colleague added that there was an "inbred disrespect of the intellectual capacity of females lurking somewhere in there," a sentiment he believed was reinforced by the historic absence of women on the bench.[48] John Brooke, a judge on the court Wilson joined, added laughingly, "They had no exposure to practising law with women. They had never been beaten by a woman in a courtroom!"[49] The naysayers seemed mystified as to how women could possibly fit.

None, even in their wildest imaginings, voiced the most preliminary questions about what it meant that "maleness" was so inextricably tied to judging.

CHAPTER 10

Claire L'Heureux-Dubé and the Quebec Superior Court

laire L'Heureux-Dubé's move into the Quebec courthouse was an intimidating prospect: one woman setting up an office alongside twenty male judges.[1] It represented a next step in exposing the maleness of law, but the preliminary challenge was simply to survive the entry. Instead of the flattering welcome traditionally offered during a judge's swearing-in ceremony, Chief Justice Frédéric Dorion ignored his new colleague and delivered a tirade against union leaders, irresponsible college students, and the demise of Christian society.[2] The chief justice was a man of "severe standards," who railed against divorce and abortion, and was rumoured to harbour pro-Nazi sentiments.[3] His brusqueness may have related to L'Heureux-Dubé's divorce practice, her long-time professional connection with Sam Bard, and her gender.[4]

Sam Bard, who might have been able to smooth her entry, was unfortunately transferred away to the Montreal Superior Court, and many of Dorion's colleagues shared his strong objections to a woman in their midst. L'Heureux-Dubé described the prevailing environment: "I was looked on by my peers as some kind of special animal. It was my impression that they felt I would never be able to do the job [trans]."[5] The angry muttering circulated so widely that even

Chief Justice Frédéric Dorion, circa 1965.

L'Heureux-Dubé heard the disgruntled verdict of her peers: "[T]hey can't *stand* her. She knows *nothing*."[6] As she explained, it felt as if she were "received like a dog in a china shop."[7] It seemed that her colleagues must be wedded to the idea that even one woman could fatally sully the sanctity of the male circle.

Even the titles did not fit. Male judges were referred to as *le juge*. The French word was masculine and required the article *"le."* L'Heureux-Dubé objected to being addressed as *Monsieur le juge*, the term most often blurted out by the lawyers who appeared in her courtroom. "I said, 'You can do anything to me, but don't change my sex,'" she recalled. Instead, she selected *Madame le juge*, a combination of gender opposites. "It took a long time before they got used to calling me Madame *le juge*," she added. "I was called Monsieur *le juge* for years, and I just joked about it." Some years later, Quebec feminists would insist upon "Madame la juge" in an attempt to disrupt traditional male-centric language. It was not a change with which L'Heureux-Dubé agreed. By the time the feminine article "*la*" became commonplace, she professed to be "too old to change."[8]

The baptism by fire continued. One of the first cases she was assigned involved a complicated application for an interlocutory injunction. It was a legally technical matter that pitted a water purification company, which needed to haul heavy equipment to the St. Lawrence River, against the port authority that had refused access to Crown land. The rumour was that Dorion was playing a "dirty trick" on her with such a tough assignment. The lawyer for the plaintiff dropped by L'Heureux-Dubé's chambers

Claire L'Heureux-Dubé at her swearing-in ceremony for the Quebec Superior Court with her male colleagues, 1973.

to insist that it was "not fair" to ask a new judge to adjudicate such an onerous case. He offered to go to the chief justice and "ask that another judge be appointed." Undoubtedly meant kindly, it underscored the dubious position of the region's first female judge. Although she was anxious about the case, she was more troubled by the offer to remove her. Hubris triumphed over apprehension, and she replied, "I'm going to preside over this and judge it. Forget it."[9]

Things worsened when she stepped into the courtroom and saw nine men seated in the front row, the full membership of the board of directors of the water purification company. "When they saw a woman, they panicked," she recalled. "Women don't know anything. She's known for family law. [It's] terrible. I could see it in their faces."[10] She took full notes of the arguments, and laboured for hours in the library researching the law. Then she penned a twenty-three-page judgment granting the injunction. It was a decisive opinion on a hotly contested matter, something that would become characteristic of her career as a judge.[11]

JUDGING ON CIRCUIT

In addition to her Quebec City trials, L'Heureux-Dubé was assigned cases throughout the Lower St. Lawrence. Her circuit hearings were primarily in Rimouski and Rivière du Loup, although she also sat less frequently in Baie Comeau, Sept-Îles, Îles-de-la-Madeleine, Chicoutimi, Beauce, and Trois Rivières. She loved driving to the far-flung courthouses, even on the narrow winding roads of the time. She would leave at 6 a.m. and drive three hours to Rivière du Loup, starting court at 9 a.m. Because Rimouski could take an extra hour, she would delay court until 10 a.m. Baie Comeau and Sept-Îles required a plane ride and a week-long stay. When weather grounded the planes, she would spend the weekend there.

Her heavy workload was complicated further by the sexist

culture in which she moved, where status and behaviour were always being filtered through the lens of gender. In each new town and courtroom, L'Heureux-Dubé was confronted with litigants, witnesses, lawyers, judges, and court staff for whom her femaleness was startling. "Being a pioneer is, in the end, having to prove oneself at every opportunity rather than being accepted on the face of one's previous achievements [trans]," she explained.[12] Discriminatory presumptions about women's incapacities followed her everywhere.

Claire L'Heureux-Dubé on the bench in traditional white tabs.

Some observers voiced concerns that L'Heureux-Dubé was tough on the lawyers who appeared in her courtrooms. It reflected the stereotypical assessment that men who were uncompromising were properly "assertive," while strong-minded women were unfairly "aggressive." It may also have been at least partly accurate. L'Heureux-Dubé's daughter, Louise, recalled riding in the courthouse elevator, embarrassed at overhearing several lawyers criticize her mother's severe treatment of counsel.[13] In 1979, a *Le Soleil* reporter noted, "She has a reputation for being demanding of lawyers when they appear before her." L'Heureux-Dubé's quick retort was, "It is because I am demanding towards myself [trans]."[14] The young girl from the convent who had incessantly quizzed nuns and classmates, peppering them with questions until she was satisfied, had not changed her tune.

It was something about which she was happy to defend herself:

> We had a party one day at [my former partner's] and one lawyer [told me] "lawyers don't like you." I said, "I can't stand bad lawyers." "You didn't do your job," I would say. "I know the file better than you. You go out and study it and when you're ready, I will come back to you." I was rough. I was not tender. I've never been tender on the bench. I was strict because the litigants had a right to be represented correctly, and I couldn't accept that a lawyer couldn't do his job. But good lawyers loved me.[15]

L'Heureux-Dubé found the most rigorous judicial task to be writing decisions. Here she drew upon her convent training in the classical French humanities to create a structural format in which she divided her reasons into sections labelled "facts," "law," and "solution."[16] She prided herself on efficient scheduling and on never wasting time: "I was never late for court. I was never late in writing a judgment."[17] She also found her judicial responsibilities easier to manage than her law practice, where the hours were unpredictable. "At the courts, it was nine to five," she explained, and then she would write decisions "until eleven." The "best thing" about being a judge, she added with laughter, "was you didn't have to bill your clients."[18]

THE DOCKET OF CASES

Quebec Superior Court had jurisdiction over a varied docket. L'Heureux-Dubé adjudicated marital separations, dealt with divorcing spouses, settled alimony obligations, and ruled on child custody. She sorted out the intricacies of registering civil judgments, assessed employment claims, dealt with zoning and property disputes, issued interlocutory injunctions against striking union members, and heard a variety of contract disputes. She quantified damages for motor vehicle collisions, ruled on personal injury suits, dealt with insurance indemnity suits, settled estate matters, and decided debt and bankruptcy disputes.[19]

She restricted herself to civil cases, the field she knew well from her years of practice. She mostly avoided criminal trials because she worried that her lack of prior experience hampered her, adding, "I was afraid of it. Probably the defence lawyers who criticized me [later in my career] would laugh to hear me say that."[20] Recognition of self-limitations rarely deterred male judges, many of whom adjudicated cases that were far removed from their earlier practices. And it did not deter reporters from questioning the lone female judge about her views on criminal justice. In front of the Press Club of Rimouski, she pronounced herself against the death penalty and in support of criminal rehabilitation. The reporters extolled her as "one of the notable personalities not only of Quebec's legal milieu but also in the 'clan' of Quebec society reformers [trans]."[21]

Her years on the Superior Court reveal a judge in full control of her courtroom. Cases arrived as a tangled mess of conflicting evidence, with litigants who were frightened, confused, combative, sometimes recalcitrant, and often bitter. She separated contested from non-contested facts and gave each case her thoughtful attention. Her decisions were carefully organized, tightly reasoned, and clear. Her opinions, almost all in French, were beautifully written. Under her proficient hands, the decisions emerged as a tribute to the rationality of the judicial art.[22] For those who feared that women's biology and socialization rendered them too emotional for a judicial role, it should have offered a stark rebuke.

What observations can be drawn from L'Heureux-Dubé's years on the trial court? Some of her rulings in family law demonstrated an early recognition of women's equality and a growing disregard for the sexual double standard. She delved more deeply into family disputes than other judges, calling children into her chambers for consultation in custody disputes, poring over expert reports from social workers and psychologists, and closely inspecting the financial implications of alimony claims. On the other hand, the rulings showed little evidence of iconoclastic tendencies. She spoke out in support of the separate responsibilities of the legislators and the courts: the former to create the law, the latter to apply it.[23] She was not opposed to paternal custody or to relieving some men from the burdens of alimony payments.[24] This was not the output of a radical reformer. It was the dossier of an intelligent, industrious judge, whose solid decisions were generally in conformity with established standards.

CHAPTER 11

Claire L'Heureux-Dubé: Family tragedy and the Quebec Court of Appeal

he stress of combining a judicial schedule with two children and a spouse, who left most of the parenting to her, posed many challenges for Claire L'Heureux-Dubé. There was no provision for maternity leaves for judges and she took just fifteen days off with each birth. After that, she hired full-time caregivers. She micro-managed the household chores and the meals. If the floors needed cleaning, she rose early in the morning to wash them. She settled for a sleep regimen of four hours a night.[1] She juggled multiple roles at a time when many insisted that female professionals could never successfully combine careers and domesticity.[2] Her family braved the prurient speculation of the neighbours and the press, who wanted to know how husbands coped without a stay-at-home wife and how a working mother could possibly measure up.[3]

Significant health issues worsened the situation. Both children, Louise and Pierre, suffered from severe asthma, necessitating frequent emergency trips to the hospital. Then Pierre was diagnosed with schizophrenia and bipolar disorder. A battery of specialists examined the sensitive and erratic boy, but none could offer effective treatment. He experimented with drugs, was arrested for stealing at age twelve, and was expelled

L'Heureux-Dubé family in 1969, posing for a *Le Soleil* story.

from school. Police officers called repeatedly to check on his whereabouts. L'Heureux-Dubé was summoned back from her judicial circuit time and again because of Pierre's transgressions.[4]

ARTHUR'S DOWNWARD SPIRAL

Meanwhile, Arthur was dealing with a deepening depression by self-medicating with alcohol, which intensified his illness. His university lectures impeded his drinking in the morning, but he would return home before noon and drink continuously until bedtime. Efforts to connect him with Alcoholics Anonymous failed. On July 11, 1978, eighteen-year-old Louise went downstairs to the basement to discover that her father had shot himself to death with his hunting rifle. Fourteen-year-old Pierre followed her down and witnessed the blood and destruction. The tragic news was relayed to their shocked mother, who aborted her trial in Rivière-du-Loup and drove home in agonized grief.[5]

L'Heureux-Dubé family at home in December 1977.

Memories of Arthur and Claire in happier times.

Word of Arthur's death became the source of relentless gossip: the blood-spattered basement ceiling, the consternation of young Louise and Pierre discovering the body, his wife's frantic drive home.[6] Yet L'Heureux-Dubé steeled herself to get through it. Family and friends rallied to offer support and Arthur's Laval colleagues arranged the funeral, but her sister Louise noted that "most of [Claire's] strength came from within, from herself."[7]

L'Heureux-Dubé insisted that there should be no pretence about the cause of death, which surprised her friends and colleagues.[8] Years later, she mused about the stigmatization attached to suicide: "Why do people hide suicide? [I guess that] it's the perception that it is a sin. I cannot see any other reason for societal condemnation of suicide. Since I'm not religious, [I] don't have those barriers."[9] It was a courageous decision that helped to forge a path for wider disclosure and compassion generally, although it would eventually lead to greater public scrutiny than she ever imagined at the time.

Determined to honour the brilliant man she had loved so much, she created a scholarship in Arthur's name and emphasized that no one should lose sight of the positive memories. "I think he was happier the twenty-two years he lived with me than he would have been otherwise," was her final comment.[10] It was a view that Arthur's brothers and sisters-in-law wholeheartedly endorsed.[11]

L'Heureux-Dubé threw herself back into her work. "[It helped me] to be busy intellectually. I think it was the greatest strength of my life, to be able to close off one aspect, and turn to my work. There was no point dwelling upon the suicide. And, of course...I had two children depending on me," she explained.[12] Her daughter, Louise, added, "[My father] struggled his entire life with depression and alcohol. I don't think he had a plan [or] knew what he wanted. He was just trying to survive. He ultimately failed at that. That part is just really sad." Years later, Louise also marvelled at her mother's capacity to continue, adding, "I don't know how she survived."[13]

ELEVATION TO THE COURT OF APPEAL

L'Heureux-Dubé did more than just survive. On October 16, 1979, three months after the anniversary of Arthur's death, she was appointed to the Quebec Court of Appeal, the first woman on that bench and, after Bertha Wilson, the second in Canada.[14] No applications were required and so, once again, L'Heureux-Dubé had no idea the appointment was coming.

A few months earlier, Prime Minister Joe Clark had led the Progressive Conservatives to their first government, albeit a minority one, in sixteen years and several influential Conservatives promoted her candidacy for the judicial vacancy. Martial Asselin, a senator in Clark's Cabinet, remembered L'Heureux-Dubé fondly from their shared Laval school days. Clark's Justice Minister Jacques Flynn, a lawyer from Quebec City, was well aware of her solid reputation as a lawyer and judge.[15] But the most important factor seems to have been the desire of both Prime Minister Clark and his feminist lawyer wife Maureen McTeer to find more female judges.[16]

Reporters seized upon the gender angle, a point that left L'Heureux-Dubé uneasy. She disclaimed any "special mission" and insisted that all she wanted was to be "a good judge," adding, "I have always claimed and affirmed that women had no special role to play in the Bar, in practice, and on the bench. A jurist is a jurist; a judge is a judge; a lawyer is a lawyer, whether a woman or a man [trans]."[17] But, demanded one reporter, was she appointed because she was a woman? L'Heureux-Dubé ducked the question, repeating that she did not agree with appointing women simply because of their gender: "I also think it is very bad *for women* to appoint a woman because of her gender. I believe that we must appoint any person, woman or man, strictly on the basis of competence [trans]."[18]

Yet suspicions were afoot that women had suddenly become the only candidates of choice. One Quebec lawyer described the perception by saying, "[T]he government wanted women. If a woman wanted to be nominated, she could just walk into that path. She was offered the spot."[19] It was correct on one level and L'Heureux-Dubé's success can certainly be attributed in some measure to that. But it was also not correct. For decades, competent women had been overlooked and women who could have distinguished themselves as lawyers, judges, and chief justices were blocked from entry. Finally, the urgent demands of the politically powerful feminist movement had motivated the politicians to search for women to appoint. Because there were just a few women who had the requisite qualifications, they got the offers. But to suggest that they were *un*meritorious ignored the toil and fortitude it had required to transcend stiff barriers in a resolutely male world. Some observers may have thought that the promotions for the first women came easily. That discounted what it had taken to rise to an eligible position in the first place.

L'Heureux-Dubé found the swearing-in ceremony a pleasant change from her painful experience at the Superior Court six years earlier. The warm speech from Chief Justice Édouard Rinfret, so different from the frosty remarks of Chief Justice

The Quebec Court of Appeal swearing-in: Claire L'Heureux-Dubé with her children, 1979.

Pictured with her former law partners, Jacques Philippon, Christine Tourigny, Sam Bard, Roger Garneau, 1979.

Dorion, reflected the success she had attained in diminishing the skepticism of her male colleagues.[20] In an emotional moment during her own remarks, L'Heureux-Dubé expressed deep sadness that her husband was not there to share in the occasion, his death still a searing memory for the family and friends who were gathered together in the courtroom.[21]

Judges of the Quebec Court of Appeal. Front row (left to right): George H. Montgomery, Marcel Crête, Chief Justice G. Édouard Rinfret, George Robert Whittey Owen, and Jean Turgeon; standing row (left to right): Rodolphe Paré, Laurent E. Bélanger, John A. Nolan, Claire L'Heureux-Dubé, Antonio Lamer, Amédée Monet, Fred Kaufman, Yves Bernier, François Lajoie, André Dubé, and Albert Mayrand.

A (MOSTLY) COLLEGIAL
APPEAL COURT EXPERIENCE

Unlike trial courts, where judges sat on their own, in the Court of Appeal judges sit in panels of three. Although some of L'Heureux-Dubé's new colleagues were supportive of her presence, a few obstreperous judges remained. George W.R. Owen was one of the latter, a "big bulldog of a man" who "hated the idea of women on the bench."[22] L'Heureux-Dubé had prepared carefully for one of her early hearings with Owen. After the lawyers presented their arguments, she asked them some questions for clarification. Owen made an exaggerated show of checking his watch; he had an appointment for lunch at 12:30 p.m. "Madam Justice L'Heureux-Dubé withdraws the question," he exclaimed and, jabbing her in the side, he motioned the panel to adjourn. Outside the courtroom, he exploded, shouting, "I'm not going to endure you asking questions like this." It was a flagrant display of bullying and, almost at the point of tears, L'Heureux-Dubé asked no more questions that day.[23] Justice Amédée Monet, a judge with a reputation as a serious drinker, also had an upsetting habit of challenging anything she said.[24] The tensions mirrored other disruptive interactions L'Heureux-Dubé would experience later on the Supreme Court of Canada.

As a rule, however, L'Heureux-Dubé was determined not to let minor incidents ruffle her. In a gesture apparently meant to be playful, Fred Kaufman, a judicial colleague she liked and admired, once gave her a quick slap on the buttocks.[25] The other judges regaled him with cries of, "Fred, you'll be sued!" L'Heureux-Dubé just laughed and said, "Oh, it's so nice. Oh, Fred…I miss it." Years later, she added, "I was the only one. I was not going to alienate everybody there."[26] It was a strategy that eventually won her the reputation of *"une femme attachante"* (an endearing woman).[27] She hosted dinners for her colleagues, she participated in the new pan-Canadian language-training programs being offered to French and English judges, and she entertained many of the legal and judicial visitors to the city. One colleague commented on how many of the judges came to like her personally, appreciating how much she "loved discussion, dinners with other people, [and that] she was just fun to be with."[28]

It was at a judicial education conference that Rosalie Abella, later appointed to the Supreme Court of Canada, first met L'Heureux-Dubé. "I heard her before I saw her," laughed Abella.

Claire L'Heureux-Dubé with white blouse and glasses, 1986.

"I was sitting having breakfast and there was a table of male judges from Quebec. I just heard one female voice and I looked up, and there was a woman going up and down the row—it was a long table, six guys on each side—just going around to each person, hugging, kissing, and laughing with each of them. She was irresistible. It wasn't something you normally saw at a judicial conference."[29]

The essence of the job was learning how to cooperate on decision-making panels, where three judges had to consult, negotiate, and compromise on the judgment. The best appeal judges had to be able to "act as a group," recognizing that it was problematic to be the "lone wolf."[30] As the "lone woman," L'Heureux-Dubé was at even greater risk of isolation. Failing to achieve agreement would be self-defeating, rendering her influence minimal. L'Heureux-Dubé's colleagues observed that she learned to excel at this process. As one explained, "We have to be a mixer to a certain extent, to exchange our ideas in a correct way, to be able to accept the other opinions of others, [and] to convince others that ours are quite good. I think she had all [those] qualities."[31]

There was little foreshadowing of the title she would attract at the Supreme Court as "the Great Dissenter." However, there were subtle hints in family-law cases when she sat with Owen and Monet. In alimony disputes, she felt her colleagues offered insufficient financial protection to ex-wives, and she insisted that lump sum awards were preferable to unreliable periodic payments from ex-spouses. When Owen and Monet claimed that lump sums should only be awarded in "exceptional" circumstances, she complained that they were wrong in law and went on to recommend lump sums whenever she felt they were appropriate.[32] She also rejected the historical preference for paternal authority within the family, ruling that the "wellbeing of the children" should be the deciding factor in child custody.[33]

For someone who had heard no criminal cases in the lower court, one of the new challenges was the large volume of criminal appeals. Here L'Heureux-Dubé generally agreed with her colleagues, issuing mostly unanimous rulings from three-person panels. In the few dissents, her opinions were evenly balanced between the Crown and the defence. There was no intimation of the reputation she would later develop as a judge who strenuously protected victims' rights in sexual assault. Nor was there anything to signify the equality rights champion she would later become. [34]

L'Heureux-Dubé's rulings on the Court of Appeal were essentially "formalist"—accepting the law as given, with the judge's task simply to apply recognized legal doctrines to the facts at hand. American jurist Richard Posner's explanation of "formalism" fit her decisions to a tee: outlining the opinion of the court below, noting the positions of the parties, summarizing the facts, locating the applicable legal rules, making detailed references to authoritative texts, and applying the rules extracted from these sources to the parties' arguments.[35] Her decisions were notable for their logical format, tidy organization, and succinct conclusions. As she had in the lower court, she continued to write almost entirely in French, a language she had perfected under the painstaking tutelage of the nuns.

L'Heureux-Dubé became, by all accounts, a highly successful appellate judge. Eventually, she even came to think of most of her colleagues as family. She praised them for their wisdom, empathy, and intellectual rigour. In retrospect, she would describe her years on the Quebec Court of Appeal as the "happiest time of my life as a judge."[36] Despite the glimpse of reform-mindedness in family-law cases, and the occasional dust-ups with a few colleagues, she overcame much of the outsider stigma that shadowed her earlier years as a judge. And she left behind a body of decisions that bore little imprint of the jurisprudential mark she would make in the future. Apparently, she was still just getting her feet wet.

CHAPTER 12

Bertha Wilson and the
Ontario Court of Appeal

ertha Wilson was spared family crises such as suicide
and juvenile criminality, but faced parallel skepticism in her first judicial appointment. Like Claire
L'Heureux-Dubé, she trod gingerly.

A CHALLENGING RECEPTION

Wilson's swearing-in ceremony was warmer than L'Heureux-
Dubé's at the Quebec Superior Court, but suffused with
references deemed appropriate to the fair sex. Chief Justice Bill
Gale welcomed three new judges that day. His speech about
the two men, Duncan Gordon Blair and Horace Krever, was
filled with references to their military contributions, brilliant
academic achievements, and public service. "And now we come
to our debutante," was his opening comment about Wilson.[1]

He identified her Scottish birthplace while adding that the
profession had been "invaded" from "all points of the compass."
The judiciary was anything but diverse at the time, but some
invaders were obviously more welcome than others, and Gale
remarked that he hoped Wilson's "delightful" Scottish accent
would "never wane." Although he said nothing about the two

"New justices sworn in." Standing left to right: Duncan Gordon Blair and Horace Krever, and Bertha Wilson, *Toronto Star*, 1976.

men's spouses, he emphasized that Wilson was a married woman who had followed her husband, a minister, to Halifax. It was a description bound to reassure the curious about her status as the dutiful wife of a man of the cloth. "Madam Justice Wilson is a person who has enormous intelligence and is blessed, up to this point, with a charming personality," he concluded.[2]

The title "Madam Justice" mirrored the dilemma that L'Heureux-Dubé had faced with *Monsieur le juge*. Gale's choice followed an earlier struggle over terminology. The first woman appointed in 1971 to the Ontario Superior Court in Toronto, Mabel Van Camp, had objected to the customary title "Mister Justice." Because she was unmarried, some suggested she be called "Miss Justice." This struck others as a short slip away from "injustice" and Van Camp had settled upon "Madam Justice" without an "e."[3] Wilson thought "Madam" too reminiscent of a bordello and would have preferred "Madame." Nonetheless, Van Camp's version stuck.[4]

Like L'Heureux-Dubé, Wilson later confessed that she had correctly suspected that not all her new colleagues were "receptive."[5] Apparently Gale had objected to having his court serve as the guinea pig to test the first female judges, preferring that the experiment "commence somewhere else."[6] He called a special meeting to give the male appellate judges a heads' up that the new appointee would be a woman. When Wilson's name was read out, "a chorus of *Bertha Who?*" rose in unison from the assembled group.[7] Wilson would later be quick to excuse the response as understandable due to her "behind the scenes" law practice.[8] But she was more concerned when she learned that one of the senior judges had "added balefully, 'No woman can do my job.'"[9]

Years later, John Brooke observed that his judicial colleagues were mostly former "litigation counsel," all of them from "the same mould," adding, "It was really quite a surprise. I don't think she'd ever really been in a courtroom. It must have been quite a shock to her, because it was a shock to us. [It] took a while, standing back and wondering about her."[10] Wilson was invading an all-male zone. Her professional path did not match the members of the club.

Brooke vividly recalled Wilson's first day in court, when she sat on a panel with him and Gale. The chief justice took him aside and said, "John, you look after her." "I didn't know what to do," explained Brooke. "So I walked with her into the courtroom and held her chair while she sat down. And she blushed and she turned around, put up her index finger and said, 'Don't you ever do that again.' The front row...all Queen's Counsel, just broke right out laughing." The room recovered, the case commenced, and Brooke emphasized that Wilson was ultimately "a great sport about it."[11]

Despite Wilson's ability to smooth it over, it was of a piece with Gale's swearing-in speech, graced with references to "charm," Scottish accents, and the peculiar allusion to a "debutante," more reminiscent of a coming-out ball for an ingénue. Gale, who was by all accounts amiable and gregarious, and Brooke, also a man of impressive and impeccable reputation, were both stumbling through new uncertainties over the rules of etiquette.[12] As Brooke explained, "I was always brought up to respect a woman. I would have held Bertha's chair whether sitting down at my dining room table, or sitting down in a courtroom, simply because I respected her. She was a lady."[13]

It may seem a minor thing to have provoked confusion and anxiety, a simple recognition of traditional rules of chivalry. And it was certainly preferable to the bullying L'Heureux-Dubé faced. But women who were struggling to become full participants in a male venue often felt that being singled out for "lady-like" treatment detracted from equal stature. As feminists would explain, women would happily open their own doors in return for a fair shot at a professional job or equal pay. Horace Krever, who observed that the chair-holding anecdote was retold in legal circles for years, understood the difficulty. As he remarked, Brooke "meant well," but "didn't realize that she was now a judge and not just a woman."[14] It was an astute comment. Judicial status seemed to have altered the essence of gender in some significant aspects. Whether gender might alter the essence of judging was less clear.

Mabel Van Camp had also fallen victim to scrambled signals at her first judicial meeting. The chief justice had asked her, the only woman in a room of men, to take notes. She interpreted the request as a gender-based deprecation of her new status as a trial judge. So she flatly refused and took no steps to soften her refusal afterwards. The male judges perceived her action as wrong-headed and the widely circulated story served to harden her outsider status. One judicial colleague described the general feeling as "Look, Mabel, get off it." In contrast, he stressed that Wilson "never had that edge about her. She didn't have any of this sort of brittle feminist approach."[15] It is possible that Van Camp's behaviour that day may have sealed any hopes for her elevation to the court of appeal. Musing about why Wilson received the first appellate appointment and not Van Camp, another male judge ventured that Van Camp was "perhaps a little bit set in her ways."[16]

Still, observers recalled that there was uneasiness over Wilson's presence and that colleagues exhibiting the "usual prejudice" would indulge in "all kinds of conversations when she was not around."[17] Arthur Jessup stood out among the judges as overtly hostile. Referring to Wilson as "*that woman*," he objected to sitting on panels with her specifically because of her gender. Wilson recalled his "great skill in ignoring her completely" along with his "stony-faced stare." At one point Jessup asked the chief justice to replace her on a complicated contracts case involving concurrent wrongdoers. The matter was "too complex for her to grasp," he told her. Wilson was upset, certain that the corporate-commercial expertise she had amassed during her years at Oslers uniquely qualified her for the case. "I think I know a bit about the subject," was her terse reply and she took her seat on the panel.[18]

"Strangely enough," reflected Wilson, "I found this quite distressing as I had great respect for his abilities as a judge."[19] As always, Wilson couched her observation in polite terms, but Jessup was one judge she was not prepared to forgive. The other male judges were. None of the men appears to have intervened with Jessup, upbraiding him for his sexist behaviour and chiding him to behave. Here the traditional rules of chivalry had no sway. Although they conceded that Jessup was a "rude" and "difficult" man who could be "negative about people," they looked the other way and were quick to emphasize that he had been a "good lawyer," had seen artillery service during the war, had a son who committed suicide, and was struggling with alcoholism.[20]

Arthur Martin, the judge famous for his encyclopedic knowledge of criminal law, presented different challenges.[21] Wilson's years at Oslers had not exposed her to criminal practice and she made a side remark one day to the effect that she did not find criminal cases "all that interesting." Her quip got back to Martin, who took umbrage over what he interpreted as a curt dismissal of his life's work. Wilson was upset to learn that a comment she thought had been confidential had been passed on to Martin. Her colleague John Arnup urged Wilson to seek forgiveness by asking Martin to tutor her until she could get "up to speed."[22]

It bothered Wilson that no one ever suggested to the male judges that they were deficient in specific areas of law, although in reality all of them were. It also rankled that no male judges were subjected to similar catch-up regimens.[23] But after Wilson worked her way through the copious texts and cases Martin assigned, they came to a rapprochement. With customary graciousness, she later described the experience by saying, "He was kind enough to prescribe me a course of reading, both textbooks and leading judgments, and to spend a great deal of his precious time responding to what must have seemed to him the most elementary questions."[24]

Things unravelled once more when the two sat together

on a murder appeal involving drug dealers, *R. v. Olbey*. On a panel composed of Wilson, Martin, and Charles Dubin, Martin took the lead. His judgment affirmed the trial conviction and dismissed the arguments of self-defence, provocation, and intoxication. Dubin, regarded as one of the most intellectually brilliant members of the court, enthusiastically signed on. Wilson did not. Instead, she wrote a strong dissent asserting that if the court had considered the relationship between intoxication and provocation subjectively, a lesser verdict of manslaughter might have been fairer. It set tongues wagging, an upstart female having the effrontery to dissent from Arthur Martin and Charles Dubin, and it too became a story that made the rounds for years. "I think she had a certain kind of stubbornness," noted Krever, who sourced the dissent as the cause of another rift with Martin.[25]

The Gale court, 1976. Bertha Wilson is fifth from the left in the standing row.

Judgment is reserved in property squabble by unmarried couple

OTTAWA (CP) — The Supreme Court of Canada reserved judgment yesterday on whether it can impose a trust on property that unwed couples accumulate during their relationships.

The request from Rosa Becker of Hawkesbury, in the Ottawa Valley, east of Ottawa, is the first to come before the Supreme Court of Canada and involves three farms used for beekeeping that the couple purchased during their nearly 20 years of living together.

Miss Becker was originally awarded 40 beehives from Lothar Pettkus and $1,500. The Ontario Court of Appeal varied the judgment, imposing a constructive trust and awarding Miss Becker a half interest in the farms.

Lawyer Barry Swadron, appearing for Mr. Pettkus, said there had never been any agreement that the two would share in the farms. Mr. Pettkus had his own bank account, all of the property was in his name only and the evidence was that Miss Becker herself didn't expect any property, he argued.

The two immigrated to Canada in 1955 and shortly afterward began sharing an apartment rented by Miss Becker. Evidence was that she paid most of the expenses while he saved enough money to buy the first farm.

The evidence also showed she took an active part in the beekeeping business and herself dug a trench for their septic tank.

They parted briefly in 1973 after a falling-out and the court was told that Mr. Pettkus "literally threw" $3,000 at Miss Becker. She also took an old car. She returned a few months later with $1,900 remaining. They parted permanently in 1974.

Ontario's Family Law Reform Act of 1978 recognizes the right of a married spouse to share in property built up during a marriage. It also gives a right to unwed partners to obtain maintenance.

Mr. Pettkus' lawyer said the courts should not intrude in areas where Parliament or provincial legislatures have acted, such as Ontario in the present appeal.

He also said that the courts should not impose a trust on any family where there is no legal document on which to base it.

Sidney Lederman, appearing for Miss Becker, said there was evidence that Mr. Pettkus was enriched unjustly at the expense of the work and money put into the business by his client.

He said the business could be viewed as a joint venture and Miss Becker was entitled to a fair share.

Mr. Justice Roland Martland asked what the case would be if a employer were enriched unjustly by paying poor wages to an employee. He wondered whether the lawyer would argue that the employee was entitled to a property settlement.

The lawyer for Mr. Pettkus said the appeal was similar to the Murdoch case in Alberta in which the court ruled against a wife who had worked building up a ranch.

News clipping of the Pettkus case, *The Globe and Mail*, June 24, 1980.

At this early stage, it was already clear that Wilson could take an innovative approach to law. *Becker v. Pettkus*, in 1978, dealt with the separation of family property.[26] Rosa Becker and Lothar Pettkus had lived as common-law spouses for decades, working side-by-side in a bee-keeping business. Rosa paid for the couple's rent, food, clothing, and living expenses. Lothar invested their business profits in land and separate bank accounts, all registered in his name. When the relationship dissolved, Rosa claimed half the accumulated assets. Lothar argued that the land and the business were his. Since title was in his name, traditional legal analysis would have dismissed Rosa's claim.

The infamous *Murdoch* case, decided by the Supreme Court in 1973 to national dismay, had refused another wife's similar request.[27] Wilson knew that Bora Laskin had dissented in favour of the wife in that case and she decided to give it a second try. Borrowing from Laskin's dissent, she used the doctrine of "constructive trust" to hold that Lothar should not benefit from "unjust enrichment." She split the capital and revenue of the business in half between two spouses whose joint effort had fostered the financial success.[28] Her sense was correct that the time for transformation had arrived. The Supreme Court unanimously affirmed her judgment.[29]

The *Bhadauria* case, in 1979, became even more notorious, one of the "best known judgments" of Wilson's career.[30] Pushpa Bhadauria was a Canadian citizen of East Indian origin who had a doctorate in mathematics, an Ontario teaching certificate, and seven years of teaching experience. Over four years, she applied ten times for positions at Seneca College. She was never interviewed. She claimed that each time the college hired someone of lesser qualifications who was not of East Indian heritage. Bhadauria had explored her options with the Ontario Human Rights Commission, an agency mandated to enforce legislation prohibiting employment discrimination. Bhadauria's experience

A landmark human rights ruling

For the first time in any country ruled by English common law, an act of unlawful discrimination is regarded with the same seriousness as a broken contract, physical injury or slander.

That's the meaning of the landmark decision rendered by the Ontario Court of Appeal in the case of an East Indian woman who claims she was denied employment by Seneca College because of her race. The court's ruling has nothing to do with whether the claim of discrimination in this case is or is not well-founded; that will have to be determined when the case returns to a lower court.

What the court has established, rather, is the right of any individual to seek remedy in the courts for alleged discrimination. It has decreed that racial discrimination is so pernicious, so dangerous to peace and order in society that its expression must be contained by making the perpetrator compensate the victim by paying damages.

Until now, the usual recourse open to someone who believed he was suffering racial discrimination in Ontario was to file a complaint with the Ontario Human Rights Commission, a procedure lawyers regard as a "second-class remedy."

The commission is a necessary and worthwhile agency, but lawyers see it as an administrative remedy, subject to changes in policy and emphasis with changing governments. In other words, when the commission is overseen by a minister who is militant in his support of human rights, the commission may be likely to accept more difficult cases. When the minister is uninterested, the commission may define its role more narrowly.

The right to sue, however, does not depend on the outlook of a minister or the priorities of his staff. The courts are available to every citizen without the need to ask anyone's permission. It is for the courts to decide whether the case has merit or the evidence is adequate. It is the expense of a lawsuit that prevents the launching of whimsical suits.

When the woman in the Seneca College dispute took her case to court, the college's defence was that there is no precedent establishing racial discrimination as a ground on which a person can sue.

The judge agreed with the college and ruled that. her only recourse was through the human rights commission. But this week's ruling by the Ontario Court of Appeal says the judge was wrong. Just because there was no precedent, doesn't mean that it can't be done.

But history shows that the effects of such court rulings in discrimination cases are much more profound than they first appear. When Mr. Justice Keiller Mackay, in another landmark Ontario decision, struck down restrictive covenants on the sale of private property in 1945, he helped set the stage for today's climate of tolerance and understanding.

Without that decision, our cities today would probably be divided into racially segregated neighborhoods, each at war with the other.

The essence of Mackay's decision was that no matter how precious property rights might be, they must yield to the higher demands of human rights.

Similarly, last week's decision makes clear that, according to the most fundamental and enduring law of the land, racial discrimination can no longer be regarded as a private matter, a question of personal preference. Assuming that the Supreme Court approves this ruling if it's appealed, this is a large step forward.

News clipping of the Seneca College case, *Toronto Star*, December 18, 1979.

with the agency, like many other claimants at the time, was hampered by its lack of resources, delay, and mismanagement. So she hired a lawyer to push the boundaries of the common law to establish a new "tort of discrimination."

The issue was whether the common law could be stretched to encompass this innovative claim despite the lack of precedents. Canadian judges rarely dared to develop new causes of action, but Wilson was undeterred by the novelty of the case. Writing for a unanimous panel, she noted that although no authority had yet recognized a "tort of discrimination," none had "repudiated" it. Then she added, "If we accept that 'every person is free and equal in dignity and rights without regard to race, creed, colour, sex, marital status, nationality, ancestry or place of origin' as we do, then it is appropriate that these rights receive the full protection of the common law."[31] It was a courageous position, that the right to equality deserved newfound protection under the common law, and it inspired an outpouring of support from legal scholars and lawyers.[32] Unfortunately, the same Bora Laskin who had sided with her earlier family law ruling overturned the judgment when the appeal from Wilson's decision came before the Supreme Court in 1981.[33]

Like L'Heureux-Dubé, Wilson recognized that she had to shoulder the difficult task of proving herself as the lone woman on the bench. She worked assiduously on her judgments, participated in working lunches and dinners at Osgoode Hall (the magnificent nineteenth-century building that housed the law society and the courts), attended decision-writing seminars, took French tutoring, and embedded herself into the culture of the court.[34] Where L'Heureux-Dubé's manner was effervescent, Wilson's was a study in courteous composure. As a male colleague explained, "She just put everybody at ease. People could say, 'Look at Bertha Wilson. Don't worry about another female appointment. They're fine.'"[35] Where L'Heureux-Dubé's judgments gave little hint of her future jurisprudence, Wilson's forays into uncharted territory offered more premonition of what would come. Brooke's characterization captured the dichotomy that Wilson presented. She was "always thoroughly prepared" and "someone who did her level best to fit in," he said, but also "firm," "opinionated," and someone who could be "very difficult." "She was a Scot," he quipped. "That's the easiest way for me to put it."[36]

CHAPTER 13

Appointments to the Supreme Court of Canada, 1982 and 1987

he top court represented the final barrier. In 1982, at the age of fifty-eight, it was Bertha Wilson who took the title of "first."

THE FIRST

One year earlier, Sandra Day O'Connor had been appointed the first woman on the United States Supreme Court, prompting MP Flora MacDonald to demand that Canada match that record. Justice Minister Jean Chrétien's reply in the House of Commons, that the government could find no qualified female, had provoked gales of protest.[1] The National Action Committee on the Status of Women struck a "Women Are Persons" medallion and vowed to store it for safekeeping until it could be presented to the first female appointed to the Supreme Court.[2] Feminist lobbying had helped to shape the patriation of the constitution.[3] The *Charter of Rights and Freedoms*, set to come into force in April 1982, transferred "sweeping powers" over social policy to the judiciary.[4] The unprecedented equality guarantee that followed in 1985 heralded a new era in the judicial engagement with human rights. Pressure intensified to appoint women judges.

CHAPTER 13 *Appointments to the Supreme Court of Canada, 1982 and 1987* | 147

The Supreme Court is a geographically representative body: three spots are marked for Quebec, three for Ontario, two for the West, and one for the East. The spot that opened in 1982 was for Ontario.[5] Of the names that surfaced in the press as rumoured contenders, the front-runners were Charles Dubin, Gerald Le Dain, and Bertha Wilson.[6] Dubin was thought to be the most distinguished jurist on the Ontario Court of Appeal. Bora Laskin, now Supreme Court Chief Justice, had been trying to orchestrate Dubin's appointment for years.[7] Le Dain was a bilingual, bi-juridical judge of the Federal Court of Appeal who had served as an influential dean at Osgoode Hall Law School and chaired the path-breaking inquiry into the non-medical use of drugs.[8] In a move that astonished many, Bertha Wilson edged ahead of both.

Dubin's star was the first to recede, although it is unclear whether this was because he preferred to remain in Toronto or because Prime Minister Pierre Elliot Trudeau disliked his ties to the Conservative Party.[9] Le Dain was the more durable

Pierre Elliott
Trudeau, 1975.

contender and the initial choice of the prime minister. It would take a series of interventions to get Trudeau to shift his sights to Wilson, the flagship candidate for those who wanted a woman.[10]

By law, Supreme Court judges are appointed by the Governor-in-Council (the Cabinet), but in practice, the decision-making power lies in the Prime Minister's Office.[11] And Trudeau was uncertain about appointing a woman. His government had charted the way in naming women to other courts, but the Supreme Court of Canada was of a different magnitude. Trudeau turned to Allen Linden, an Ontario Superior Court judge and long-time Liberal party adviser, to seek reassurance. He mentioned that he had been "thinking of appointing a woman" and was reading through Wilson's judgments. He asked Linden, "Is she the best person?" Linden, an expert in Canadian tort law, knew of Wilson's efforts in the *Bhadauria* case to create a new cause of action for human rights. "Wow, how fabulous!" he recalled telling Trudeau. "She's fantastic and a great writer. She has done great work on the court and knows a lot of law."[12]

But there was also a chorus of opposition. The same gender-based prejudices that had greeted Wilson and L'Heureux-Dubé's earlier judicial appointments surfaced anew. "Women judges have no place in the Supreme Court of Canada" was a refrain repeatedly voiced in public.[13] A senior political advisor recalled that the "establishment" in the Ontario legal community had been "shameless in making the case that [Wilson] wasn't 'ready,' and that there were other (male) candidates who were better 'qualified.'"[14] As so often transpired, terms such as "merit" were baldly asserted without further analysis.

The rumours dismayed Edward Ratushny, the former special adviser on judicial appointments, who was now a law professor at the University of Ottawa. He sent a confidential letter to the prime minister, emphasizing that Trudeau would have to face blunt questions if he did *not* select Wilson. Reminding Trudeau of Wilson's innovative *Bhadauria* decision, Ratushny urged Trudeau to dismiss any spiteful gossip from the "close fraternity of barristers," and added that the views of the bar "had nothing to do with the capacity of a Supreme Court of Canada Justice to carry out his or her duties." He urged Trudeau to "make history."[15]

What transpired around the Cabinet table where the order-in-council was signed remains a mystery. Ratushny was told that Trudeau simply announced his straightforward decision for Wilson, asked if anyone had "any objections," and then signed the order-in-council.[16] Others gossiped that Trudeau "wasn't that keen" and that "at least three members of the Cabinet fought manfully" against the appointment "because of a feeling Wilson was being appointed over more qualified men."[17] Without naming names, *Saturday Night* magazine speculated that, "The women in his office got to him."[18]

Two of the female ministers at the table offered first-person accounts. Judy Erola, minister of the status of women, recollected that Trudeau had initially announced his preference for Gerald Le Dain that day. She interrupted to stress that Wilson was the choice of equality rights champions inside and outside of government. Then Monique Bégin, minister of health and welfare, raised her hand to say, "I fully support that. It's about time." Both women recalled that Jean Chrétien interjected next, saying, "Prime Minister, the girls are right. You should appoint her." And with that, the tide had turned. Erola praised Chrétien's intervention, but emphasized that the victory was attributable to "the women of this country" who had demonstrated that they were "capable of incredible political force."[19] Her words gave well-deserved recognition to the feminist lobby that had successfully mobilized thousands of women across Canada to demand gender equality during the patriation of the constitution and the framing of the *Charter*.[20]

Jean Chrétien recalled that he had advocated for Wilson prior to the Cabinet meeting, but failed to convince Trudeau, who was just "not ready" to appoint a woman. When Trudeau arrived at the Cabinet meeting prepared to sign the order-in-council for someone else, Chrétien had challenged him:

I said to my colleagues, "I have a disagreement with the Prime Minister." Everybody was shocked when I said that. It was a bit gutsy on my part, to confront the PM in front of my colleagues. I said, "We cannot miss the opportunity to name a woman to the Supreme Court of Canada." It was not a long discussion. The cabinet supported me. In front of the cabinet, Trudeau backed down and we got Bertha Wilson.

Trudeau had promised the Chief Justice [Bora Laskin] that it was to be somebody else. He was embarrassed by that, so he asked me to call the Chief Justice myself: "You inform him, not me." The Chief Justice was pretty unhappy. [He] tended to be kind of stubborn about it. He wanted somebody else. He put down the phone on me.[21]

Undeterred, Chrétien phoned Wilson next, reaching her in Arizona where she was on holiday with her husband, and she accepted the position.[22] At the end of the day, Trudeau was the person who would go down in history for appointing Bertha Wilson. Le Dain would receive the next appointment to the top court two years later.

THE SECOND

In 1987, when a Quebec slot opened, the appointment was up to Brian Mulroney, who had been elected as Conservative prime minister in 1984. Many names were bandied about, but Montreal lawyer Yves Fortier, an Oxford-trained Rhodes scholar and former president of the Canadian Bar Association, got the first nod.[23] Despite his close friendship with Mulroney from the days when the two had practised together at the same law firm, Fortier turned the prime minister down.[24]

Behind the scenes, the feminist lobby that had been so

Bertha Wilson, Supreme Court of Canada portrait.

important to Wilson's appointment moved into overdrive. In 1985, women's leaders had expressed disappointment with Mulroney's first Supreme Court appointment, Gérard La Forest, concerned that the government not leave Wilson isolated and perpetually outnumbered by eight male judges.[25] Although it had not been his first impulse to select a woman, Mulroney objected to being cast as averse to the notion. "I think that the record will show that I appointed more women to Cabinet and to the bench than any prime minister in history," he claimed. "I thought it was an important thing to do." After Fortier's refusal, he instructed Justice Minister Ramon Hnatyshn that he "wanted to do this with a woman."[26]

According to the press, Claire L'Heureux-Dubé was the leading female contender, stronger than the other two under scrutiny: Louise Mailhot of the Superior Court and Montreal lawyer Michèle Audette Filion.[27] Mulroney was well aware of L'Heureux-Dubé's reputation since he too had graduated from

Prime Minister
Brian Mulroney.

Laval law school and practised in Quebec.[28] Partisan politics had no role to play, emphasized Mulroney: "I did not ever allow politics to enter the consideration in terms of Supreme Court of Canada appointments. I have no idea whether [Claire] was Conservative, NDP, or Liberal. I didn't ask."[29]

There was one final check with Chief Justice Brian Dickson, who had replaced Bora Laskin in 1984. "[B]elieving in no surprises, I always talked to Brian before I made an appointment," explained Mulroney. "[I] had him over to 24 Sussex for coffee, [and] said, 'Look…I'm down to a choice here for the Supreme Court…. [W]e have [a few] candidates and I think I am going to go with [L'Heureux-Dubé]. What is your view?'"[30] Dickson was not one to support affirmative action in judicial appointment. "I don't think it is any compliment to the particular group that we will have a minimum of, say, three women on [the court]," he would later say. "If they aren't the best persons to be sitting as judges of the court, then I think you cheapen the court…. If it is a woman who is truly outstanding in competition with any man, I think that is wonderful."[31] L'Heureux-Dubé, also a staunch opponent of affirmative action, would not have disagreed, although it was not a principle applied to the designation of seats based on geography, which seemed to have passed muster for generations without cheapening the court.[32] Nor did it address the multiple ways in which the concept of "merit" was riddled with discriminatory perspectives. In any event, Dickson must have approved Mulroney's choice because the next day the prime minister took the plunge.

On the evening of April 14, 1987, Mulroney reached L'Heureux-Dubé by phone. Unlike Wilson, who had accepted the offer outright, L'Heureux-Dubé was hesitant. She told the prime minister that she was happy at the Court of Appeal and preferred living in Quebec City to Ottawa. With his characteristic self-confidence, Mulroney insisted, "I'm going to appoint you and you are going to accept." He told her she had until 8 a.m. the next morning to decide. Years later, he explained that decisiveness was "one of the important elements in a magistrate," and if you "offer somebody an appointment to the Supreme Court and she is going to need weeks to decide, you've called the wrong person."[33] He was also anxious to make the announcement on the fifth anniversary of the *Charter*, three days away, a point that would later be heralded in the media.[34]

Upset by the haste, L'Heureux-Dubé agonized over the pros and cons all night. Before dawn the next morning, she placed a call to the Ottawa home of Supreme Court Justice William McIntyre, whom she knew well from his participation in judicial education circles. He bluntly advised her that "rumours were flying" that she was "trouble" and would "not be welcomed" at the Supreme Court.[35] This would soon become public knowledge when *Maclean's* magazine reported that her appointment had been "opposed by some Supreme Court judges."[36]

Claire L'Heureux-Dubé's former law partners, Roger Garneau, Jacques Philippon, and Sam Bard at the Supreme Court of Canada swearing-in ceremony, May 4, 1987.

L'Heureux-Dubé marked the phone call with McIntyre as "the turning point." "[I] never backed down from a challenge," she explained. "[I] decided right then to accept the appointment."[37] Mulroney met his *Charter* anniversary deadline with ease and took delight in announcing that fifty-nine-year-old L'Heureux-Dubé was one of three women appointed that day.[38] Her former judicial adversary, George W.R. Owen, was less pleased. Sitting in the judicial dining room in Montreal, he snorted, "They have appointed three women. Next time, dogs."[39]

Claire L'Heureux-Dubé with her children at the Supreme Court of Canada swearing-in.

CHAPTER 14

Contrasting family lives

They reached the pinnacle through parallel pathways. Yet their presence side-by-side on the top court cloaked diametrically opposed family lives. In this, the two women could not have been less similar.

BERTHA WILSON:
A DOMESTIC PARTNERSHIP OF EQUALS

"For many years, Bertha was happy to go where I went and to look after me," explained John Wilson. After the Supreme Court appointment, he felt it was "her turn."[1] Wilson had followed her husband from Aberdeen to Macduff, then from Renfrew to Halifax to Toronto. John had transitioned from parish work as a Presbyterian minister to a career in ecumenical church fundraising. By 1985, the couple had abandoned regular church attendance and John was working with the Consumers' Association of Canada. It was a post he left to accompany his wife to the nation's capital.[2]

And so, the Wilsons uprooted themselves from their modest stucco home in Toronto to a "fixer-upper" stucco house in Ottawa. The move entailed shifting their massive library, a

John and Bertha Wilson at home over tea, July 1985.

bibliophile's dream of books stacked wall-to-wall and floor-to-ceiling, with volumes on theology, poetry, philosophy, literature, law, political economy, and sociology, leavened with atlases, bird books, and murder mysteries.[3] A feature on Bertha Wilson in *Saturday Night* magazine extolled John's "magnificent collection of illustrated first editions of the Book of Job."[4] The couple shared a love of intellectual pursuits, read voraciously, and debated philosophical ideas that others found impenetrable. After one visit, their nephew recalled that the Wilsons had spent "days mulling over a single passage from Heidegger."[5]

In marked rejection of the "separate spheres" ideology, John and Bertha lived life as an egalitarian couple, even in their domestic division of labour. Bertha insisted upon doing the housecleaning as long as her chronic rheumatoid arthritis permitted, while John handled the grocery shopping and cooking.[6] They spent their summer holidays in a tiny, rented one-room boathouse in Bobcaygeon in Ontario's Kawartha Lakes district, listening to music and quietly reading through the classics from Austen to Shakespeare. The two enjoyed nothing more than cerebral conversations over John's home-cooked meals, complemented with good wines and occasional snifters of single-malt Scotch.[7] Bertha's cookbook contained their favourite recipes scripted in tidy penmanship: Tomato Juice Cocktail, Bean Pickles, Kidneys, Liver Casserole, Grilled Fresh Black Pudding, and Stuffed Haddock Fillets. Swiss Milk Fudge was one of multiple entries for fudge, clearly a Wilson favourite.[8]

In Ottawa, where Bertha was inundated with a flood of legal briefs, John volunteered for more tasks. He compiled a "clipping service" on legal and other domestic and world affairs that he felt should be brought to his wife's judicial notice. He chauffeured Bertha to and from court in their little silver Toyota, toting heavy briefcases laden with her documents.[9] One of Wilson's law clerks recalled that when John came to collect Bertha, he would linger in her chambers, chatting about where to find a good butcher, the excellent Rideau Bakery bread, and what to cook for dinner. Occasionally, he lamented that doing laundry cut into his time in the National Library researching left-wing social movements of the past.[10]

Some people described John Wilson as a "house-husband," a role bound to draw attention in late-twentieth-century Canada, where this remained an oddity. In fact, after her Supreme Court appointment, to the outside world looking in the couple reverted to something approximating the separate spheres, only reversed. Not only had Bertha Wilson dared to invade the court's all-male stronghold, but she was violating gender norms in the private sphere as well. When men were expected to be the breadwinner and wives the primary helpmate, this led to sexist assumptions about toppled gender roles. The Wilsons were not perceived as an egalitarian "power couple," but as spouses with the traditional sex roles reversed. Some regarded it with a "scarcely concealed tone of incredulity."[11] Even supportive observers typically

The Wilsons at the International Association of Women Judges dinner,
Chateau Laurier, 1998.

described John as a "sweetheart" and "lovely," endearing terms more frequently used for women. The *Saturday Night* feature had characterized John as a "kind of intellectual Mr. Pickwick," a reference to a fictional Charles Dickens' character who is loyal, protective, and gallant, but also unworldly, somewhat simple, and innocent.[12]

People often presumed that Bertha was the brains behind the two. One male judge who knew the Wilsons from social encounters in Ottawa offered his opinion: "John didn't really do that well in his profession. He never really got a major church. I have a feeling that she was much smarter than he was, and he knew it, but he was grateful she was with him [and] he looked after her with love and support."[13] A former Osler partner described John as a "solid sort of guy," adding that he was "a good fellow, but we can't all be stars."[14] The assessment was not accurate, but reflective of stereotyped notions about men deemed less successful than their wives. It was not a sentiment that Bertha would have shared. To the extent that she was aware of this, it may also have upset her, although from all accounts it never bothered John. An executive legal officer at the Supreme Court observed that John "felt he had married an extremely intelligent woman" who could "really achieve a lot in the law and he thought that would be a wonderful thing for her. It worked for him and it clearly worked for her."[15] Another former law partner added that he had "known husbands who resented their wives' accomplishments," but that John was not one of them.[16]

It was John's task to serve as the "first male spouse" at the Ontario Court of Appeal and the Supreme Court; he became a male judicial "consort" before anyone had tangled with such notions before. John accompanied his wife to unending official engagements: receptions, state dinners, lawyers' conferences, and judicial education seminars. When the Wilsons were introduced, everyone automatically mistook John as the judge and Bertha as the spouse, requiring endless correction. At the judges' seminars, there was typically a "little extra program" for the "ladies," excursions to cultural and scenic venues deemed of interest for female guests.[17] One male judge recalled that John would take his place in the "ladies' program" and "completely charm all the wives." He added that John deserved a lot of credit for this. "He reminded me somewhat of Prince Philip, who was there one step behind, but her constant companion and supporter."[18] Others reported that John's status could cause "awkwardness," with some unfairly inclined to offer "a few snickers" and "look down their noses at him" because he was a "house-husband."[19]

Although the Wilsons were a "very private couple," John outshone his wife in sociability.[20] A friend who often celebrated New Year's Eve with the Wilsons recalled John as "charming" and "animated."[21] Others described him as a person with a "great memory for names," who "could come into a room and light it up," someone who was "the raconteur and the life of the party" while "Bertha was happy to sit back and let John talk."[22] Then, inevitably, she would join in with her "wonderful laugh."[23]

Jeannie Thomas, a family friend, with John and Bertha Wilson, Ottawa, undated.

That the Wilsons had no children was something that drew widespread curiosity but was almost never openly discussed. A former law clerk recalled that there were "all sorts of things people wanted to know" about Wilson, including speculation about why she had no children, but added that Wilson "was very guarded."[24] It took an audacious journalist to voice a speculation that the couple's childlessness was "not by choice."[25] It was a comment given credence in John Wilson's obituary, where it was noted that the Wilsons "deeply regretted having no children."[26]

Saturday Night described the Wilsons as "well-matched" partners who "grew together as they grew up," and their marriage as both "thoroughly old-fashioned" and "supremely modern."[27] The couple had survived a complete transformation, from Bertha the minister's wife to John the judge's house-husband, and those who knew them pronounced them "completely devoted to each other," something that was "quite lovely to see."[28] Rosalie Abella described them as "intellectual soulmates" and "as close a couple" as she had ever seen.[29] It was a relationship that indisputably buoyed up Bertha Wilson's success.

CLAIRE L'HEUREUX-DUBÉ:
UNENDING TRAUMAS AND TRAGEDIES

L'Heureux-Dubé's personal life was a study in contrast. She watched her parents' marriage unravel when her father, Paul, left her mother, Marguerite, for Montreal and a new life partner. Then Marguerite's multiple sclerosis immobilized her in a wheelchair. Marguerite's death in 1983 left L'Heureux-Dubé bereft of the individual who had been the "greatest influence" on her life.[30] L'Heureux-Dubé's daughter, Louise, studied law and practised briefly in Quebec City before moving away in an effort to cope with her grief over her father's suicide.[31] But it was the tortured behaviour of her son, Pierre, that brought the greatest misery to the emotionally over-burdened family.

"Pierre became impossible after Arthur's suicide," recalled L'Heureux-Dubé.[32] His schizophrenia worsened. He went on glass-smashing binges. He sought solace in alcohol and drugs. He skipped school so often that he never learned to read properly. At age sixteen, he was charged with breaking and entering. When he was sentenced to juvenile detention, he escaped. His mother pinned her hopes on the Montreal adolescent re-education centre where Pierre was sent in the early 1980s, but her son successfully obtained judicial release. All efforts at mental health counselling failed.[33] Throughout it all, L'Heureux-Dubé never lost hope. "She was so optimistic," explained her sister Louise. "Pierrot would get better. She was going to get control of that. Pierrot would straighten out."[34]

Pierre's problems added enormously to the strain of his mother's Ottawa years. Louise Dubé recalled how her brother would extract large sums from his mother: "She gave him $25,000 one time, and $10,000...it was awful."[35] L'Heureux-Dubé's sister Nicole remembered Pierre's threats. "[Claire] was a Supreme

Pierre Dubé, Quebec City.

Court judge. He was going, 'If you don't give me this, I'm going to say all these bad things to the journalists about you.' [He] threatened her all the time."[36] L'Heureux-Dubé's fellow judges observed Pierre's outbursts first-hand when he became disruptive inside the Ottawa courthouse.[37] Her former law partners, family, and friends worried that Pierre might possibly even kill his mother.[38]

In the fall of 1991, Pierre arrived at his mother's townhouse high on drugs and desperate for more. He drew a gun and started firing at the TV. L'Heureux-Dubé was so frightened that she fainted. An alarmed Pierre called 911 and the police arrived. "I was so under strain," L'Heureux-Dubé explained, "I don't remember if they asked me something or what, but they said, 'I think we better take him with us.' I didn't resist. I think I was at the end of the line."[39] Afterwards, she phoned her sister and wept.[40]

Pierre was charged with possessing a weapon for purposes dangerous to the public.[41] In October 1992, he pleaded guilty to the lesser crime of mischief. It helped that his mother testified that her son was experiencing severe depression and that she never believed her life was endangered. Pierre's defence counsel submitted a medical report stating that Pierre was making progress toward "turning his life around." Pierre received three years' probation. Reporters hovered over the details. It would have been hard enough to bear in private. The intrusive public glare made it more horrific.[42]

Within a year, Pierre was arrested again for threatening a shop-manager with a knife during an armed robbery. He contracted an infection in prison and in the winter of 1994, he was moved to a locked rehabilitation facility in Trois Rivières, where the authorities diagnosed flesh-eating disease.[43] Pierre was only thirty years old, but his body was succumbing to the deadly illness. L'Heureux-Dubé was notified and rushed to her son's bedside for what turned out to be the last week of his life. Pierre died on March 7, 1994.[44]

It took L'Heureux-Dubé four years before she began to recover from an all-consuming grief.[45] Her court attendant, who drove her to functions, remembered watching her sob in the back seat. "She would ask me to go around the block, and then she'd say, 'Let's get on with it, I'm okay now.' I think she got her strength from her mother. Claire was always talking about how positive her mother was. When things got tough, she'd swallow and say in French, 'Turn the page.'"[46] L'Heureux-Dubé's sister Louise agreed: "[Claire] had this really important job. Once she got into work, she must have wiped it all out. Just like my mother.... She developed a mechanism for turning things on and off."[47]

Her colleagues on the Supreme Court recalled how careful L'Heureux-Dubé was not to let her grief show in public. Gérard La Forest remembered that she "kept on working away—enough that many of us didn't even know about what happened."[48] Jack Major concurred, saying, "I think she was the most resilient person that I've met. That's the one thing Claire never did was seek sympathy."[49] Pierre's death was not something that L'Heureux-Dubé was able to discuss, even with Bertha Wilson.[50] The loss of her son on top of so many tragedies was a life-long wound, but she steeled herself to surmount every setback: "I was busy intellectually. I think that was the greatest strength in my life." L'Heureux-Dubé was, as she called herself, "a survivor."[51]

CHAPTER 15

Chilly reception at the
Supreme Court of Canada

Surviving their entry to the top court would require significant fortitude and tenacity from the first two women judges. Commotion attended Bertha Wilson's appointment from the start. When dozens of news outlets badgered her for interviews, she replied that any comments from her would be judicially "inappropriate." The press then regaled readers with a cartoon captioned "Mum."[1] Women's groups applauded her elevation as a "supreme decision" but critical voices soon surfaced.[2] Prominent law professors expressed concern that campaigns for women impeded consideration of "outstanding male judges and lawyers."[3] A leading political scientist told the *Toronto Star* that the female candidates had not presented "a bumper crop."[4] Claire L'Heureux-Dubé met much the same commentary. *The Globe and Mail* described her appointment as "not without detractors."[5]

Both women faced unprecedented speculation about their merit. The *Toronto Star* reported that some people were "privately questioning" whether Wilson had the "best qualifications for the job."[6] The newspaper quoted an Ottawa lawyer who labelled her "able but not spectacular."[7] One law professor claimed that if she were not female, Wilson "wouldn't even have been considered."[8] As for L'Heureux-Dubé, the *Star* advised

"Mum" cartoon, *The Globe and Mail*, March 10, 1982.

that "according to the experts," she might not have been "the most qualified jurist in the province."[9] A Montreal lawyer told *Maclean's* that L'Heureux-Dubé was "strong on facts but short on law."[10] A McGill law professor characterized her appointment as "controversial."[11]

These sentiments were rarely voiced about men appointed to the top court—many with varying attributes and talents themselves—who were customarily greeted with effusive praise from lawyers who jockeyed for position to celebrate new male judges. It represented a backlash over the very idea of female judges, a warning that entry itself would not signal a full victory for gender equality. No one publicly explored the baseline for the concept of merit, which was never articulated, debated, or applied across the board. Feminists saw it as an underhanded way of insisting that female candidates could never measure up.

EARLY DAYS AND UNEASY
JUDICIAL COLLEAGUES

Wilson and L'Heureux-Dubé had worked hard to find collegiality on their previous courts. Now all the signs indicated that they would be starting afresh. At Wilson's swearing-in ceremony, Chief Justice Bora Laskin's nervousness over her appointment was "disappointingly obvious."[12] At L'Heureux-Dubé's, Chief Justice Brian Dickson's demeanour was "cool and peremptory."[13]

Obviously, any newcomer to an elite institution is uneasy upon arrival. Those who represent "firsts" carry additional burdens. What would it have meant to make the first women truly welcome? Both Wilson and L'Heureux-Dubé acknowledged that their colleague William McIntyre distinguished himself in this respect, visiting them in their offices and conversing congenially as an equal.[14] Other colleagues failed. Perhaps they had no inkling that their actions unsettled the first two women

Supreme Court of Canada judges as a group, 1987. Front row (left to right):
William McIntyre, Jean Beetz, Brian Dickson, Willard (Bud) Estey, and
Antonio Lamer; back row (left to right): Gérard La Forest, Bertha Wilson,
Gerald Le Dain, and Claire L'Heureux-Dubé.

Chief Justice
Brian Dickson.

and were unaware that the masculine court environment was exclusionary. Perhaps they were mystified about what sort of welcome might have smoothed the path.

Some of the judges, however, were simply awful. Willard (Bud) Estey was disrespectful to Wilson in front of their colleagues and refused to speak with L'Heureux-Dubé for the first three months. "After that," recalled L'Heureux-Dubé, "he sent me a note saying, 'You've passed your probation.'"[15] Some relationships improved over time, particularly with Brian Dickson, whom both women came to regard with reverence and who came to appreciate his female colleagues in turn.[16]

Interactions with Antonio Lamer were more complicated. The first day that Wilson entered the judges' conference room, all the men rose in unison. All but Lamer. The woman who had objected earlier to being helped into her courtroom chair must have winced over the misplaced chivalry of the seven standing judges and wondered simultaneously what point the eighth was making.[17] When L'Heureux-Dubé arrived, the court

Antonio Lamer.

William McIntyre.

reverberated with rumours that Lamer had threatened to resign, vowing that she would be appointed "over his dead body." The law clerks overheard prurient gossip about L'Heureux-Dubé's sexual reputation and Lamer's quip that menopause made her unfit for the job.[18] Wilson would find that her relations with Lamer improved when she sided with his views on the rights of accused in criminal law and disintegrated when she chaired the Canadian Bar Association's Task Force on Women in the Legal Profession.[19] L'Heureux-Dubé would find her relationship with Lamer only worsened, to the point of open hostility.[20]

A CULTURE MARKED BY
GENDER AND ETHNICITY

The culture of the court reflected its traditional male milieu. Chief Justice Dickson never failed to address his colleagues as "gentlemen."[21] When the judges gathered in the conference room to discuss cases, some left the door ajar when they used the adjoining bathroom and male locker-room humour could surface.[22] Corridor talk turned mostly to male-dominated sports—hockey, football, and baseball. Wilson's efforts to turn the conversation to the symphony and ballet invariably faltered and she retreated into silence.[23] Both women found themselves left out of behind-the-door consultations with their peers.[24] Taken individually, these incidents might seem trivial. Repeated over and over, their impact was isolating.

Gender is never one-dimensional and ethnicity also affected perceptions. In Wilson's case, her Scottish roots gave her a leg up, softening her colleagues' regard somewhat.[25] Often describing it incorrectly as a "Highland accent," an "Edinburgh brogue," and a "Glaswegian lilt," people loved to mimic her accent.[26] Wilson's Aberdeen burr charmed her Canadian listeners—unlike, say, a Caribbean, Eastern European, or Asian accent might have done. One of her law clerks suggested that she was a "safe immigrant," whose success story could vindicate Canada's narrative "as a settler society."[27] "It made her different," explained another, "not as someone exotic or scary, but in an acceptable 'tea and cookies' kind of way."[28]

L'Heureux-Dubé was, by contrast, a francophone from Quebec, bilingual with a trace of French accent. Although she was descended from Canada's earliest settlers, her Québécoise identity amplified her outsider status in Ottawa. She experienced the court as composed of "two solitudes" with the English-speaking judges having virtually "no knowledge" of Quebec or its jurisprudence.[29] One of her law clerks emphasized that the dominant anglophone environment at the court exhausted francophones, who were required to operate within completely unfamiliar cultural references.[30] Another recalled that the anglophone clerks nicknamed L'Heureux-Dubé "Happy-Doobie," their irreverent translation of her name.[31]

When L'Heureux-Dubé entered a room, she greeted people effusively, embracing and kissing each on the cheeks in the traditional Québécois manner, causing some of her anglophone colleagues to shrink back in discomfort.[32] Her colourful and occasionally overwhelming mannerisms were attributed to

Supreme Court of Canada conference room.

her ethnicity. Some described her as a match for Lamer, with both Quebec judges perceived as "vivacious," "flamboyant," and "Latin."[33] But the reaction to those attributes was gendered. People saw Lamer as an outgoing man, displaying jovial *bonhomie*. L'Heureux-Dubé was understood as transgressive because of her gender.[34]

RESPONDING TO THE CHILLY CLIMATE

Wilson was well aware that as the first trailblazer, she would be closely watched. A formidable work ethic was one means she used to prove herself.[35] Her gruelling pace brought her in early and kept her immersed in preparation on the weekends. She drafted decisions in the morning, debated the law with her clerks in the afternoons, and then combed through countless legal references for hours.[36] One law clerk described her as "the most disciplined worker" he had ever seen, a judge who began each morning with a row of freshly sharpened pencils and then worked them down to dull stubs through rigorous editing of draft decisions she had dictated the day before.[37] L'Heureux-Dubé was notorious for burning the midnight oil.[38] She would get up at 6 a.m. swim, eat breakfast, and then work at the court from 8 a.m. to 2 a.m. She astonished her colleagues by moving a cot into her chambers. As she confessed to the press, she needed "very little sleep—just four hours a night."[39] Matching work ethics would eventually win both of them grudging recognition from their colleagues.

Whereas Wilson was seen as scholarly and reflective, L'Heureux-Dubé was perceived as mercurial and rebellious. Wilson took a deliberately cerebral, philosophical approach to judging. Reflecting a very different approach when asked how she decided cases, L'Heureux-Dubé pointed at her gut and said, "It comes from here."[40] Even their gift-giving habits were polar opposites. L'Heureux-Dubé provoked generalized astonishment when she bought a lacy Christian Dior negligée for her female law clerk. Wilson politely shook hands with her male clerk and handed him a box of shortbread.[41]

Wilson's philosophy was never to make a frontal attack on the culture of the court, but to work as "constructively as possible," refusing to let the "regrettable behaviour of others" influence her and trusting that things would "change over time."[42] One of Wilson's law clerks sensed that she might have been angered by the lack of respect from her colleagues, but never let it show. The same female clerk speculated that Wilson "shut down" parts of her persona in order to survive. It was a "sad" even "tragic" consequence of being "the first woman to shatter the glass ceiling," she added wistfully. "I remember thinking, there's just no soft landing here."[43]

Observers perceived that L'Heureux-Dubé "battled against that culture" more overtly.[44] One law clerk recalled that "things could get a little nippy at times," when Lamer and L'Heureux-Dubé exchanged "unpleasant emails, the judicial equivalent of Armageddon." The trademark charm that had subdued many others ultimately failed to mollify Lamer. The meltdowns occasionally grew so intense that the law clerks quailed over the shouting in the hallways.[45]

L'Heureux-Dubé was not afraid to request systemic change. She voiced concern that the judges were not provided with the lawyers' written briefs until the day before the hearing. Despite Wilson's warning that the judges were "set in their ways," L'Heureux-Dubé requested earlier distribution of the materials. In the judges' conference room, she stood up to lament that there was insufficient time for a personal life. Then she exclaimed, "What should I do with *my lovers*?" The startled judges laughed in unison, the written materials were produced earlier, and L'Heureux-Dubé described it as her "first adventure in change." It was a victory of sorts for the unconventional judge who took pride in her reputation as a *femme fatale*, and Wilson came by her chambers later to confess that she had loved the "s" at the end of "lovers."[46]

Yet, by all accounts, there was little opportunity for female comradeship. Wilson had apparently been disappointed when she met Sandra Day O'Connor, the first woman on the United States Supreme Court. She hoped they might have a chance to speak about shared experiences, but found the American judge reluctant to engage on the topic.[47] L'Heureux-Dubé found much the same with Wilson. Although Wilson was a "source of comfort," she was "reserved and a bit distant by nature," "not very talkative," and there was little day-to-day sociability.[48] Recalling that Wilson would leave the hearings and conference discussions to go directly "back to her quarters," L'Heureux-Dubé felt that while the two had "great respect" and "admiration" for each other, the prospect of a closer friendship and shared emotions was not on the table.[49]

In fact, nothing could fully overcome the weight of the outsider status. The executive legal officer at the Supreme Court saw first-hand the "stress" that Wilson experienced, describing it as "a little bit of an undertow" that he believed occasionally made her feel "hurt and mistreated as a woman."[50] In one of her rare press interviews, Wilson admitted that she never imagined "that the male judges took it for granted" that she was going to be "able to do the job," adding, "I think, maybe, that the view was contrary."[51] She was upset that her male colleagues bypassed her when they wrangled over decisions and wondered where on earth their private discussions took place. As she said to one of her law clerks half in jest, "I just don't know where they discuss it. It must be in the washroom!"[52] When Lamer learned that Wilson had criticized her exclusion from informal "closed-door consultations" of the male judges, he lashed back. Publicly denying that "cliques" had ever existed, he added that there was no point in "going to Bertha's office" because "she was stubborn as a mule."[53]

Characteristically forthright, L'Heureux-Dubé never shied away from criticizing the "very severe atmosphere" on the court. "We felt isolated," was how she summed it up. "We were not part of the gang."[54]

CHAPTER 16

Bertha Wilson's
Supreme Court decisions

The disrespect that confronted the first women was exacerbated by the unsettled times. Bertha Wilson's appointment coincided with the first year of the *Charter* and the advent of the court's responsibilities as the final arbiter of Canada's fundamental rights and freedoms. The *Charter* upset critics who complained that unelected judges were usurping the powers of a democratic parliament. Others cheered its potential to protect minority rights from the tyranny of the majority.

Faced with unprecedented demands, the judges struggled over their decisions. On the top court, they sat in larger panels, often with a full bench of nine but sometimes as few as five. In some cases, they all agreed and released a unanimous ruling. Other times they split and issued a "majority" decision along with a "dissent." The majority ruling determined the law, but dissents sketched possibilities for the future. Occasionally, a judge might vote with the majority on the result but for different reasons and then write a separate opinion called a "concurrence." The author of more dissents and concurrences than any of her male colleagues, Wilson drew upon the innovative legacy she left at the Ontario Court of Appeal and moved additional steps beyond.[1]

Bertha Wilson in her
Supreme Court of
Canada robes.

Some extolled Wilson as a principled, pragmatic, compas-
sionate jurist who put flesh on the bones of the new *Charter*.
Others decried her as a judicial activist who improperly trampled
upon parliamentary supremacy. Her jurisprudence has spawned
an outpouring of legal writing.[2] This chapter delves into a few
cases related to gender equality.

DOMESTIC RIGHTS:
SPOUSAL SUPPORT AND SELF-DEFENCE

In her earlier *Becker v. Pettkus* decision, Wilson endorsed an
equal division of property between spouses. In *Pelech v. Pelech*
in 1987, she examined spousal support.[3] When the fifteen-year
Pelech marriage ended in divorce in 1969, the spouses retained
separate lawyers to negotiate a support agreement. Under the
legislation at the time, Mrs. Pelech was entitled to ongoing,
permanent support payments. Mr. Pelech, a general contractor
agreed to pay his ex-wife a lump sum of $28,760 in resolution of

all future claims for maintenance. That agreement, signed by both spouses, was court-approved and implemented. Then their lives began to diverge dramatically. Mr. Pelech's net worth increased to $1,800,000 while his ex-wife was reduced to living on welfare due to psychological and physical illness. In 1982, she asked the court to order her ex-husband to pay additional support.[4]

Wilson heard the case with six male colleagues; Claire L'Heureux-Dubé had joined the court too late to join in. All seven judges agreed on the outcome and Wilson wrote their majority decision. To the surprise of those who had predicted that a female judge would demonstrate greater sympathy for divorced women's needs, she rejected the request for more spousal support. Hers was a decision to prioritize the need for certainty in marriage breakdown, to respect the autonomy of ex-spouses, and to herald a "clean-break" philosophy in divorce. In an opinion that few hailed as an advance for women, Wilson wrote:

> I believe that every encouragement should be given to ex-spouses to settle their financial affairs in a final way so that they can put their mistakes behind them and get on with their lives. It seems to me that where the parties have negotiated their own agreement, freely and on the advice of independent legal counsel…and the agreement is not unconscionable in the substantive law sense, it should be respected.
>
> Absent some causal connection between the changed circumstances and the marriage, it seems to me that parties…should thereafter be free to make new lives for themselves without an ongoing contingent liability for future misfortunes which may befall the other…. [T]he obligation to support the former spouse should be, as in the case of any other citizen, the communal responsibility of the state.[5]

It was a perspective rooted in "formal equality," based upon a belief that women and men were fully capable of negotiating contracts and equally capable of supporting themselves after divorce. Wilson was concerned about stereotyping women as inherently vulnerable, which she cautioned might "reinforce" biases that left them even more unequal.[6] It was also a vision of egalitarian marriage that reflected her own domestic situation.

Critics of Wilson's decision preferred "substantive" over "formal" equality, based upon a belief that sameness of treatment could result in unfair outcomes when individuals were rooted in different circumstances. They argued that support awards should take account of the financial consequences of marriage, disparate child-rearing responsibilities, bargaining inequities in family-law negotiations, and discriminatory education and workplace opportunities. The issue of who should rescue the financially vulnerable—the family or the state—also came under contention. *Pelech* was indicative of how complicated concepts of equality could be. It provoked fierce divisions inside the women's movement as socialist feminists, radical feminists, liberal feminists, and others debated the principles, practices, and strategies of equality.[7]

The *Lavallee* case in 1990 was more widely heralded as a leap forward in the legal treatment of battered women.[8] Twenty-two-year-old Lyn Lavallee was living in a common-law relationship with a man who had battered her for years. She had suffered severe bruising, a fractured nose, and multiple contusions. She claimed that she was terrorized and unable to break free of the relationship. One night, her partner pulled her from the bedroom closet where she was hiding, pushed and slapped her, tossed her his gun, and taunted her with the threat of "either you kill me, or I'll get you." She shot him in the head as he was leaving the bedroom. She was charged with murder, raising the question of whether her actions were justified as self-defence.

Initially, the Supreme Court judges thought that self-defence did not apply, with Chief Justice Dickson suggesting it was an

Bertha Wilson
at the Canadian
Bar Association
Annual Meeting,
1988.

"open and shut case."[9] The criminal law permitted recourse to
self-defence only if individuals were "under reasonable apprehension of death or grievous bodily harm," and believed "on
reasonable and probable grounds" that they could not preserve
themselves otherwise.[10] In this case, the attack was not in progress or imminent when Lavallee fired the shot. The prosecution
insisted that she could have saved herself by leaving the abusive
relationship.

But Wilson fastened upon the word "reasonable." How
should a court decide what conduct was "reasonable"? Should
the standard be the typical male barroom brawl? What would
self-defence look like if it reflected the reality of a battered
woman? She saw the need to dispel "myths and stereotypes" that
jurors might incorrectly hold. Her decision explained:

It is commonly thought that battered women are not really beaten as badly as they claim, otherwise they would have left the relationship. Alternatively, some believe that women enjoy being beaten, that they have a masochist strain in them. Each of these stereotypes may adversely affect consideration of a battered woman's claim to have acted in self-defence in killing her mate....

If it strains credulity to imagine what the "ordinary man" would do in the position of a battered spouse, it is probably because men do not typically find themselves in that situation. Some women do, however. The definition of what is reasonable must be adapted to circumstances which are, by and large, foreign to the world inhabited by the hypothetical "reasonable man."[11]

She noted later, with some surprise, that this case caused her to recognize for the first time that traditional self-defence law had been "essentially male oriented."[12] All-male judges had created all-male laws.

Wilson's colleagues initially thought she was "mad to think that there was anything that could even be said in [Lavallee's] favour."[13] Yet she asserted that the standard should be that of a reasonable battered woman caught up in a cycle of violence. Would such a woman have believed that killing a violent partner was the only way to save her life? On that test, Wilson concluded, Lavallee deserved an acquittal. L'Heureux-Dubé readily agreed. More surprisingly, Wilson was able to obtain support from the male judges for her landmark decision revising the rules of self-defence.[14] That she managed to change Dickson's mind, in particular, was seen as a powerful indication of her influence. As Dickson later stated, Wilson's contributions convinced him and others to see "how much weaker our legal culture has been for the dearth of women lawyers and judges."[15] Although some critics worried that the ruling opened up a "licence to kill," *Lavallee* was celebrated as a "triumph of gendered analysis in criminal law."[16]

CONSTITUTIONAL RIGHTS:
PROSTITUTION AND ABORTION

The *Prostitution Reference* represented one of Wilson's most important constitutional decisions, a dissent that offered a first step toward decriminalizing sex work in 1990.[17] At issue was whether the *Charter* could be used to strike down the criminal offence of "communicating," a charge typically laid against prostitutes who were negotiating with men in public for the sale of sexual services.[18] The male judges dismissed the *Charter* challenge, holding that although the provision infringed freedom of expression and liberty, it was a "reasonable limit" that was "demonstrably justified in a free and democratic society." Writing for herself and L'Heureux-Dubé, Wilson dissented.

The contemporary debate over prostitution was in its preliminary stages. Some argued that sex work should be decriminalized to remove all criminal penalties attached to the commercial sale of sexual services. Others argued for the abolition of sex work, their objective being to eradicate the prostitution system as a form of exploitation on the basis of sex, race, and class.[19] Wilson did not take a stance either way, noting that she could see the "economic purpose" for prostitution, but adding that it was a "degrading way for women to earn a living" and that the "real victim of prostitution" was the prostitute. Since Canada had never made prostitution itself a crime, she concluded that the "communicating" offence constituted a violation of freedom of expression, freedom of association, and the right to liberty. She would have struck down the offence as a disproportionate effort to prohibit the "social nuisance arising from the public display of the sale of sex."[20] Her dissent was an early harbinger of what the Supreme Court would later do in *Bedford*, decriminalizing the public sale of sex in 2013.[21]

Morgentaler, which decriminalized abortion in 1988, was often cited as Wilson's most "stirring" decision.[22] Dr. Henry Morgentaler had been performing abortions in his clinics in

Dr. Henry Morgentaler, 1984.

Montreal, Winnipeg, and Toronto for decades. He openly defied the *Criminal Code* provisions that made the procedure illegal except in an approved or accredited hospital and only after a therapeutic abortion committee of three physicians had certified that the pregnant woman's life or health was in danger.[23] Morgentaler had been subject to death threats, numerous prosecutions, and months in jail. With the introduction of the *Charter*, he claimed that section 7, which protected life, liberty, and security of the person, should be applied to strike down any law that compelled a pregnant woman to carry a foetus to term against her will.[24]

During oral submissions, the federal government lawyers argued that the only access to abortion should be through the duly constituted therapeutic abortion committees. In the question period, Wilson mentioned that she had "difficulty understanding" why the government thought it sufficient that there were "plenty of committees in Toronto" when there were "so few" in other parts of the country.[25] It was a salient point that underscored the glaring inequalities throughout Canada: many hospitals had no committees, some had committees that never met, some committees met but refused all applicants, most committees used wildly varying standards to define "health," and the process injected lengthy delays into an operation where time was of the essence.[26]

Six male judges sat with Wilson.[27] The majority struck down the criminal abortion law. Four of the men found that section 7 had been violated. Two dissented.[28] Wilson agreed with the four that the law could not withstand *Charter* scrutiny, but her separate concurrence went further. She concluded that the law violated women's right to liberty and freedom of conscience substantively, not just on procedural grounds.

Using language similar to *Lavallee*, Wilson wrote from a distinctly female perspective:

> This decision [to terminate a pregnancy] is one that will have profound psychological, economic and social consequences for the pregnant woman.... It is a decision that deeply reflects the way the woman thinks about herself and her relationship to others and to society at large....
>
> It is probably impossible for a man to respond even imaginatively to such a dilemma not just because it is outside the realm of his personal experience (although this is, of course, the case) but because he can relate to it only by objectifying it, thereby eliminating the subjective elements of the female psyche which are at the heart of the dilemma....
>
> The right to reproduce or not to reproduce...is properly perceived as an integral part of modern woman's struggle to assert *her* dignity and worth as a human being.... In essence, what [the present legislative scheme] does is assert that the woman's capacity to reproduce is

"When does life begin?" cartoon, *The Hartfort Courant*, 1981.

not to be subject to her own control.... Can there be anything that comports less with human dignity and self-respect? How can a woman in this position have any sense of security with respect to her person?[29]

Wilson's endorsement of women's reproductive autonomy was balanced against the state interest in regulating later stages of pregnancy. In early pregnancy, she believed that "woman's autonomy" should be "absolute." In later stages, perhaps "somewhere in the second trimester" of pregnancy, the state's "compelling interest in the protection of the foetus" could justify "prescribing conditions." Wilson chose to leave the timing "to the informed judgment of the legislature."[30] In fact, Parliament was unable to agree on new criminal prohibitions and Wilson was reportedly "very happy that this was the case."[31]

It was an outcome cheered in some circles, but not all. A *Lawyers Weekly* reader labelled her judgment a "straightforward feminist polemic."[32] A letter in *The Globe and Mail* complained that her reasons read "more like a feminist tract than an interpretation of law."[33] A flood of rancorous hate mail poured into Wilson's Supreme Court office, combining grisly death threats with "gruesome pictures of mutilated and aborted foetuses." Metal detectors and RCMP security were introduced for the first time in the court's history.[34] Although she found the hostility "discouraging," John's support bolstered her ability to withstand the venom. He reassured her that such challenges made "character."[35]

Wilson's singular voice marked a noteworthy harbinger of change.

Bertha Wilson.

Bertha Wilson receiving an honorary doctorate at the Dalhousie convocation on May 22, 1980.

CHAPTER 17

Claire L'Heureux-Dubé's
Supreme Court decisions

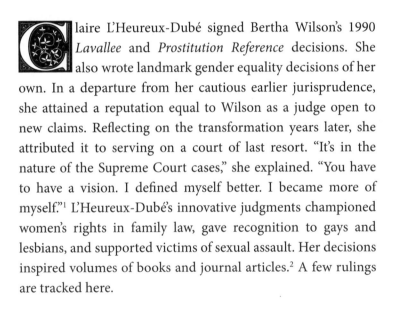laire L'Heureux-Dubé signed Bertha Wilson's 1990 *Lavallee* and *Prostitution Reference* decisions. She also wrote landmark gender equality decisions of her own. In a departure from her cautious earlier jurisprudence, she attained a reputation equal to Wilson as a judge open to new claims. Reflecting on the transformation years later, she attributed it to serving on a court of last resort. "It's in the nature of the Supreme Court cases," she explained. "You have to have a vision. I defined myself better. I became more of myself."[1] L'Heureux-Dubé's innovative judgments championed women's rights in family law, gave recognition to gays and lesbians, and supported victims of sexual assault. Her decisions inspired volumes of books and journal articles.[2] A few rulings are tracked here.

FAMILY LAW: FROM SUPPORT
FOR EX-SPOUSES TO INCLUSIVE FAMILIES

In *Moge v. Moge* in 1992, she delivered a judgment on spousal support.[3] Its effect was to reverse *Pelech*, Wilson's earlier decision espousing a "clean break" upon divorce.[4] Because Wilson had

Claire L'Heureux-Dubé's official photo, Supreme Court of Canada.

retired the year before, there is no way of knowing what she would have decided in *Moge*. But Canada's first two female Supreme Court judges appear to have held opposing positions. It underscored the divisive debates over family law.[5]

Zofia and Andrzej Moge, a married couple from Poland, settled in Winnipeg in the 1950s, separated in 1973, and divorced in 1980. The court ordered Andrzej, a welder, to pay $150 a month to support his ex-wife. Zofia, who cared for their three children, worked night shifts as a hotel maid. Child care responsibilities prevented her from obtaining language training or skills upgrading, and when her job terminated, she could no longer make ends meet. Since Andrzej was now earning four times the income of his former wife, the lower court ordered a small increase in his spousal support payments. In 1989, he requested that these obligations end.[6]

The *Winnipeg Free Press* quoted Andrzej as saying he had given Zofia "ample time to become self-sufficient." He asked the court to affirm Wilson's earlier clean-break analysis, insisting that his ex-wife did not deserve a "pension for life."[7] If women were pressing for equality, it meant standing on their own two feet when marriages ended. L'Heureux-Dubé disagreed. Social science data had demonstrated what she knew from her family law practice, that many women suffered financial devastation upon divorce, and that a "sink or swim" approach had contributed to the "feminization of poverty."[8] She wrote:

> Women have tended to suffer economic disadvantages and hardships from marriage or its breakdown because of the traditional division of labour within that institution.... These sacrifices often impair the ability of the partner who makes them (usually the wife) to maximize her earning potential because she may tend to forego educational and career advancement opportunities. These same sacrifices may also enhance the earning potential of the other spouse (usually the husband)

who, because his wife is tending to such matters, is free to pursue economic goals.[9]

Zofia Moge's responsibility for the children had eroded her ability to become economically self-sufficient, but family law could play a "limited role in alleviating the economic consequences of marriage breakdown."[10] In what commentators described as a "revolutionary" approach, *Moge* renounced the clean-break model and opted for long-term compensatory spousal support. Family law experts cited L'Heureux-Dubé's decision as one of the Supreme Court's "most important judgments in family law in one hundred years."[11]

Mossop was the first LGBT case to reach the top court in 1993, well before the rights of lesbian, gay, bisexual, and trans people were recognized in law.[12] Brian Mossop and Ken Popert, two gay

Ken Popert and
Brian Mossop,
Toronto, 1974.

activists from Toronto, sought inclusion in the legal definition of "family." They failed in that quest. But L'Heureux-Dubé's dissenting judgment, which cemented her reputation as "the Great Dissenter," spoke to the "aspirations and possibilities" of LGBT communities even if the law "wouldn't yet open the door."[13]

Mossop worked as a translator for the federal government. Under his union contract, employees could obtain bereavement leave to attend the funeral of an "immediate family" member. When Popert's father died, Mossop applied, indicating that Popert was a "lover (male) of ten years with whom I reside." If he and Popert had been heterosexual married or common-law partners, he would have been entitled to the leave. But his request was denied and he lodged a human rights complaint.[14] Neither Mossop nor Popert were supporters of same-sex marriage because they believed marriage to be a "repressive institution."[15] But they wanted to be recognized as a "family" in law.

Brian Mossop and Ken Popert at a gay rights rally, Toronto, 1994.

Lamer, by then chief justice, wrote the majority decision denying Mossop's claim. He emphasized that the federal government had not yet amended the human rights legislation to prohibit discrimination based on sexual orientation. Lamer believed that the denial of leave was based on Mossop's status as a gay man and he should not be allowed to side-step the gap by claiming a benefit indirectly under "family status." He refused to consider the definition of "family" further.[16]

By contrast, L'Heureux-Dubé's dissent drew upon contemporary values to redefine the family. Not all Canadians lived in traditional family formations, she noted, but all families—including Mossop and Popert's—should be enabled to function "free from discrimination." L'Heureux-Dubé criticized Lamer's decision as based on an underlying assumption that the grounds of "family status" and "sexual orientation" were "mutually exclusive." To ignore overlapping categories was to misconceive "the reality of discrimination."[17]

Claire L'Heureux-Dubé and Tony Lamer on the bench.

Mossop and his partner, Popert, later mused that by failing to fold gays and lesbians into protections offered under "family status," the judicial system had "missed a huge opportunity to nip the whole anguished gay marriage thing in the bud."[18] Mossop admitted that he had not expected to win the test case, but emphasized that he was particularly pleased with L'Heureux-Dubé's dissent.[19] On the eve of her retirement, when reporters asked L'Heureux-Dubé which judgment she was most proud of, *Mossop* topped the list.[20]

SEXUAL ASSAULT: PRIOR SEXUAL HISTORY AND IMPLIED CONSENT

It was her decisions on sexual assault, however, that brought L'Heureux-Dubé her greatest notoriety, transforming her into an icon and a lightning rod at the same time. It began with *Seaboyer*, her 1991 dissent on cross-examination in sexual assault trials.[21] Historically, the law had permitted defence lawyers to question women about their reputation for "chastity" and extramarital sexual acts. This deterred women from laying complaints and fed into a high rate of acquittals even when they did.[22] A feminist outcry led to reform in 1982, when the *Criminal Code* was amended to include a "rape shield law" that restricted the range of inquiry but did not preclude all questions. It was a compromise that satisfied neither feminist reformers nor defence lawyers.[23] Defence lawyers launched a court challenge in *Seaboyer*, claiming that the reforms violated the *Charter* rights of accused men.

The majority of the Supreme Court agreed, striking down the rape shield law on the basis that there needed to be *more* scope to cross-examine on prior sexual history. Beverley McLachlin had been appointed the third female judge in 1989, but Bertha Wilson had retired in 1991, again leaving just two women on the top court. To the astonishment of many, it was

McLachlin who wrote the majority decision (signed by six male colleagues) to permit wider cross-examination. It gave rise to soul-searching among those who insisted that women judges would create greater gender equality in the law.

In a ringing dissent signed by one other male colleague, L'Heureux-Dubé castigated the evidentiary rules that treated sexual assault victims "with suspicion and distrust."[24] Premised on the belief that "extramarital sexual activity was abnormal for women," courts had historically expressed "contempt for the unchaste female accuser," turning the inquiry away from the offender's conduct to the "moral worth" of the complainant. Women who had had "consensual sex outside of marriage" were presumed to have "a dual propensity: to consent to sexual relations at large and to lie." The problem, L'Heureux-Dubé explained, was rooted in gender inequality:

> Sexual assault is not like any other crime. In the vast majority of cases the target is a woman and the perpetrator is a man.… Unlike other crimes of a violent nature, it is for the most part unreported.… The prosecution and conviction rates for sexual assault are among the lowest for all violent crimes. Perhaps more than any other crime, the fear and constant reality of sexual assault affect how women conduct their lives and how they define their relationship with the larger society.[25]

The rape shield law should be unassailable under the *Charter*, she argued.

If anything, the range of cross-examination was still overly broad.[26] According to *The Globe and Mail*, the "passionate eighty-six page" opinion made L'Heureux-Dubé "an instant hero to women."[27] It also inspired the retired Bertha Wilson to pen a short personal note to her dissenting colleague: "*Dear Claire: Re Seaboyer—great judgement! I feel more relaxed about having left—hope you carry the day but not overly optimistic! Bertha.*"[28]

The next blockbuster came in 1998 with the infamous *Ewanchuk* case.[29] Ewanchuk, a forty-four-year-old man with four previous sexual assault convictions, lured a teenager to a trailer in a mall parking lot, under the pretext of interviewing her for a sales-booth marketing job. He asked her to give him a massage, which made her anxious, but she complied. Then he pushed her backwards, lay on top of her, and ground his pelvis into hers. He took his penis out of his shorts and stuck it between her legs, while rubbing against her vaginal area on top of her underwear. Throughout the ordeal, she repeatedly exclaimed "No!" and "Just stop!" often through tears. She eventually escaped and reported it to the police.[30]

When Ewanchuk was tried for sexual assault, the lower courts acquitted him. Wesley John (Buzz) McClung of the Alberta Court of Appeal dismissed the teenager's repeated cries of no, stressing that she lived in a common-law relationship and had born a child out of wedlock. He stated that "in a less litigious age, going too far in the boyfriend's car was better dealt with on site—a well-chosen expletive, a slap in the face, or, if necessary, a well-directed knee." He depicted Ewanchuk's advances as "clumsy passes" in aid of "romantic intentions" that were more "hormonal" than "criminal." He rebuked the teenager for dressing in shorts, adding that she did not enter Ewanchuk's trailer "in a bonnet and crinolines."[31]

When the appeal reached the Supreme Court, all nine judges concluded that the acquittal, based upon a notion of "implied consent," was wrong in law. Although it was a unanimous outcome, the judges issued three separate decisions. Jack Major's was signed by five male colleagues. Beverley McLachlin wrote a brief concurring opinion of her own. But L'Heureux-Dubé, who was incensed at McClung's intemperate and insulting language, wrote the lengthiest judgment. Charles Gonthier, the judge who signed her decision in *Seaboyer*, was the only one to join her this time as well.

L'Heureux-Dubé criticized the sexism in the lower court

Feminist demonstration at the Supreme Court of Canada, 1991.

ruling, which she attributed to "mythical assumptions" that portrayed women who said no as "really saying 'yes,' 'try again,' or 'persuade me.'" She objected to McClung's comment that the victim was an unwed mother living with her boyfriend. Did he intend to suggest that the young woman was "of questionable moral character?" She took exception to McClung's suggestion that a woman should have to "fight her way out" of sexual assault. She wrote:

> Complainants should be able to rely on a system free from myths and stereotypes, and on a judiciary whose impartiality is not compromised by these biased assumptions…. It is part of the role of this Court to denounce this kind of language, unfortunately still used today, which not only perpetuates archaic myths and stereotypes about the nature of sexual assaults but also ignores the law.[32]

Her spirited endorsement of female sexual autonomy was greeted with waves of support from women across Canada.[33] But McClung was infuriated. He sent an "open letter" to the *National Post* the next day. It was an unprecedented move for a sitting judge to criticize a Supreme Court decision in a public forum.[34] Yet McClung accused L'Heureux-Dubé of "feminist bias" and a "graceless slide into personal invective," asserting that "personal convictions" delivered "again from her judicial chair" could be responsible for the "disparate (and growing) number of male suicides being reported in the Province of Quebec."[35] The reference to suicide struck many as inexplicable until readers discovered that L'Heureux-Dubé's husband had committed suicide.

Some speculated that McClung's outburst cloaked an underlying opposition to women's entry into the judiciary. Supreme Court colleague Jack Major described the Alberta Court of Appeal as "an old boys' club," where "after a session [the judges] retired to somebody's office and mulled over the case [with] a

John Wesley "Buzz" McClung.

drink of scotch."[36] "When women started to invade that world,"
he explained, "they just [didn't] feel comfortable."[37]

Edward Greenspan, a famous Toronto defence lawyer, also
wrote to the *National Post* insisting that no Supreme Court judge
had "the right to pull a lower court judge's pants down in public
and paddle him." His letter continued:

> By labelling Judge McClung, in effect, the male chau-
> vinist pig of the century, the chief yahoo from Alberta,
> the stupid, ignorant, ultimate sexist male jerk, Judge
> L'Heureux-Dubé did an unnecessary and mean-spirited
> thing.... It is clear that the feminist influence has
> amounted to intimidation, posing a potential danger to
> the independence of the judiciary....
>
> Feminists have entrenched their ideology in the
> Supreme Court of Canada and have put all contrary

views beyond the pale. Judge L'Heureux-Dubé was hell-bent on re-educating Judge McClung, bullying and coercing him into looking at everything from her point of view.[38]

Greenspan's conclusion that L'Heureux-Dubé had "disgraced the Supreme Court" disparaged a judge in terms rarely heard in Canada before. One *Globe* columnist queried whether Greenspan would have "hit the same tone had the opinion been written by the guy," adding, "Bullying has its rules, just like a courtroom."[39] As if to prove his point, the name of Charles Gonthier never came up.

Some observers believed that Chief Justice Lamer should have come to L'Heureux-Dubé's public defence, protecting his court by publicly condemning McClung for his tirade. That was certainly L'Heureux-Dubé's view. Others felt that he should remain silent.[40] Lamer chose to hold his peace.

CHAPTER 18

The conundrum of feminism and the complexities of race

Bertha Wilson and Claire L'Heureux-Dubé were excoriated as feminists but persistently distanced themselves from the label. Wilson's biographer described her as "emphatically" and "avowedly not a feminist."[1] Wilson herself spoke of uneasiness with feminists who "demanded" that she should "use her position on the court to battle for women's rights."[2] L'Heureux-Dubé insisted, "I never belonged to a movement of feminists. I had plenty on my plate to work and have children. It was enough." And she added, "It's absolutely true I didn't want to be called a feminist because the perception was 'anti-men.' I am not anti-men at all."[3]

Both emphasized their domesticity. The *Toronto Telegram* had quoted Wilson explaining that she "loved to do housework," which she found to be a "nice change from legal responsibilities."[4] L'Heureux-Dubé cooked eggs over a hot stove for her family every morning, and got up early to wash the floors.[5] When *Action Québec* profiled her as an impeccable hostess presiding over a gracious home, it noted that, "She never felt the need to join the ranks of 'Women's Lib'.... 'For me, discrimination has never been a problem. I admit that it exists and that such movements can awaken the population, but I am under the impression that no one really believes in these movements,' she said. [trans.]"[6]

Claire L'Heureux-Dubé at the Supreme Court of Canada.

It was a message that U.S. Supreme Court Justice Sandra Day O'Connor also emphasized, reminding audiences that she had come "with her bra and her wedding ring."[7] Insistence upon feminine deportment and an aversion to the label "feminist" was a hallmark of many early female lawyers and judges.

Why might women who faced such significant sexism oppose feminism? In the first place, it must have been obvious that there were risks to self-identifying as feminist. Politicians were reluctant to appoint women's rights advocates to judgeships. Maureen McTeer, the feminist spouse of the Prime Minister Joe Clark, who had supported L'Heureux-Dubé's candidacy for the Quebec appellate court, acknowledged that "it would have been a barrier" if the nominee had been a feminist.[8]

The resistance may also have reflected a misapprehension of what feminism itself represented; opponents of the movement often portrayed it in skewed and pernicious ways. The early women lawyers and judges may also have disagreed with some of the strategies that feminist activists adopted and been puzzled by the diverse philosophies produced by feminism.[9] They

Claire L'Heureux-Dubé with her children, Louise and Pierre.

may have felt that dwelling on discrimination would just lead to anger and depression. Perhaps denying feminism was also a way of making themselves more acceptable to male colleagues. The institutions they joined barely tolerated the first women. Quite possibly it was so hard to find a foothold that proclaiming feminism became unthinkable.

Their aversion may also have reflected acquiescence to the notion that feminism was a form of "bias." Wilson asserted that if she went around "displaying a bias" it would make her "totally useless as a judge."[10] This assumed that judges operated from a value-free, point-of-viewless perspective. It masked the fact that a legal system constructed entirely by men may have passed for "objective" but often reflected masculinist ideals. It also misrepresented feminism, a movement that sought to eradicate sexist bias, not to establish a new hierarchy of female dominance.

SLINGS AND ARROWS

Yet distancing themselves from feminism did little to prevent attack. REAL Women of Canada was an anti-abortion group that opposed pay equity, universal daycare, and LGBT rights. L'Heureux-Dubé's *Ewanchuk* decision provoked the group to complain to the Canadian Judicial Council (CJC), an organization that reviewed judicial misconduct. REAL Women demanded L'Heureux-Dubé's removal from the bench, claiming that she had "consistently promoted her own feminist bias in her judgments." When asked about Charles Gonthier, who had signed the *Ewanchuk* judgment too, the group's spokesperson retorted that she had "no quarrel with him."[11]

REAL Women targeted Wilson as well. It complained to the CJC in 1983 when Wilson gave a lecture in Winnipeg on "The principle of sexual equality."[12] In 1990, it complained about her keynote address in Toronto titled "Will women judges really make a difference?" In the latter speech, Wilson delved into the

Bertha Wilson speaking at a Canadian Bar Association event, 1990.

question of whether women might have a positive influence on the law by infusing it "with an understanding of what it means to be fully human."[13] Ultimately equivocal on the answer, Wilson repeated some of the language about distinct female perspectives from her decisions. Despite Wilson's characteristic "dry" and "measured" delivery, her cautious presentation had a "magical" effect upon an overflow audience, who "erupted into a standing, cheering ovation."[14] REAL Women rushed to call for Wilson's removal from the bench.[15]

REAL Women also complained about Wilson's *Morgentaler* ruling, lambasting the lone female judge although a majority of her male colleagues had ruled for the same outcome. Wilson was a "childless woman," the group insisted, so she could not "possibly understand anything about childbirth."[16] A different anti-abortion group complained when the National Action Committee on the Status of Women awarded Wilson a medallion to commemorate the historic "Persons Case."[17]

Canada

REAL Women file protest against high court justice

By Stephen Bindman
Southam News

The conservative group REAL Women filed a formal complaint Tuesday against Madame Justice Bertha Wilson of the Supreme Court of Canada over her remarks last week about male bias in the law.

The self-described pro-family organization has asked the Canadian Judicial Council to recommend the removal of Wilson from the top court because of her "biased and improper" comments in a speech last week.

"Her presence on the court representing the views of a special-interest group instead of impartially and objectively applying the law on behalf of all Canadians is unacceptable," the group said.

Wilson, the first woman appointed to the Supreme Court, said some aspects of Canadian law are so biased in favor of men, they are "little short of ludicrous" and cry out for change.

Bertha Wilson
Cited male bias in legal system

Wilson also called for more courses for judges on gender issues, warning recent events have led to the inescapable conclusion that "in some respects our existing system of justice has been found wanting."

Wilson cited American studies that show sexism is the underly-

ing premise in many judgments and that "gender-based myths, biases and stereotypes are deeply embedded" in the attitudes of many male judges. Others have found that female lawyers are often subject to sexist comments and inappropriate jokes, Wilson said.

But REAL Women (Realistic, Equal, Active for Life) said Wilson's failure to understand that the "views of a few vocal feminists" do not represent the views of all Canadian women is "deeply disturbing.

"(It) indicates her inability, or alternately, her unwillingness to properly carry out her duties to impartially and objectively interpret the law as is her responsibility.

"Those who do not support Madame Justice Wilson's feminist interpretation of the law cannot enjoy any confidence in her impartiality but rather have been placed at a grave disadvantage because of her apparent bias."

"Real Women File Protest." *Ottawa Citizen*, February 14, 1990.

The CJC eventually dismissed all the complaints, but first, both women had to file responses and endure intrusive media coverage.[18]

Wilson and L'Heureux-Dubé became lightning rods for a movement to which they did not belong. Yet their objections to feminism belied the role of the women's movement. Without it, the law schools and the legal profession would not have opened their doors to women. Both women owed their judicial appointments to the burgeoning feminist movement that championed women on the bench. Feminist legal theorists produced the equality research and analysis that underlay Wilson and L'Heureux-Dubé's important Supreme Court decisions. On the cusp of significant changes in the status of women, ahead of the movement that so assisted their careers, like many professional women of their generation immersed in the trail-blazing effort to succeed, they did not claim feminism on the way up.

The National Action Committee on the Status of Women present the "Women Are Persons" medallion to Bertha Wilson, Ottawa, circa 1982. Left to right: Wendy Lawrence, Rosemary Billings, Doris Anderson, Bertha Wilson, Pat Hacker, and Michelle Swenarchuk.

Canada

THE GAZETTE   FRIDAY, MARCH 30, 1990

Complaint against woman judge is dismissed

No grounds for action over speech about male bias in law, council says

STEPHEN BINDMAN
SOUTHAM NEWS

OTTAWA — The Canadian Judicial Council has dismissed a complaint of bias against Justice Bertha Wilson of the Supreme Court of Canada made by the conservative group REAL Women.

The self-described pro-family organization had asked the council of judges to recommend the removal of Wilson from the top court because of "biased and improper" comments she made in a speech last month about male bias in the law. But a spokesman for the council said yesterday that no formal investigation was warranted and the file is considered closed.

"The chairman of the judicial conduct committee concluded that the complaint contained no information to suggest that a formal investigation by the coun-

cil . . . was warranted," the spokesman said.

Although the council, composed of all federally appointed chief justices, normally does not discuss its investigations, it agreed to respond to inquiries about Wilson because REAL Women issued a statement when it made its complaint.

Wilson, the first woman appointed to the Supreme Court, told a Toronto audience that some aspects of Canadian law are so biased in favor of men, they are "short of ludicrous" and cry out for change.

She also called for more courses for judges on sexual issues and warned that recent events have led to the inescapable conclusion that "in some respects our existing system of justice has been found wanting."

But REAL Women (Realistic, Equal, Active for Life) said Wilson's failure to understand that the "views of a few vocal feminists" do not represent the views of all

Canadian women was "deeply disturbing."

"It indicates her inability, or alternately, her unwillingness to properly carry out her duties to impartially and objectively interpret the law as is her responsibility," the group said in a letter to the council.

"Those who do not support Madame Justice Wilson's feminist interpretation of the law cannot enjoy any confidence in her impartiality but rather have been placed at a grave disadvantage because of her apparent bias."

In her speech at Osgoode Hall Law School in Toronto, Wilson cited U.S. studies which show sexism is the underlying premise in many judgments and that "gender-based myths, biases and stereotypes are deeply embedded" in the attitudes of many male judges. Others have found that female lawyers are often subject to sexist comments, Wilson said.

"Complaint against woman judge dismissed," March 30, 1990.

INSENSITIVITY ON ISSUES OF RACE

Although racism had riddled Canadian society for centuries, the law had never done much to dismantle it. Judges typically ignored racial disparities in favour of "race-less" perspectives that cemented past injustices and perpetuated ongoing discrimination.[19] The Supreme Court had never had a non-white judge and the first two women were no exception. The feminist movement that lifted women forward had not set out equal demands for racially diverse judges, and the anti-racism movement had not yet made independent headway on judicial appointments.

The "colour-blind" patterns began with the lawyers' arguments and moved to the judges who rarely asked questions about race. For instance, Lyn Lavallee, the abused woman who shot her spouse in *Lavallee*, was Métis. Her defence counsel did not raise the issue and the opportunity was missed to inquire how her Indigenous status might have contributed to her plight.[20] If, as Wilson concluded, women could understand peril differently from men, the court might equally well have asked whether Indigenous women had a life experience that affected that assessment as well.

Racine v. Woods was a 1983 child custody case where Indigeneity *was* on the record and Wilson's gaps in understanding were evident.[21] Linda Woods, an Ojibway woman in Portage la Prairie, Manitoba, had given birth to a daughter, Leticia. Woods was experiencing addiction problems and the Children's Aid Society seized the child six weeks later, placing her in a foster home with two white parents. The foster parents divorced and the white foster mother re-partnered with a Métis man. When a legal dispute erupted over who should have custody, the reconfigured foster couple, Sandra and her second husband Allan Racine, sought to adopt Leticia. The birth mother, who had made progress toward addiction recovery and educational upgrading, wanted her daughter back within her extended family in the Ojibway community.

Writing for a unanimous court, Wilson ruled for the foster couple. Applying the "best interests of the child" rule, she concluded that the psychological bonding that Leticia had experienced in the extended time she lived with the white foster mother was more important than her Ojibway birth mother's culture and heritage. Woods was devastated and, understandably, not mollified by the foster father's Métis heritage, a culture at significant variance from the Ojibway. She was adamant that she did not want her daughter growing up in the "predominantly white neighbourhood" where the Racines lived.[22]

Wilson dismissed the birth mother's plea not to cut Leticia off from her Indigenous roots. She noted that the trial court had seen "danger signals" in the "venom" of Woods' "anti-white feelings." It was a peculiar comment, turning the anger of an Indigenous mother about a white society that had done much to destroy her community against her own custody rights. As for the foster parents, Wilson described them as "fully sensitive to the special problems of raising a native Indian child in a predominantly white environment." Wilson's assurance that the foster parents were "well able to cope with any identity crisis Leticia might face as a teenager" was not something that most Indigenous people would have taken for granted. But Wilson claimed that "interracial adoption, like interracial marriage" was "now an accepted phenomenon in our pluralist society."[23]

The decision made no mention of Canada's efforts to assimilate generations of Indigenous children through forced removal to abusive residential schools. It made no mention of the "Sixties Scoop," in which upwards of 20,000 Indigenous children had been adopted out to non-Indigenous families, often without the knowledge or consent of their parents. It made no reference to the theft of land that created the poverty and inadequate housing that made Indigenous parents the targets of middle-class white agencies that seized their children. It ignored the devastation of Indigenous languages and cultures inflicted by such removals, and how children were intricately tied to the future survival of

Indigenous communities.[24] Wilson was not the only judge to miss these crucial dimensions, but her custody decision reflected a serious lack of race awareness.

L'Heureux-Dubé manifested similar insensitivities. In 1973, she accepted an appointment to take a leave from her trial court to chair a commission of inquiry into sexual improprieties within the Montreal immigration office. She heard extensive evidence about immigration officers soliciting sex from women wishing to settle in Canada. Six male officers were disciplined, but L'Heureux-Dubé's report neglected to note that all the officers were white while, with few exceptions, all the women sexually targeted were Black. Despite testimony about racist comments in the workplace, she explicitly absolved the department of racism.[25] This was another lost opportunity to address racism in a city that was no stranger to racial hostility. Four years earlier, complaints of racism at Sir George Williams University had led to outbursts of anti-Black hatred and street riots in Montreal.[26] L'Heureux-Dubé's inquiry passed into history as a race-less episode of unsavoury behaviour on the part of a few offensive officers of unspecified race.

Baker was another illustrative case.[27] Mavis Baker, an African-Caribbean single mother who worked as a housekeeper, had been living in Toronto since 1981 without proper immigration status. Her life was strewn with challenges: the birth of four children, postpartum psychosis, and the subsequent loss of her job. Ordered deported in 1992, she sought discretionary admission as a landed immigrant. A white immigration officer summarily denied her application without a hearing. His bombastic note recommended deportation to Jamaica because of Baker's mental illness, receipt of welfare, lack of skills, and large number of children. "This case is a *catastrophy*," he wrote (misspelling in the original).[28]

In a majority decision that was, at first blush, helpful to Baker, L'Heureux-Dubé overturned lower court rulings that the duty of fairness here was "minimal." She concluded that

Mavis Baker with two of her children, Toronto 1998.

discretionary decisions must be exercised in accordance with "the principles of the rule of law, the principles of administrative law, the fundamental values of Canadian society, and the principles of the *Charter*."[29] She set aside the deportation order and returned the matter to the government for "redetermination by a different officer."[30] Mavis Baker subsequently obtained landed immigrant status.

But the case again rendered race invisible. The officer had said nothing directly about race in his note, but Baker was one of a large number of Black single-mother deportees and the Toronto African-Canadian community understood that racist stereotypes were at the root of it.[31] Roger Rowe, the African-Canadian poverty lawyer who represented Baker, hoped to raise racism at the Supreme Court. Dismayed to discover that he was the only African-Canadian in a courtroom filled with white judges, he chose not to make race explicit, a decision he would regret for years: "[L]ooking at the complexion of the court, [I thought] they are totally out of touch with…the reality of most black people…. So in terms of how we framed the case, we had to think, 'Do we want to make this about race?'—which we all know it's really about—or 'Do we want the best chance of getting the largest number of judges on side?'"[32]

What does it say about a legal system in which lawyers fear to raise legitimate arguments related to racism for fear of negative repercussions against their clients? What does it say about a multicultural country with an entirely white Supreme Court bench? In *Baker,* the court sidestepped the issue of race, pinning blame on another race-less "rogue immigration officer," who simply needed to conduct himself more objectively.[33]

Is it unfair to complain of judicial insensitivity to racism in an era when this was the norm? It raises the questions of when, and in which era, it does become fair and who pays the price for the damage done in the meantime. And it ignores the hard evidence of inequality and the multiple voices contesting racism at the time. Canadian legal authorities overlooked racism unless there was overt name-calling. It was something that neither of the two first women judges understood or strove to change.

CHAPTER 19

Retirement and after

Bertha Wilson retired from the Supreme Court on January 4, 1991, at the age of sixty-seven. Claire L'Heureux-Dubé retired on July 1, 2002, two months before reaching the compulsory retirement age of seventy-five. Their leave-taking was a study in contrasts.

Wilson took her leave simply and quietly. *The Globe and Mail* reported that the "notoriously press-shy" judge wrote a brief statement indicating that the task of judging the disputes of her fellow citizens had been a "truly humbling experience."[1] Some speculated that the early retirement related to increasing unhappiness with Antonio Lamer's chief justiceship.[2] Others pointed to her arthritis, a long-standing illness that she had borne stoically until it placed too heavy a toll to deny.[3] Wilson herself explained she wanted time for a "normal domestic life" with John.[4] Dalhousie Law School held a conference in her honour. The familiar bagpipes greeted the guests, and Nova Scotia musicians premiered a piece of Celtic music commissioned for the occasion.[5]

L'Heureux-Dubé departed in a blaze of controversy and glory. Gossip surfaced in the press that the feud with Lamer had escalated to a point where the two judges were jockeying to outlast each other on the court, a tug-of-war L'Heureux-Dubé

The unveiling of Bertha Wilson's portrait by artist Mary Lennox Hourd, with outgoing Chief Justice Lamer and incoming Chief Justice McLachlin.

won by two-and-a-half years.[6] The *National Post* profiled the attacks of critics depicting her as a "threat to the very foundations of Anglo-Canadian legal tradition."[7] But her supporters stole the show. Raucous celebrants regaled the retiring judge at gala dinners, festive receptions, and a bevy of workshops and conferences, oblivious to the small group of demonstrators protesting her decisions at the door. The homage outdistanced anything yet seen for a retiring judge. L'Heureux-Dubé had become a rock-star within the staid halls of the nation's top court.[8]

Beverley McLachlin coined the phrase a "cascade of Clairefests" to describe the adulation, but she was concerned that not enough had been done to commemorate Wilson. She arranged to commission an oil portrait of Canada's first female judge, which was belatedly hung in the halls of the Supreme Court in December 1999.[9]

Bertha Wilson welcoming Frank Iacobucci, who replaced her on the Supreme Court, 1991.

Canadian Lawyer cartoon of Claire L'Heureux-Dubé with the sword
of justice in "*retraite.*"

POST-RETIREMENT ACTIVITIES:
WILSON'S EXPANDING RECOGNITION
OF INDIGENEITY AND GENDER

Wilson's hopes for a sedate retirement were soon dashed. In April 1991, the Canadian government created a Royal Commission on Aboriginal Peoples (RCAP) and appointed former Chief Justice Brian Dickson to set it up. When he called on Wilson to serve as a commissioner, she could not resist.[10] It would develop into a formidable five-year assignment necessitating travel to ninety-six far-flung, remote Indigenous communities. It taxed her arthritis to the breaking point and her health was further sabotaged by the onset of shingles and neuralgia.[11] Yet, by all accounts, she was shocked to discover dishonoured treaties, the theft of Indigenous lands, the suppression of Indigenous cultures, and the damage of residential schools.[12] She also found herself immersed in Indigenous spirituality. Describing it as a profoundly moving experience, she said it had "completed my baptism into the Canadian society and in a strange way...made me whole."[13]

Speaking later to a conference of Canadian women judges, Wilson described how meaningful it had been to sit in a circle of elders, adding that she had never "known wisdom as deeply" as she did "in that moment."[14] It was a striking statement for a woman who had sought after wisdom all her life and the poignancy of her remarks moved many of her transfixed listeners to tears.[15] In the final RCAP report, Wilson and the other commissioners called upon Canada to recognize Indigenous peoples as sovereign nations with the inherent right to self-government. They proposed the overhaul of Indigenous education, health, and housing; the reinvigoration of Indigenous languages and culture; and the transfer of land and resources back to Indigenous communities.[16]

The report's description of the devastating harms caused by cross-cultural foster placement and child adoption must have given Wilson some pause.[17] Her biographer believed that the *Racine v. Woods* case came to resonate as one of the most wrenching of her career.[18] A former law clerk observed that the RCAP hearings constituted a "profound engagement with race" for the retired judge.[19] A law professor who attended a Hong Kong conference with Wilson in the early 1990s was struck by her "sense of humility" in the face of her RCAP experiences.[20] The distressing thing was that ten years after the report was released, the year of Wilson's death in 2007, the Assembly of First Nations advised that Canada's implementation of it had been an abject failure.[21]

Wilson's perspectives on sex discrimination also expanded after she agreed to chair the Task Force on Gender Equality in the Legal Profession that the Canadian Bar Association established in 1991. The task force organized a frenzy of meetings with women lawyers and feminist legal organizations, where Wilson "shone in her capacity" to listen and ask perceptive questions.[22] Its report concluded that gender discrimination permeated

Bertha Wilson at a CBA meeting in 1993.

the profession, skewering women's employment opportunities, complicating family responsibilities, and fomenting sexual harassment.[23] Although Wilson observed that discrimination was "more subtle" than when she had started out in the 1950s, she spared no punches in her conclusions, stating, "A *white* view of the world is not neutral. A *masculine* view of the world is not neutral. A *heterosexual* view of the world is not neutral."[24] The statement drew upon her speech "Will women judges really make a difference?" and moved the discussion further still.

Some of the report's most controversial sections dealt with women judges, whose numbers had doubled from 4 per cent to 9 per cent between 1982 and 1990.[25] Wilson had identified two hundred female judges and sent each one a confidential questionnaire under her signature, asking if they had personally encountered sex discrimination on the bench. The replies were sobering. Forty-four per cent listed problems such as discriminatory work assignments, isolation, exclusion from informal networking, and sexual harassment from male judges.[26] Shocked over the data, Wilson was doubly upset when an angry Chief Justice Lamer demanded that she reveal the names of the women judges who claimed to be victims and the alleged culprits. Wilson stood by her guarantee of confidentiality and refused. Lamer then wrote to all the women judges asking them to name names. Not surprisingly, he got no responses. In the end, his public repudiation of the report did much to bolster the profession's resistance to its findings.[27]

The recommendation that female judges should meet to discuss issues of mutual interest did come to fruition, although not without initial resistance from a generation disinclined to identify as "women judges." Wilson's preliminary efforts to create an association solely for women judges failed.[28] Then the executive director of the Canadian Judicial Council (CJC), a body newly charged with taking responsibility for judicial education, began organizing small dinners for women judges in the Ottawa area. Lamer, who chaired the CJC, expressed reservations,

Women judges' dinner at the Supreme Court of Canada, May 1997. Left to right: Dolores Hansen (National Judicial Institute, previously Federal Court of Canada), Alice Desjardins (Federal Court of Appeal), Bertha Wilson, Claire L'Heureux-Dubé, Louise Charron (Ontario Court of Appeal), and Judith Bell-Oyen (Ontario Superior Court).

Women judges' dinner with Norma Wikler, April 1991. Left to right: Louise Charron (Ontario Court of Justice General Division), Norma Wikler, and Bertha Wilson.

Women judges' dinner, Ottawa, January 1997. Left to right (top row): Jeannie Thomas, Rosalie Abella (Ontario Court of Appeal), and Beverley McLachlin; (seated): Claire L'Heureux-Dubé and Bertha Wilson.

asking whether they were "all going to talk about the male judges."[29] But the dinners were a great success, with Wilson and L'Heureux-Dubé among the most enthusiastic attendees. One evening the group played host to Norma Wikler, a sociology professor who had helped to establish judicial gender-bias task forces across the United States. Newly energized by the growing interest in the challenges facing women judges, the Canadian chapter of the International Association of Women Judges (IAWJ) came into being some years later.[30]

Although the Task Force report was hailed as a milestone, the backlash it spawned within the profession did much to torpedo its momentum. The suggestion that law firms must restructure to accommodate responsible parenting struck some of the more outspoken opponents as absurd. Wilson found herself on the receiving end of vituperative, humiliating, public repudiation. In retrospect, she characterized her work on the task force as "enormously painful" and an "unequivocal and deeply personal experience of gender discrimination."[31] The statement marked a growing recognition that sexism cut close to home for her, even as a retired Supreme Court judge.

L'HEUREUX-DUBÉ'S EXPANDING INTERNATIONAL PROFILE AND NEW CONTROVERSIES IN QUEBEC

The public explosion that attended the *Ewanchuk* decision launched L'Heureux-Dubé onto the international stage. With heightened recognition that judges needed more training to deal with sexism, reformers from around the world sought her intervention. Although still a controversial figure in Canada, she led successful workshops for judges in India, Sri Lanka, Bangladesh, Nepal, Pakistan, and Palestine, while giving lectures and forging ties with other judges in Australia, New Zealand, Serbia, Croatia, Taiwan, Zimbabwe, and South Africa.[32]

In the international setting, she began to speak more freely about the impediments that sex discrimination had imposed upon her own career. Struck by her honesty and humour, UK Baroness Helena Kennedy QC marvelled at L'Heureux-Dubé's talent to "charm old patriarchal judges into rethinking their attitudes."[33] Naina Kapur, a Uganda-born lawyer who ran a feminist organization in India, helped to organize a South Asia Pacific judicial program in which L'Heureux-Dubé became a central participant. Working with her was wonderful, Kapur said, because "Claire had the ability to evoke respect just by telling the truth."[34] The founders of the IAWJ described L'Heureux-Dubé as a "star attraction," a "whirlwind" whose influence stretched worldwide. At its 2012 UK conference in London, the organization presented her with its highest honour, the Human Rights Award.[35]

Claire L'Heureux-Dubé with Pakistani judges in the Judicial Education Program.

Just as Wilson had found with her task force work, these activities brought L'Heureux-Dubé into closer contact with feminist activism. She was confronting male judges internationally with the need to acknowledge how their background and social upbringing influenced their values and beliefs. She was enthusiastically recruiting female judges to join the new international organizations of women. In doing so, L'Heureux-Dubé acknowledged her own personal history and called it by name: sex discrimination. Yet she drew the line at identifying as feminist. Throughout retirement, she continued to insist that she was "not a feminist" and that feminism was "unnecessary."[36]

Rosalie Abella, who knew both women well and would later follow them onto the top court herself, tried to explain the difference between Wilson and L'Heureux-Dubé. She described L'Heureux-Dubé as a woman who "promoted women's issues and women judges" but "disavowed feminism." She saw Wilson as less inclined to "disavow feminism," citing in particular the "Will women judges make a difference?" lecture. In Abella's opinion, Wilson was willing to take a position about the inter-connectedness of gender and judging, while L'Heureux-Dubé was a woman who would have contested that to the end.[37]

There was another difference that came to the fore in retirement. Wilson's understanding of how racism had devastated

International Association of Women Judges meeting in London, UK, 2002.

Indigenous communities grew significantly. It was something her contemporaries remarked upon.[38] For L'Heureux-Dubé, her international activities also brought her greater exposure to the damage done by racism, causing observers to praise her effectiveness in cross-cultural settings.[39] But in the years after she left the court, L'Heureux-Dubé's perspectives on religious and ethnic discrimination created more controversy. The woman who had grown up chafing against the stranglehold of the Roman Catholic Church had come to prize secularism. And it brought her to the centre of attention when she objected to face-coverings for Muslim women as incompatible with sexual equality.[40]

L'Heureux-Dubé argued that a secular state was essential in a society where centuries of Catholic domination had wreaked havoc:

> My public position on the neutrality of the state is precisely a fight against what was imposed on women during my life by the Catholic religion: submission of women to their husbands, denying abortion and divorce, and I can go on.... [D]iscrimination against women, gays, etc., was what I fought during my practice at the bar and on the bench. Discrimination against women by religion, whatever religion, is to me unacceptable and as such must be denounced.[41]

When successive Quebec governments introduced legislation to prohibit the wearing of face-coverings for individuals giving or receiving public services, human rights advocates objected.[42] They characterized it as a blatant attack against an ethnic and religious minority group and an unlawful contravention of equality rights. L'Heureux-Dubé spoke to the media in support of the face-covering ban, arguing that "minorities" should "adapt to common values such as sexual equality," and that this would "ensure that immigrants become like us."[43] When she testified before a Quebec legislative committee that the proposed measure was lawful, the press described her as "the most prominent jurist to argue for the constitutionality of the ban."[44]

It landed her into another hotbed of debate, with some applauding her efforts to promote "*laïcité*" (secularism), while others insisted that L'Heureux-Dubé had betrayed her own belief in equality law and taken a position that could encourage anti-Muslim hate-crimes against a vulnerable minority community.[45] The media reported that the prospect of a face-covering ban had "roiled Quebec," bringing thousands out to march in the streets—pro and con. Anti-Islam graffiti was scrawled over mosques and Muslim businesses; hijab-wearing women reported being stopped on the streets and told to go home. The tension exploded on January 29, 2017, when a francophone Québécois man opened fire in a Quebec City mosque, killing six Muslim men and injuring nineteen more as they knelt at worship. Once again, L'Heureux-Dubé, the lightning rod, was in the thick of a controversy that embroiled Quebec City, Quebec, and the nation.[46]

In retirement, as in their earlier lives, Wilson and L'Heureux-Dubé chose difficult paths. Unleashed somewhat from the constraints of judicial office, they continued to "prove" themselves. Blazing their way through tumultuous challenges, they expanded their perspectives on issues of gender and race, at times moving forward while occasionally, in the eyes of some, faltering in the wider goal.

Conclusion

ertha Wilson, a native-born Scot descended from generations of Scots, was raised in fishing/shipbuilding towns on the northeast coast of Scotland. Claire L'Heureux-Dubé, a native-born Québécoise descended from generations of French-Canadians, was raised in port cities on the St. Lawrence River. Wilson spoke with a thick Scottish burr that never waned. L'Heureux-Dubé's mother tongue was French, although she also spoke fluent English with a trace of French accent. Both prized their ethnic heritage. Both felt themselves to be separate from mainstream Canadian culture. Wilson believed that her immigrant status had a significant impact on her life, although she recognized that her accent marked her out for favour in her adopted country. L'Heureux-Dubé found her beloved Québécois roots a source of dissonance when she was submerged in the dominant English culture.

Wilson's initial education in Aberdeen, Scotland was solid but unspectacular. She completed a master of arts degree, but carried off no academic distinctions. L'Heureux's education took place in Quebec convents under the twenty-four-hour care of Roman Catholic nuns. Nine years later, she emerged with a *baccalauréat magna cum laude* as well as the Lieutenant Governor's medal. Unlike Wilson, whose shy deportment never slipped, L'Heureux was notorious for her disruptive antics and her popularity among peers.

Wilson married her first serious suitor at age twenty-two: John Wilson, a minister of the Church of Scotland. John's desire for new horizons brought the couple to Canada, where he pursued a peripatetic career as a minister, a naval chaplain, a church fund-raiser, and a consumer advocate. The marriage produced no children but supported an intimate relationship between intellectual equals. In contrast, L'Heureux attracted numerous male admirers but rejected early proposals of marriage, cautious about settling down prematurely. Throughout a string of dalliances, she carried on a lengthy romance with Arthur Dubé, a brilliant engineering professor at Laval, whom she wed at age thirty-one. It was a tempestuous marriage, which was not stabilized by the birth of two children.

Both women enrolled in law schools at a time when their presence stirred up anxiety over affronts to traditional gender roles. Neither was prepared to succumb to the notions still in circulation that women's brains were dominated by emotion and instinct, out of sync with systems of law purportedly centred on rationality. But neither did they anticipate that a law degree would easily open up legal careers for women. Wilson's choice to enrol at Dalhousie as a mature student garnered surprise but strong support from her husband, John. L'Heureux selected law at Laval with the backing of her mother, over the protests of her father.

Both women encountered resistance inside law school. Between them, they suffered disparagement during admission, rude behaviour from some male classmates, ineligibility for scholarships, exclusion from some student social venues, ejection from sexual assault criminal law classes, and sexual harassment. Their response was to keep moving forward quietly and without complaint. Instead of protest, they chose to make discrete accommodation to traditional professional norms. Wilson doubled down on her studies with marked intensity. L'Heureux sailed through her law school years while out-socializing her classmates. Both achieved scholarly distinction, winning prizes but missing the first-place title.

Each then managed to secure an all-important first job in practice. Wilson obtained a spot as the only female lawyer in a large corporate-commercial Toronto firm. Over the next seventeen years, she developed a secure niche as a research lawyer who prepared opinions for other lawyers. It was an innovative practice that facilitated her ascent to become the first female partner. She kept a decorous distance from the rough-and-tumble of aggressive litigation, providing expert advice behind the scenes to blue-chip Toronto lawyers who valued her unique talents. L'Heureux benefitted from the generosity of one of the only Jewish lawyers in Quebec City. He hired her into his firm and she stayed for twenty years. She ran a thriving general practice and then branched into the emerging field of divorce, where her fearless litigation talents brought her visibility as the most eminent female lawyer in Quebec City.

Neither woman set out to compete for top billing in a hierarchical profession. Both sidestepped into brand-new practice directions, where there was minimal male competition but still some hope to achieve resounding success. Both women butted up against stereotypical assumptions about femininity and masculinity. Wilson neutralized her image, a proper minister's wife perceived as a Scottish "den mother" or a "great-aunt" who never rocked the boat. In contrast, the flamboyant francophone *femme fatale* frontally challenged the notion that women could not cut it in the litigation arena. *La Tigresse* forged a new zone, blending feminine and masculine characteristics and tipping traditional sex roles off kilter. Both preferred to look the other way when sexist treatment infected their workplaces. The better strategy, they believed, was just to keep forging ahead.

The two received their first judicial appointments within three years of each other. L'Heureux-Dubé became the first woman to sit in Quebec City on the Quebec Superior Court in

1973, and Wilson became the first to sit on the Ontario Court of Appeal in 1976. Much to their surprise, as well as the astonishment of others, they breached the all-male ranks of the judiciary as a result of a surging women's movement, a Liberal government wishing to ride the wings of change, a broadened judicial selection process, and a small group of influential supporters who touted their candidacies.

Both faced a dubious reception from some quarters of the bar and the judiciary, from men who objected to women judges on principle. After a period of uneasy adjustment, each amassed a solid reputation for careful adjudication. Wilson navigated her difficult reception at the Ontario Court of Appeal by demonstrating singular knowledge of law from her years of research at Oslers. She was a woman who could recite precedents with the best of them, but she also exhibited her talent as a creative judge who understood that changing societies sometimes required the remoulding of legal norms. Her innovative decisions were a sign of things to come. L'Heureux-Dubé turned her charm to advantage with her colleagues on the Quebec Superior Court and the Court of Appeal, where, with a few exceptions, she endeared herself as a *"femme attachant."* Her jurisprudence on those courts was largely "formalist," a judicial philosophy understood to be a simple application of traditionally recognized legal doctrines to the factual disputes at hand. Her rulings bore little hint of the innovations she would spearhead in the future.

The enactment of the *Charter of Rights and Freedoms* in 1982 coincided with a feminist movement in full stride that demanded more representation for women on the bench. Two prime ministers, arch-enemies Pierre Elliot Trudeau and Brian Mulroney, answered the call and elevated Wilson and L'Heureux-Dubé to become the first two women on the Supreme Court of Canada in 1982 and 1987. Both appointments elicited rumblings of discontent from the bar and vehement objections from other Supreme Court judges.

The two women who reached the rarefied heights dealt

with disparate personal lives. Bertha Wilson was married to a man who began his career as a parish minister and ended it as an intellectual soulmate and house-husband to his beloved wife. John Wilson shared his wife's interests, shouldered the domestic responsibilities, supported her path-breaking career, and never took umbrage over the anxiety his role could provoke in others. Although their childless status may have been a source of sadness, neither did they have to deal with the calamities that can befall offspring. Claire L'Heureux-Dubé was married to a man who was her intellectual equal but her opposite in terms of life-outlook. An alcoholic, a gambler, and a depressive, Arthur Dubé offered little support to the family. L'Heureux-Dubé had to navigate through his suicide, as well as their son's tragic descent into mental illness, addiction, and death in detention. She survived by burying herself in her work, and by clinging to a relentless optimism and a thirst for life and happiness.

On the top court, Wilson and L'Heureux-Dubé were enveloped in a chilly climate that signalled disrespect. The media speculated about their lack of "merit" and the male judges seemed frustratingly oblivious to the ways in which their customs and habits marginalized their new colleagues. With a few notable exceptions, the reception that greeted the two women was austere, suspicious, and, to some degree, downright hostile. Despite their efforts to prove themselves over and over again, their gender singled them out as women *first* and judges *maybe*. They responded by putting their work ethic into overdrive. They intended to put the lie to the notion that "no woman" could do the job of judging.

Ensconced in an environment that contested their very presence and vividly aware that the experiment rested heavily on their shoulders, both women recognized that they were being treated unfairly. Wilson was characteristically more restrained in her responses than L'Heureux-Dubé, who chafed increasingly over time. Yet both managed against considerable odds to produce path-breaking decisions. For Wilson, this was simply a continuation of her innovative approach from the court below, but for L'Heureux-Dubé, it was a significant transformation.

When they gave voice to female experiences, they took courageous steps toward unmasking the masculine presumptions that underlay the legal system. Between them, the two women expanded the scope of self-defence for battered women, struck down the prohibition on abortion in gendered terms, and spelled out what female sexual autonomy meant in law. In dissent, they also advocated the decriminalization of some aspects of prostitution, the extension of legal benefits to same-sex couples, and the right of women to be free from intrusive questioning about their sex lives in sexual assault trials.

The illusion that women judges would speak with one voice was disrupted by Beverley McLachlin's *Seaboyer* decision on sexual assault, as well as Wilson and L'Heureux-Dubé's differing views over the economic consequences of divorce. Women spoke with multiple voices, yet it remained incontrovertible that their diverse perspectives brought something fresh to the task of judging. Wilson and L'Heureux-Dubé's landmark decisions clarified that male-only conceptions of law failed to encompass the reality of women's lives. They premised their visions of social justice upon more gender-balanced perspectives, often expressing their ideas in language previously unheard at the Supreme Court of Canada.

Although the feminist movement was pivotal in dismantling barriers that had kept women out of law and the judiciary, it received little support from Wilson and L'Heureux-Dubé. Forced to prove themselves repeatedly in a male-centric environment, both resisted identification as feminists. In this they resembled many first generation female lawyers and judges who chose to disavow feminism for professional and personal reasons. Their careers also demonstrated insensitivity to the ways in which racism infected Canadian law and society. Wilson and L'Heureux-Dubé were descendants of the two mythical "founding nations," and both were raised within imperialist cultures

Bertha Wilson
in a traditional
Indigenous blanket,
circa 1996.

and privileged racial hierarchies.[1] They were no different from their male colleagues in failing to recognize the devastation wrought by racism. The entry of the first women heralded no victory for a vision of equality that encompassed race.

Wilson's retirement from the court was marked by restraint and decorum while L'Heureux-Dubé flamed out like the celebrity legal rock-star she had become. Neither took to needlework. Wilson shouldered new responsibilities with the Royal Commission on Aboriginal Peoples and the Task Force on Gender Equality. The two inquiries gave her new appreciation for Indigeneity and sexual equality. As one former law clerk observed, all her life Wilson never stopped "growing as a person."[2]

L'Heureux-Dubé spread her wings in the cause of judicial education, where her signature energy and charisma combined to make her Canada's most internationally influential judge. Closer to home, her commitment to secularism entangled her in a bitter debate over the place of religion in Quebec. Her support

Claire L'Heureux-Dubé with her grandson Simon in Florida.

Claire L'Heureux-Dubé in retirement at her Florida condo in 2009.

Claire L'Heureux-Dubé's grandsons, Simon and Daniel, playing by a stream.

of government efforts to ban face-coverings for individuals receiving or providing public services brought down a torrent of discord. Her opponents insisted that she was promulgating "extreme anti-Muslim bigotry" while her supporters claimed that the right to wear religious garb should be constrained for reasons of sexual equality. It was a controversial capstone to a controversial career.

Bertha Wilson's final years were dimmed by the onset of Alzheimer's and she died on April 28, 2007, at the age of eighty-three. In keeping with her wishes, her funeral was a low-key affair. Claire L'Heureux-Dubé discovered the delights of becoming a grandmother and lavished time in her later years upon her two beloved grandsons, Simon Pierre Harris and Daniel Louis Dubé Harris. In 2018, she turned ninety-one, still an active and influential legal figure throughout far-flung corners of the world.

Canada's two first female Supreme Court judges braved identical impediments as they struggled to meet the pressures of being interlopers in a male world. Yet they took divergent paths to the top. They came from dissimilar backgrounds. Their personal lives were in complete contrast. They brought to the challenges opposite personalities: one was reserved; the other rebellious. They pursued distinct strategies in negotiating their way forward: one was more deferential and disinclined to ruffle feathers; the other more flamboyant and iconoclastic. But they were both intellectually curious and driven by a desire to excel.

Did their careers change them? As practising lawyers, they discovered that sexism had confined them to narrower career paths than were available to men. Achieving success required that they adapt their behaviour to function effectively within all-male venues. Once they were appointed to the bench, their path-breaking judgments suggest that both grew in office. Wilson demonstrated a judicial independence that signalled a newfound disinclination to bend to authority. L'Heureux-Dubé's transformation was slower in coming, but she too broke away from the "rule formalist" notion that judges were completely captive to fixed legal doctrines. Neither woman disavowed traditional legal rules, but both manifested a flair for reform, recognizing that the best legal systems must incorporate diverse needs. Wilson was no longer the 1940s Aberdeen student who had been strictly obedient to hierarchical authority. L'Heureux-Dubé was no longer the 1950s Laval student tied to a vision of law as a static system of technical, black-letter rules.

Did they change the judiciary they joined? They certainly vanquished the edict that there should be "no women judges," taking the wind out of the sails of those most insistent on maintaining male supremacy. They undoubtedly facilitated the path of Beverley McLachlin, who followed them to become the first female, and longest serving, chief justice in the history of the Supreme Court of Canada. But did the elevation of Wilson and L'Heureux-Dubé to the top court signal a full victory for gender equality? No.

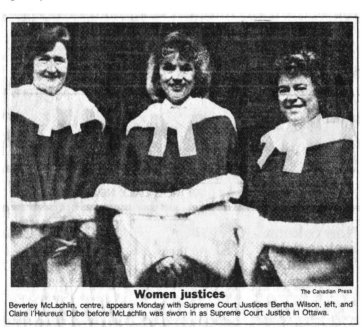

Women justices The Canadian Press

Beverley McLachlin, centre, appears Monday with Supreme Court Justices Bertha Wilson, left, and Claire l'Heureux Dube before McLachlin was sworn in as Supreme Court Justice in Ottawa.

Press clipping of Bertha Wilson, Claire L'Heureux-Dubé, and Beverley McLachlin at the McLachlin swearing-in ceremony, 1989.

Blatant and subtle variations of sexism continue to track the careers of incoming lawyers and judges. Redoubled efforts and renewed strategies remain necessary to strip away the persistent tentacles of gender discrimination. Although the two first women raised questions about the male bias embedded in law, the task of scrutinizing the full legal system for all of its sexist underpinnings remains for the future. Beyond gender itself, more urgency remains. Succeeding generations of racial and ethnic minorities, LGBTQ+ advocates, Indigenous communities, impoverished populations, and those with disabilities will need to redefine equality law to dismantle discrimination in all of its pernicious forms.

That Bertha Wilson and Claire L'Heureux-Dubé succeeded so well in the first stage should give cause for at least some optimism. Their induction into the highest rank of the Companion of the Order of Canada symbolized a fitting celebration of the extraordinary accomplishments of "two firsts," a tribute to two remarkably different Canadian women.

Claire L'Heureux-Dubé, recipient of the Companion of the Order of
Canada, April 29, 1992.

The Right Honourable Ramon John Hnatyshyn, 24th Governor General of Canada (1990–1995) presented the insignia of the Companion of the Order of Canada to the Honourable Bertha Wilson, ceremony April 29, 1992.

Endnotes

INTRODUCTION

1   Interview with Claire L'Heureux-Dubé, Quebec City, July 11, 2016. Unless otherwise indicated, all interviews were conducted by the author alone.

2   Interviews with Claire L'Heureux-Dubé, Quebec City, April 29–30, 2008; July 11, 2016.

3   The full caption read: "*Hommage à Claire L'Heureux-Dubé nommé à la Cour Suprême! Yahoo! J'arrive Bertha!*" [Tribute to Claire L'Heureux-Dubé, named to the Supreme Court! Yahoo! I'm here, Bertha!]. trans.

4   Ellen Anderson *Judging Bertha Wilson: Law as Large as Life* (Toronto: University of Toronto Press, 2001), 127, 154.

5   Interview with Claire L'Heureux-Dubé, Quebec City, April 29–30, 2008; Kirk Makin and Graeme Smith, "Gatecrashing the Old Boys' Club," *The Globe and Mail* (May 2, 2002), A8; Cristin Schmitz, "Lists former colleagues with 'beautiful minds,'" *The Lawyers Weekly* (May 17, 2002), 23.

6   Interview with Claire L'Heureux-Dubé, Quebec City, July 11, 2016.

7   See Chapter 18.

8   Bertha Wilson chapter in John Arnup, "Swearing out: An inside look, the Court of Appeal and some of its judges," Law Society of Upper Canada Archives, Toronto #2014009-001: 179.

9   Constance Backhouse, *Petticoats and Prejudice: Women and Law in Nineteenth-Century Canada* (Toronto: Women's Press, 1991).

10 Backhouse, *Petticoats and Prejudice,* Chapters 10 and 11.

11 Louise Mailhot, *Les premières! L'histoire de l'accès des femmes à la pratique du droit et à la magistrature* (Cowansville, QC: Yvon Blais, 2013), 15–19, 89–100.

12 Department of Justice Canada, "Canada's Court System" (Ottawa: Minister of Justice Attorney General of Canada, 2015), 4.

13 *Nunavut Act*, SC 1993, c. 28, ss. 31(1), 76.06(2.1).

14 Tom Belton, "Custody, control, and confusion: Legal, historical, and territorial aspects of court records in Ontario" *Archivaria* 69 (Spring 2010): 11.

15 *Courts of Justice Act*, SO 1984, c. 11, s. 25(1), as it appeared in May 1984; Superior Court of Justice, "History of the Court" (2018) online: http://www.ontariocourts.ca/scj/about/history/.

16 *An Act to Amend the Courts of Justice Act 1984*, (No 1) SO 1989 c. 55, s. 157, amending the *Courts of Justice Act*, SO 1884 c11; Ontario Courts, "Ontario Courts of Justice: A History" (2 October 2015) Project Book Working Paper ISBN: 978-0-9950133-1-5. Online: http://www.ontariocourts.ca/ocjhistory/wp-content/uploads/history-project-book.pdf.

17 Superior Court of Justice, supra note 15; Bill 79, A*n Act to improve Ontario's Court System to respond to concerns raised by charities and their volunteers and to improve various relating to the administration of Justice*, 1st Sess, 36th Leg, Ontario, 1996, cl 8 (assented to 31 October 1996).

18 *Courts of Justice Act*, RSO 1990 c. C-43, s. 1(1).

19 *Courts of Justice Act*, CQLR c. T-16, ss. 24, 25.

20 Anderson, *Judging Bertha Wilson*; Constance Backhouse, *Claire L'Heureux-Dubé: A Life* (Vancouver: University of British Columbia Press, 2017); Kim Brooks, ed., *Justice Bertha Wilson: One Woman's Difference* (Vancouver: University of British Columbia Press, 2009); Jamie Cameron, ed., *Reflections on the Legacy of Justice Bertha Wilson* (Markham, ON: LexisNexis, 2008); "Symposium to Honour the Contributions of Madame Justice Bertha Wilson" *Dalhousie Law Journal* 15 (1992), full volume; Elizabeth Sheehy, ed., *Adding Feminism to Law: The Contributions of Justice Claire L'Heureux-Dubé* (Toronto: Irwin Law, 2004); Marie-Claire Belleau et François Lacasse, eds., *Claire L'Heureux-Dubé à la Cour Suprême du Canada 1987–2002* (Montréal: Wilson & Lafleur, 2004); *Canadian Journal of Women and the Law* 15:1 (2003), full volume.

21 Justice Claire L'Heureux-Dubé, "Preface" in Brooks, ed. *Justice Bertha Wilson*, ix–xi.

22 Interview with Frank Iacobucci, Toronto, October 26, 2011.

23 Interview with Charles Gonthier, Ottawa, September 14, 2008.

24 Interview with Marie-Claire Belleau, Ottawa, December 11, 2013.

CHAPTER 1 Childhood and early schooling: Scotland and Quebec

1 Ellen Anderson, *Judging Bertha Wilson: Law as Large as Life* (Toronto: University of Toronto Press, 2001), 4; *Kirkcaldy: A History and Celebration, Francis Firth Collection (*Kirkcaldy Civic Society, 2005), 67.

2 The full birth name was Marie Marguerite Antoinette Claire L'Heureux. Her family's Quebec records stretched back ten generations. Caroline Tanguay, O.S.U., with Louise Dumais, *Une grande Québécoise: L'Honorable Claire L'Heureux-Dubé, Cour Suprême 1987–2002*, undated unpublished manuscript.

3   L. MacBean, *Kirkcaldy Burgh Records (Kirkcaldy: Fifeshire Advertiser, 1908),* 33–34, Christian Blais et al., *Québec: quatre siècles d'une capitale* (Québec: L'Assemblée nationale du Québec, 2008), 3.

4   Anderson, *Judging Bertha Wilson,* 4–8; photo caption, 74b.

5   Anderson, *Judging Bertha Wilson,* 4–18.

6   Anderson, *Judging Bertha Wilson,* 4–18.

7   Interviews with Claire L'Heureux-Dubé, Quebec City, Ottawa, Rimouski, and Clearwater, Florida, on September 17, October 30, November 1, December 2, 2007; April 29–30, May 1–2, July 23–25, 2008; March 5 and 7, April 27–28, May 10-14, 2009; interview with Nicole L'Heureux, Clearwater, Florida, May 11–12, 2009; interview with Louise L'Heureux-Giliberti, Chicago, April 20–21, 2009; Constance Backhouse, *Claire L'Heureux-Dubé: A Life* (Vancouver: University of British Columbia Press, 2017).

8   Backhouse, *Claire L'Heureux-Dubé,* 81–82, 532.

9   Anderson, *Judging Bertha Wilson,* 4–6.

10   Claire L'Heureux-Dubé, *Une vie,* undated and incomplete autobiographical manuscript. There was no network of public secondary schools in Quebec before 1954. Catholic girls who could afford to do so studied privately in convents run by nuns. Clio Collective, *Québec Women: A History* (Toronto: Women's Press, 1987), 223, 241–7; Micheline Dumont and Nadia Fahmy-Eid, *Les couventines: L'éducation des filles au Québec dans les congrégations religieuses enseignantes 1840–1960* (Montréal: Boréal Express).

11   Anderson, *Judging Bertha Wilson,* 4–6.

12   Anderson, *Judging Bertha Wilson,* 11–12.

13   Backhouse, *Claire L'Heureux-Dubé,* 102.

14   W. Hamish Fraser, *Aberdeen, 1800 to 2000: A New History* (Tuckwell Press, 2000); Norman Harper, *Spikkin Doric* (Edinburgh: Birlinn, 2009); Robert McColl Millar, *Northern and Insular Scots* (Edinburgh University Press, 2007), 116.

15   Anderson, *Judging Bertha Wilson,* 8.

16   Fraser, *Aberdeen;* Jennifer Carter, *Crown and Gown: Illustrated History of the University of Aberdeen, 1495–1995* (Aberdeen University Press, 1994); Anderson, *Judging Bertha Wilson,* 6–9.

17   Anderson, *Judging Bertha Wilson,* 10.

18   Heather Hill, "Supreme Court's first woman may give it a more liberal look," *Montreal Gazette* (March 20, 1982), B4.

19   Anderson, *Judging Bertha Wilson,* 7–9.

20   Anderson, *Judging Bertha Wilson,* 7–12; Curtis Cole, *Osler Hoskin Harcourt: Portrait of a Partnership* (Toronto: McGraw-Hill Ryerson, 1995), 119.

21   John Malcolm Bulloch, *A History of the University of Aberdeen* (London: Hodder and Stoughton, 1895).

22   Bertha Wilson, "Aspects of equality-rendering justice," unpublished speech delivered, Hull, Quebec, November 19, 1995, as quoted in Anderson *Judging Bertha Wilson,* 12.

23 Anderson, *Judging Bertha Wilson*, 7–15; Cole, *Osler Hoskin Harcourt*, 119.

24 Cole, *Osler Hoskin Harcourt*, 119.

25 Anderson, *Judging Bertha Wilson*, 17.

26 Real Bernier, *Rimouski, Métropole du Bas-Saint-Laurent*, thesis, École des hautes études commerciales de Montréal, March 1, 1941; Jeannot Bourdages et al., *Rimouski depuis ses origines* (Rimouski: Société d'histoire du Bas-Saint-Laurent, Société de généalogie et d'archives de Rimouski, 2006); Marie-Ange Caron et al., *Mosaique Rimouskoise: Une Histoire de Rimouski* (Rimouski: Le comite des fetes du cent cinquantieme anniversaires de la Paroisse Saint-Germain de Rimouski, 1979).

27 Interview with Claire L'Heureux-Dubé, Quebec City, April 27–29, 2009.

28 Between 1931 and 1961, the city welcomed only one hundred immigrants from foreign countries, principally Europe, and the city remained 98 per cent of French-Canadian origin. Bourdages et al., *Rimouski depuis ses origines*, 113–17, 232. Marguerite L'Heureux persistently identified as "French" rather than "Canadian." Interviews with Claire L'Heureux-Dubé, Quebec City, Ottawa, Rimouski, and Clearwater, Florida, on September 17, October 30, November 1, December 2, 2007; April 29–30, May 1–2, July 23–25, 2008; March 5, 7, April 27-28, May 10–14, 2009.

29 Interview with Claire's sister Louise L'Heureux-Giliberti, Chicago, April 20, 2009.

30 Backhouse, *Claire L'Heureux-Dubé*, 60.

31 The convent housed more than fifty nuns, a novitiate, *un pensionnat* for boarding pupils, and *une école normale* for the instruction of primary school teachers. Between 1906 and 1970, the first and last years of operation, the Ursulines would educate more than 20,000 young girls in Rimouski. Les Ursulines, *À Rimouski il était un monastère* (Rimouski: Les Ursulines de Rimouski, 1995); Nicole Thivierge "Les femmes dans l'histoire de Rimouski: la face cachée du développement" in Yves Michaud "L'extension du territoire urbanisé de Rimouski (de 1860 à nos jours) in « Rimouski 1696–1996 », *Revue d'Histoire du Bas-Saint-Laurent* 19:2 (49) (June 1996): 97.

32 L'Heureux-Dubé, *Une vie*; Backhouse, *Claire L'Heureux-Dubé*, 69–70.

33 Dumont and Fahmy-Eid, *Les couventines*, 203–4.

34 Backhouse, *Claire L'Heureux-Dubé*, 68–70.

35 It was an era when elite Quebeckers prided themselves on their proficiency in English, and Paul L'Heureux built upon the rudimentary English he had learned in school, purchasing and reading English literature and periodicals, to become fluently bilingual. Marguerite and the girls followed suit. Interviews with Claire L'Heureux-Dubé, Ottawa, October 30, 2007, Ottawa, November 1, 2007; interview with Louise L'Heureux-Giliberti, Chicago, April 20, 2009.

36 Tanguay with Dumais, *Une grande Québécoise: L'Honorable Claire L'Heureux-Dubé*; Backhouse *Claire L'Heureux-Dubé*, 89.

37 Interview with Claire's daughter, Louise Dubé, Boston, May 22, 2012.

CHAPTER 2 Bertha Wilson, the minister's wife

1   Ellen Anderson, *Judging Bertha Wilson: Law as Large as Life* (Toronto: University of Toronto Press, 2001), 199.

2   Sandra Gwyn, "Sense and sensibility," *Saturday Night* (July 1985), 15–16.

3   Anderson, *Judging Bertha Wilson*, 13, 17.

4   Anderson, *Judging Bertha Wilson*, 13–17.

5   Anderson, *Judging Bertha Wilson*, 14.

6   Anderson, *Judging Bertha Wilson*, 13.

7   Anderson, *Judging Bertha Wilson*, 14, 24.

8   Anderson, *Judging Bertha Wilson*, 16–18.

9   Anderson, *Judging Bertha Wilson*, 18.

10 Anderson, *Judging Bertha Wilson*, 20–27; Bertha Wilson, "In my day, Dalhousie Law School," *The Ansul* 2 (December 1977), 61.

11 Anderson, *Judging Bertha Wilson*, 20–27.

12 Anderson, *Judging Bertha Wilson*, 27–28.

13 Anderson, *Judging Bertha Wilson*, 27–28.

14 Bertha Wilson, "The Scottish Enlightenment," 1987 Shumiatcher Lecture on Literature and the Law, Saskatoon; Anderson, *Judging Bertha Wilson*, 397–98 note 7.

15 Interview with Robert Sharpe, Toronto, July 25, 2016.

16 Wilson, "The Scottish Enlightenment"; Anderson, *Judging Bertha Wilson*, 28–30, 397–98 note 7.

17 Bertha Wilson, "Aspects of equality-rendering justice," unpublished speech, Hull, Quebec, November 19, 1995, as quoted in Anderson, *Judging Bertha Wilson*, 398 note 10.

18 Anderson, *Judging Bertha Wilson*, 31.

19 Gwyn, "Sense and sensibility," 16.

20 Bertha Wilson, "One woman's way to the Supreme Court," in *Collected Speeches Delivered by the Honourable Bertha Wilson 1976–1991* (Ottawa: Supreme Court of Canada, 1992), as quoted in Anderson, *Judging Bertha Wilson*, 33.

21 Anderson, *Judging Bertha Wilson*, 33–37.

22 Anderson, *Judging Bertha Wilson*, 33–37.

CHAPTER 3 The decision to study law

1   Constance Backhouse, *Petticoats and Prejudice: Women and Law in Nineteenth-Century Canada* (Toronto: Women's Press, 1991), chapters 10–11; Constance Backhouse, "'A revolution in numbers': Ontario feminist lawyers from the 1970s to the 1990s" in Constance Backhouse and W. Wesley Pue, eds., *Essays in the History of the Canadian Legal Profession* (Toronto: Irwin Law, 2009), 265–94; "Woman's rights," *Canadian Illustrated News* (November 21, 1874), 323–34; "Female students-at-law," *The Toronto Mail* (April 6, 1892); "Women as lawyers," *The Toronto Mail* (April 7, 1892); *Canada Law Journal* 32 (June 1896), 784.

2   Wendy Mitchinson, "The medical view of women: The case of late-nineteenth-century Canada," *Canadian Bulletin of Medical History* 3:2 (Winter 1986): 207–24; Backhouse, *Petticoats and Prejudice*, 297–98.

3   "The medical aspects of female education," *Canada Lancet* 6:7 (March 1874): 233.

4   *Legal Scrap Book* (April 16, 1892), 205.

5   Backhouse, *Petticoats and Prejudice*, 32, 319, 322.

6   *Canada Law Journal* 16 (June 1980), 161; Cecilia Morgan, "An embarrassingly and severely masculine atmosphere: Women, gender and the legal profession, Osgoode Hall, 1920s–1960s," *Canadian Journal of Women and the Law* 11:2 (Fall 1996): 21; Mary Kinnear, "That there woman lawyer: Women lawyers in Manitoba 1915–1970," *Canadian Journal of Women and the Law* 5 (1992): 411.

7   Mary Jane Mossman, *The First Women Lawyers: A Comparative Study of Gender, Law and the Legal Professions* (Oxford: Hart Publishing, 2006), 87; Gilles Gallichan, *Les Québécoises et le barreau: L'histoire d'une difficile conquête 1914–1941* (Sillery, Québec: Septentrion, 1999), 101–2, 115–16.

8   *Sex Disqualification (Removal) Act, 1919*, 9 and 10 Geo. 5, c.71. Margaret Kidd was the first female member of the Scottish bar. BBC *History Extra*, "Six trailblazing women in history" (March 8, 2012); Kidd, Dame Margaret Henderson, *Oxford Dictionary of National Biography*, https://doi.org/10.1093/ref:odnb/49228.

9   The 1941 census recorded 129 women out of a total of 7,920 lawyers; Canada Department of Labour, *Occupational Trends in Canada 1931–1961* (Ottawa: 1963), 40, 45. In 1945, Statistics Canada reported higher numbers for female law students: 4.4 per cent Canadian-wide: *Survey of Higher Education and Universities: Enrolment and Degrees* cited in D.A.A. Stager with H.W. Arthurs, *Lawyers in Canada* (Toronto: University of Toronto Press, 1990), Table 4.3, 96–97. The Ontario numbers show 3.7 per cent of those called to the bar in 1945 were female: Backhouse "A revolution in Numbers," 274.

10   Gallichan, *Les Québécoises et le barreau*, 116.

11   Hélène Dumont, ed., *Femmes et droit: 50 ans de vie commune...et tout un avenir* (Montréal: Éditions Thémis, 1991), 313.

12   Constance Backhouse, *Claire L'Heureux-Dubé: A Life* (Vancouver: University of British Columbia Press, 2017).

13   Interview with Claire L'Heureux-Dubé, Ottawa, October 30, 2007.

14   Interview with Claire L'Heureux-Dubé, Ottawa, December 2, 2007.

15 Interview with Claire L'Heureux-Dubé, Ottawa, October 30, 2007. Living out their mothers' dreams was a theme that would echo for many women who took their places within the next generation of Quebec and Canadian lawyers. Backhouse, "A revolution in numbers."

16 Interview with Louise L'Heureux-Giliberti, Chicago, April 20, 2009.

17 Interview with Nicole L'Heureux, Clearwater, Florida, May 11, 2009.

18 Interview with Claire L'Heureux-Dubé, Ottawa, October 30, 2007.

19 Interview with Claire L'Heureux-Dubé, Ottawa, October 30, 2007.

20 Interview with Thérèse Dionne Lecomte, Rimouski, July 24, 2008.

21 Interview with Claire L'Heureux-Dubé, Ottawa, October 30, 2007.

22 Interview with Claire L'Heureux-Dubé, Ottawa, November 1, 2007.

23 Interview with Nicole L'Heureux, Clearwater, Florida, May 11–12, 2009. Jules-A. Brillant also loaned Claire $250 to pay for her first year of fees to the bar. She reminisced, "He loaned it to me, and then he insisted I pay it back! A multi-millionaire!" Interview with Claire L'Heureux-Dubé, Clearwater Florida, May 10–14, 2009.

24 Interview with Thérèse Dionne Lecomte, Rimouski, July 24, 2008.

25 Christie Blatchford, "Accident launched career that took her to top court," *Toronto Star* (March 5, 1982), A1.

26 Bertha Wilson, "In my day, Dalhousie Law School" *The Ansul* 2 (December 1977), 61.

27 Ellen Anderson, *Judging Bertha Wilson: Law as Large as Life* (Toronto: University of Toronto Press, 2001), 36.

28 Anderson, *Judging Bertha Wilson*, 36.

29 An additional difference was the nature of the degree. In Quebec, law schools admitted students directly from secondary school. In Nova Scotia, students typically entered law school after first completing an undergraduate university degree. Bertha Wilson had even more: a master of arts.

CHAPTER 4 Claire L'Heureux and Laval University Law School

1 The official was the university secretary, Catholic Monseigneur Alphonse-Marie Parent. The first professor she met, Marie-Louis Beaulieu, reinforced the message, adding, "This is a man's world. Don't go there. You'll never succeed. There's no future in it for you." Interviews with Claire L'Heureux-Dubé, Ottawa, November 1, 2007; December 2, 2007.

2 Interview with Claire L'Heureux-Dubé, Ottawa, November 1, 2007.

3 Sylvio Normand, *Le droit comme discipline universitaire : Une histoire de la Faculté de droit de l'Université Laval* (Québec: Les Presses de l'Université Laval, 2005), 144–47; interview with Laval classmate, Robert Auclair-Hallé, Quebec City, August 7, 2009.

4   Constance Backhouse, *Claire L'Heureux-Dubé: A Life* (Vancouver: University of British Columbia Press, 2017), Chapter 8.

5   Ten of the fifty-one graduates appointed as judges included Julien Chouinard and Claire L'Heureux-Dubé, who served on the Supreme Court of Canada; Jean Bienvenue, Paul Gervais, Ovide Laflamme, Georges Savoie, and André Trottier, who were appointed to the Superior Court; Gilles Carle and André Lévesque, who were appointed to the Provincial Court; and Robert Auclair-Hallé, who was appointed to the provincial labour court.

6   Julien Chouinard studied at Oxford, practised law in Quebec City, taught at Laval law school, and served as provincial deputy minister of justice and secretary-general of the executive council from 1968 until his appointment to the Quebec Court of Appeal in 1974. He was appointed to the Supreme Court in 1979. James G. Snell and Frederick Vaughan, *The Supreme Court of Canada: History of the Institution* (Toronto: Osgoode Society, 1985), 235, 417; Donn Downey, "Julien Chouinard Supreme Court judge was top civil servant for Quebec premier" *The Globe and Mail* (February 9, 1987).

7   Jean Bienvenue practised law in Quebec City, worked as a Crown prosecutor, and served in Premier Bourassa's cabinet before his appointment to the Superior Court in 1977. During a 1995 trial, Bienvenue incited public outcry with his sexist and Holocaust-minimizing comments during the sentencing of a female murderer. The Canadian Judicial Council recommended that the unrepentant Bienvenue be removed from the bench. He resigned in 1996. Report to the Canadian Judicial Council by the Inquiry Committee into the Conduct of Mr. Justice Jean Bienvenue of the Superior Court of Quebec in *R. v. T. Théberge.*

8   *Annuaire Général de L'Université Laval pour l'année académique 1951–52* (Québec: Université Laval, 1951), 261; interview with Judith Gamache-Côté, Quebec City, May 1, 2008.

9   Backhouse, *Claire L'Heureux-Dubé*, 107–8.

10 Jeanne D'Arc Lemay "Le droit modern et la femme," *Le Carabin* 2:4 (November 14, 1942), 8.

11 Interview with Claire L'Heureux-Dubé, Ottawa, March 10, 2010.

12 Interview with André Desgagné, Quebec City, May 10, 2010; interview with Jacques Alleyn, Ottawa, September 9, 2009.

13 Interview with Roch Bolduc, Quebec City, August 7, 2009.

14 Normand, *Le droit comme discipline universitaire*; J.E.C. Brierley, "Quebec legal education since 1945: Cultural paradoxes and traditional ambiguities," *Dalhousie Law Journal* 10 (1986–87).

15 Normand, *Le droit comme discipline universitaire*, 132–38; interview with Pierre-Gabriel Jobin, Montreal, April 23, 2010.

16 Normand, *Le droit comme discipline universitaire*, 156.

17 Interviews with classmates Martial Asselin, Quebec City, August 7, 2008; Roch Bolduc, Quebec City, August 7, 2009; and Robert Auclair-Hallé, Quebec City, August 7, 2009.

18 Interviews with classmates Roch Bolduc, Quebec City, August 7, 2009; Jacques Alleyn, Ottawa, September 9, 2009; and Robert Auclair-Hallé, Quebec City, August 7, 2009. Peter McCormack, *Supreme at Last: The Evolution of the Supreme*

Court of Canada (Toronto: Lorimer, 2000), 60; Normand, *Le droit comme discipline universitaire*, 96.

19   Interviews with classmates Roch Bolduc, Quebec City, August 7, 2009; and Robert Auclair-Hallé, Quebec City, August 7, 2009.

20   Interview with classmate Monique Perron, Quebec City, May 2, 2008, referring to Maurice Gagné, son of the Hon. Jules-Arthur Gagné.

21   Interview with André Desgagné, Quebec City, May 10, 2010.

22   Interview with Judith Gamache Côté, Quebec City, May 1, 2008.

23   Interview with classmate Monique Perron, Quebec City, May 2, 2008. In 1963, Professor Lacroix announced with embarrassment that this was the first year that sexual offences were to be taught in class to everyone together. For several years previously, Lacroix had lectured separately to the male students and taken the women students to a restaurant where he taught them in a private dining room over lunch. Interview with Pierre-Gabriel Jobin, Montreal, April 23, 2010.

24   Interview with Claire L'Heureux-Dubé, Quebec City, July 25, 2008.

25   Interview with Claire L'Heureux-Dubé, Ottawa, November 1, 2007.

26   Interview with Judith Gamache Côté, Quebec City, May 1, 2008.

27   Interviews with Roch Bolduc, Quebec City, August 7, 2009; Martial Asselin, Quebec City, August 7, 2008; and Jacques Alleyn, Ottawa, September 9, 2009.

28   Interviews with Jacques Alleyn, Ottawa, September 9, 2009; Martial Asselin, Quebec City, August 7, 2008; Roch Bolduc, Quebec City, August 7, 2009; and Robert Auclair-Hallé, Quebec City, August 7, 2009.

29   Backhouse, *Claire L'Heureux-Dubé*, 118–19.

30   Interview with Roch Bolduc, Quebec City, August 7, 2009.

31   Interview with Claire L'Heureux-Dubé, Ottawa, November 1, 2007.

32   J.E.C. Brierley, "Historical aspects of law teaching in Quebec" in Roy J. Matas and Deborah J. McCawley, eds., *Legal Education in Canada: Reports and Background Papers of a National Conference on Legal Education held in Winnipeg, Manitoba* (Montreal: Federation of Law Societies of Canada, 1987).

33   Backhouse, *Claire L'Heureux-Dubé*, 579 note 67.

34   Interview with Michèle Cloutier Mainguy, Quebec City, May 2, 2008.

35   Interview with Thérèse Dionne Lecomte, Rimouski, July 24, 2008.

36   Interview with Annette April, Montreal, June 4, 2010.

37   Backhouse, *Claire L'Heureux-Dubé*, 125.

38   Interview with Claire L'Heureux-Dubé, Ottawa, October 30, 2007.

CHAPTER 5 Bertha Wilson and Dalhousie Law School

1   Supreme Court of Canada webpage http://www.scc-csc.ca/court-cour/
    judges-juges/bio-eng.aspx?id=bertha-wilson shows her starting in 1955, which
    accords with the typed curriculum vitae held in the Osler Archives, Library
    Acquisitions and Resource Service, Toronto. Ellen Anderson, *Judging Bertha
    Wilson: Law as Large as Life* (Toronto: University of Toronto Press, 2001), 37,
    shows 1954 in concurrence with John Willis, *A History of Dalhousie Law School*
    (Toronto: University of Toronto Press, 1979), 234, noting the date of graduation
    as 1957. The latter two sources appear more authoritative.

2   Frances Fish studied from 1915–1918 and was admitted to the Nova Scotia bar as
    its first woman. Willis *Dalhousie Law School,* 76–77.

3   Glube was married and pregnant during her Dalhousie legal studies. She was
    appointed to the Nova Scotia Supreme Court Trial Division in 1977 and became
    its chief justice in 1982. Louise Mailhot, *Les premières! L'histoire de l'accès des
    femmes à la pratique du droit et à la magistrature* (Cowansville: Éditions Yvon
    Blais, 2013), 122–24.

4   Ian Donaldson "Six women among Dal law grads" cited in Anderson, *Judging
    Bertha Wilson,* 398–99; George Inrig, "In my day, Dalhousie Law School," *The
    Ansul* 2 (December 1977), 64.

5   G.V.V. Nicholls, "In my day, Dalhousie Law School," *The Ansul* 2 (December
    1977), 69.

6   Bertha Wilson, "In my day, Dalhousie Law School" *The Ansul* 2 (December 1977),
    61.

7   Wilson, "In my day, Dalhousie Law School," 61.

8   Wilson, "In my day, Dalhousie Law School," 61.

9   Four of the other women were single; Lilias Toward was widowed. Anderson,
    Judging Bertha Wilson, 37, 398; Sandra Gwyn, "Sense and sensibility," *Saturday
    Night* (July 1985), 16.

10 Anderson, *Judging Bertha Wilson,* 37–38.

11 Willis, *Dalhousie Law School,* 6, 10, 19–21.

12 Willis, *Dalhousie Law School,* 14, 78–80, 121, 150.

13 A "life-long devotee of Harvard," Read later added a Harvard doctorate. At
    Dalhousie, his course-load included the more theoretical jurisprudence, Roman
    law, conflicts, and international law. He taught at the University of Minnesota law
    school from 1934 to 1950 before returning to Dalhousie as dean. Willis, *Dalhousie
    Law School,* 88, 97–99, 106–7, 120–1, 173, 183, 197, 203.

14 Christie Blatchford, "Accident launched career that took her to top court," *Toronto
    Star* (March 3, 1982), A4; Anderson, *Judging Bertha Wilson,* 37.

15 Anderson, *Judging Bertha Wilson,* 43; Willis, *Dalhousie Law School,* 183, 234.

16 Constance Backhouse, *Petticoats and Prejudice: Women and Law in
    Nineteenth-Century Canada* (Toronto: Women's Press, 1991), Chapter 10.

17 Cecilia Morgan, "An embarrassingly and severely masculine atmosphere: Women,
    gender and the legal profession, Osgoode Hall, 1920s–1960s," *Canadian Journal*

of *Women and the Law* 11:2 (Fall 1996), 51; Cameron Harvey, "Women in law in Canada," *Manitoba Law Journal* 4 (1970), 13; Mary Kinnear, "That there woman lawyer: Women lawyers in Manitoba 1915–1970," *Canadian Journal of Women and the Law* 5 (1992), 414, 426; Ian C. Pilarczyk, *A Noble Roster: One Hundred and Fifty Years of Law, McGill* (Montreal: McGill University Faculty of Law, 1999), 65–66; interview with Suzanne Labbé, Ottawa, August 12, 2009.

18 Anderson, *Judging Bertha Wilson*, 39.

19 Gwyn, "Sense and sensibility," 13, 17; Charlotte Montgomery, "Bring compassion to Charter rulings: Wilson," *The Globe and Mail* (September 24, 1982); Anderson, *Judging Bertha Wilson*, 36.

20 Anderson, *Judging Bertha Wilson*, 39–43; Gwyn, "Sense and sensibility," 13, 16–17; Willis, *Dalhousie Law School*, 181.

21 Obituary, *The Globe and Mail* (May 9, 2000).

22 Anderson, *Judging Bertha Wilson*, 44–45; Gwyn, "Sense and sensibility," 17.

23 Wilson stood seventh out of seventy in first year, fourth out of fifty-seven in second, and seventh out of fifty-eight in third. Anderson, *Judging Bertha Wilson*, 44–6, 399.

24 Anderson, *Judging Bertha Wilson*, 39–40; Willis, *Dalhousie Law School*, 67, 172–83, 220. Willis noted (174) that the practitioner's approach was designed to prevent any straying "from strict law into such 'irrelevant' things as history, philosophy, medicine, penology, civil liberties and so forth." Offered a more contextual approach, Wilson might have become more interested in criminal law at an earlier stage.

25 Anderson, *Judging Bertha Wilson*, 341–42; Willis, *Dalhousie Law School*, 164, 173, 178; Bertha Wilson, "The ideal teacher," tribute to William Lederman, Queen's University Symposium, quoted by Anderson, 399.

26 Anderson, *Judging Bertha Wilson*, 39, 48.

27 Judith Richards Hope, *Pearls and Pinstripes* (New York: Scribner, 2003), 17.

28 Anderson, *Judging Bertha Wilson*, 48.

29 Gwyn, "Sense and sensibility," 17.

30 Willis, *Dalhousie Law School*, 159, 165. Willis's history referred to faculty members as "a full-time man," "a first-year man," "men of unusual distinction," and "the boys." In a brief reference to "women behind the law school" he focused on the secretaries, and repeated the description of one, offered by a "post-war student," as "supremely efficient and stunningly attractive." 102, 117, 145, 168, 239, 302.

31 Willis, *Dalhousie Law School*, 195. Read did hire Eunice Beeson, a woman doubly qualified in both law and library science, as the law librarian. Dalhousie would have to await a new dean before it hired its first full-time female law lecturer, Patricia Hyndman, in 1965. Correspondence from Dalhousie Law Dean Innis Christie to Mary Jane Mossman, November 18 and December 6, 1988.

32 Interview with Alice Desjardins, Ottawa, July 2, 2009.

33 Wilson and John Charters shared the Smith Shield for mooting in front of three judges in their third year. Anderson, *Judging Bertha Wilson*, 46.

34 Transcript of interview between Curtis Cole and Bertha Wilson, December 18, 1989, Osler Archives, Library Acquisitions and Resource Service, Toronto.

35 Wilson, "In my day, Dalhousie Law School," 62. Bissett had previously hired one of the early Jewish articling students, Samuel Margolian of Yarmouth. Bissett and Clarke were well acquainted as Conservative political activists. Philip Girard and Jeffrey Haylock, "Stratification, economic adversity, and diversity in an urban bar" in Constance Backhouse and W. Wesley Pue, eds., *The Promise and Perils of Law* (Toronto: Irwin Law, 2009), 75, 96.

36 Anderson, *Judging Bertha Wilson*, 46. Bissett had also represented Viola Desmond in her unsuccessful challenge to racial segregation in 1946; Constance Backhouse, *Colour-Coded: A Legal History of Racism in Canada, 1900–1950* (Toronto: Osgoode Society and University of Toronto Press, 1999).

37 Transcript of interview between Curtis Cole and Bertha Wilson, Osler Archives.

CHAPTER 6 L'Heureux-Dubé's practice in Quebec City and marriage

1 Less than a third of the first twenty female Laval graduates found jobs in private practice, mostly through family connections. Constance Backhouse, *Claire L'Heureux-Dubé: A Life* (Vancouver: University of British Columbia Press, 2017), Chapter 11.

2 Ginette Fournier was admitted to the bar in January 1951 and opened her office in late 1951 or early 1952. *Canadian Law List, 1952–56* (Toronto: Cartwright & Sons, n.d.) shows her practising in her own firm. She disappeared from the *Canadian Law List, 1957.*

3 Backhouse, *Claire L'Heureux-Dubé*, 123–25, 141, 150.

4 Interview with Donald Carr, Toronto, September 10, 2009; interview with André Desgagné, Quebec City, May 10, 2010; interview with Melvin Rothman, Montreal, August 12, 2008; interview with Monique Perron, Quebec City, May 2, 2008; interview with Raymond Lessard, Île d'Orléans, Quebec, May 11, 2010; interview with Brauna Hendler, Montreal, July 26, 2010; interview with Jacques Philippon, Quebec City, April 28, 2009; interview with Roger Garneau, Quebec, April 28, 2009.

5 Interview with Joel Bard, Boston, July 8, 2010; interview with Perry Bard, Montreal, August 23, 2010; interview with Roger Garneau, Quebec City, April 28, 2009; "Bard, Samuel Schwarz" in Dr. Eli Gottesman, ed., *Who's Who in Canadian Jewry* (Montreal: Jewish Institute of Higher Research, 1965), 55.

6 Backhouse, *Claire L'Heureux-Dubé*, Chapter 11; Constance Backhouse, *Colour-Coded: A Legal History of Racism in Canada, 1900–1950* (Toronto: University of Toronto Press, 1999), Chapters 4 and 5.

7 Alan Davies, ed., *Antisemitism in Canada: History and Interpretation* (Waterloo: Wilfrid Laurier University Press, 1992); Pierre Anctil and Gary Caldwell, *Juifs et réalités juives au Québec* (Québec: Institut québécois de recherché sur la culture, 1984); Morton Weinfeld, "The Jews of Quebec: Perceived antisemitism, segregation, and emigration," *Jewish Journal of Sociology* 22:1 (1980): 5–20; Harold Troper, *The Defining Decade: Identity, Politics, and the Canadian Jewish Community in the 1960s* (Toronto: University of Toronto Press, 2010), 9–10.

8   Interview with William Tetley, Montreal, April 23, 2010.

9   Interviews with Claire L'Heureux-Dubé, Quebec City, April 27–28, 2009; Clearwater, Florida, May 10–14, 2009.

10   Interview with Claire L'Heureux-Dubé, Quebec City, April 27–28, 2009.

11   Interviews with Claire L'Heureux-Dubé, Ottawa, November 1, 2007; Ottawa, December 2, 2007; Quebec City, July 25, 2008.

12   Interviews with Claire L'Heureux-Dubé, Quebec City, July 25, 2008; Quebec City, April 27–28, 2009.

13   Interviews with Claire L'Heureux-Dubé, Ottawa, November 1, 2007; Ottawa, December 2, 2007; Quebec City, July 25, 2008; interview with Joel Bard, Boston, July 8, 2010.

14   Interview with Perry Bard, Montreal, August 23, 2010.

15   Interview with Joel Bard, Boston, July 8, 2010.

16   Interview with Louis LeBel, Ottawa, July 8, 2010. He practised in Quebec City in the same era and later joined her as a judicial colleague at the Supreme Court of Canada.

17   Statutes of Lower Canada 1865, c.41, article185. Separation from bed and board was the only remedy. A man could obtain it with proof of his wife's adultery. A woman had to prove that her husband was keeping "his concubine in their common habitation." Article 187–8.

18   *Divorce Act*, S.C. 1968, c.24.

19   Interview with Julien Payne, Ottawa, July 7, 2009; interview with Jacques LeMay, Quebec City, May 5, 2010; interview with Roger Chouinard, Quebec City, May 11, 2010.

20   Interview with Claire L'Heureux-Dubé, Ottawa, June 30, 2010.

21   Interview with Claire L'Heureux-Dubé, Quebec City, April 27–28, 2009.

22   Interview with Claire L'Heureux-Dubé, Ottawa, March 10, 2010.

23   Interview with Claire L'Heureux-Dubé, Quebec City, April 27–28, 2009.

24   Interview with Claire L'Heureux-Dubé, Quebec City, April 27–28, 2009.

25   Paul-André Crépeau, *La réforme du droit civil canadien : Une certain conception de la recodification, 1965–1977* (Montréal: Éditions Thémis, 2003); interview with Paul-André Crépeau, Montreal, October 1, 2010.

26   Civil Code Revision Office, *Report on the Family, Part I* (Montréal: Québec Official Publisher, 1974), 12, 16, 141, 148.

27   *Civil Code of Québec*, S.Q. 1991, c.64.

28   Louise Mailhot became the first woman appointed to the Montreal bench of the Quebec Court of Appeal in 1987. Interview with Louise Mailhot, Gananoque, May 20, 2009.

29   Interview with Roger Garneau, Quebec, April 28, 2009.

30   Interview with Claire L'Heureux-Dubé, Clearwater Florida, May 10–14, 2009.

31 Interview with Georges-Henri Dubé, Rimouski, July 24, 2008; interview with Yves Dubé, Ottawa, September 18, 2008; interview with Jean Drapeau, Rimouski, July 24, 2008.

32 Interview with Claire L'Heureux-Dubé, Ottawa, November 1, 2007.

33 Interview with Claire's sister Louise L'Heureux-Giliberti, Chicago, April 21, 2009.

34 Interview with Claire L'Heureux-Dubé, Clearwater Florida, May 10–14, 2009.

35 Interview with Claire L'Heureux-Dubé, Quebec City, April 29–30, 2008.

CHAPTER 7 Bertha Wilson's practice in Toronto

1 In Halifax, John and Bertha had joined the United Church and both remained active with the United Church in Toronto. John's first Toronto job was with the interdenominational church fundraising organization, Wells Canada. When the United Church later created an internal fundraising operation, John took over the management of it. Ellen Anderson, *Judging Bertha Wilson: Law as Large as Life* (Toronto: University of Toronto Press, 2001), 52, 75–77.

2 Transcript of interview between Curtis Cole and Bertha Wilson, December 18, 1989, Osler Archives, Library Acquisitions and Resource Service, Toronto, 1–2.

3 Interview with Edward Saunders, Toronto, July 22, 2016; *Canadian Law List* (Toronto: Cartwright and Sons, 1958); transcript of interview between Cole and Wilson, 1–2. Blake, Cassels, Graydon, the other Toronto firm that Wilson applied to, had one woman lawyer in the thirty-two-lawyer firm in 1958, D.M. (Margaret) Grimshaw, called in 1946. *Canadian Law List* (Toronto: Cartwright and Sons, 1958).

4 Transcript of interview between Cole and Wilson, 2. Gordon (Swatty) Wotherspoon, the individual quoted, was still known around the firm as "the Brigadier." Interview with Timothy Kennish, Toronto, July 21, 2016.

5 Janet MacFarland, "Purdy Crawford was the firm hand on Canada's business tiller," *The Globe and Mail* (August 15, 2014).

6 Transcript of interview between Cole and Wilson, 2. There had been several female articling students prior to Wilson, although none between 1954 and 1958, and none had been asked to stay on. Senior partner Hal Mockridge's opposition to women was evident some years later when women were first admitted as undergraduate students to Princeton University. A former Princeton grad, Mockridge resigned his membership in the Princeton Club in protest. Interview with Edward Saunders, Toronto, July 22, 2016; interview with Timothy Kennish, Toronto, July 21, 2016; Angela Fernandez and Beatrice Tice, "Bertha Wilson's practice years (1958–1975)" in Kim Brooks, ed., *Justice Bertha Wilson: One Woman's Difference* (Vancouver: University of British Columbia Press, 2009), 15, 16.

7 Transcript of interview between Cole and Wilson, 3; Anderson, *Judging Bertha Wilson*, 53.

8 Interview with Bill Bryden, Guelph Ontario, August 29, 2016, advising that he was upset when he discovered Wilson's articling term would terminate before she could finish his research and that he convinced Wotherspoon to offer Wilson a

permanent post. Wilson's memory was that it was Wotherspoon whose research necessitated her continuing employment. Transcript of interview between Cole and Wilson, 5.

9   Backhouse, *Claire L'Heureux-Dubé: A Life* (Vancouver: University of British Columbia Press, 2017), Chapter 11.

10 Clara Brett Martin had been called to the bar in Toronto in 1897. Constance Backhouse, *Petticoats and Prejudice: Women and Law in Nineteenth-Century Canada* (Toronto: Women's Press, 1991). In addition to Blake's Margaret Grimshaw, Margaret P. Hyndman, Janet Boland, and Mabel M. Van Camp were among the women practising in 1958. *Canadian Law List* (Toronto: Cartwright and Sons, 1958).

11 There was one Roman Catholic and one Jehovah's Witness; there were no Jews. Curtis Cole, *Osler, Hoskin & Harcourt: Portrait of a Partnership* (Whitby: McGraw-Hill Ryerson, 1995), 92–115; interview with Maurice Coombs, Toronto, July 22, 2016.

12 Interview with Timothy Kennish, Toronto, July 21, 2016.

13 Cole, *Osler, Hoskin & Harcourt*, 92–94, 113–14, 132–33, 294.

14 The three lawyers often credited with the modernization of Osler were Purdy Crawford (the rainmaker), Allan Beattie (the conciliator and consensus-maker), and Bertha Wilson (the in-house lawyer's lawyer). Anderson, *Judging Bertha Wilson*, 58.

15 Interview with Dennis Lane, Haliburton, ON, August 26, 2016.

16 Interview with Edward Saunders, Toronto, July 22, 2016.

17 Anderson, *Judging Bertha Wilson*, 61.

18 Interview with Ron Ellis, Toronto, October 12, 2016.

19 Interview with Timothy Kennish, Toronto, July 21, 2016.

20 Fernandez and Tice, "Bertha Wilson's Practice Years," 26–30; interview with Edward Saunders, Toronto, July 22, 2016.

21 Interview with Timothy Kennish, Toronto, July 21, 2016; Anderson, *Judging Bertha Wilson*, 56–57.

22 Interview with Curtis Cole, Toronto, October 13, 2016.

23 Sandra Gwyn, "Sense and sensibility," *Saturday Night* (July 1985), 13, 17.

24 Anderson, *Judging Bertha Wilson*, 64.

25 Interview with Dennis Lane, Toronto, August 26, 2016; Anderson, *Judging Bertha Wilson*, 59–65, adding that if someone presented a position that troubled Wilson, "she might seek him out the following day and let him know her opinion privately." Anderson, 63.

26 Fernandez and Tice, "Bertha Wilson's practice years," 31.

27 In 1962, *The Globe and Mail* mentioned her presentation at the "first Ontario women's conference of the New Democratic Party" in which she advocated for governmental action on public housing. "Lawyer criticizes poor housing," *The Globe and Mail* (May 7, 1962), 14. In 1971, Wilson was one of a small band of Osler lawyers who spearheaded a proposal to set up a pro bono storefront legal aid clinic, a project that the partners rejected after it resulted in political divisions

within the firm. Her principled positions led her colleague Allan Beattie to characterize her as the "conscience of the firm." Interview with Ron Ellis, Toronto, October 12, 2016; interview with Jack Ground, Toronto, 2016; Anderson, *Judging Bertha Wilson,* 63; transcript of interview between Cole and Wilson, 12.

28 Interview with Bill Bryden, Guelph, August 29, 2016.

29 Fernandez and Tice, "Bertha Wilson's practice years," 24; transcript of interview between Cole and Wilson, 4; interview with Dennis Lane, Toronto, August 26, 2016; interview with Maurice Coombs, Toronto, July 22, 2016.

30 Interview with Dennis Lane, Toronto, August 26, 2016; interview with Jack Ground, Toronto, October 12, 2016; interview with John Morden, Toronto, July 20, 2016.

31 Interview with Maurice Coombs, Toronto, July 22, 2016.

32 Transcript of interview between Cole and Wilson, 6.

33 Interview with Dennis Lane, Toronto, August 26, 2016.

34 Interview with Timothy Kennish, Toronto, July 21, 2016 and speaking notes of Timothy Kennish, Bertha Wilson portrait unveiling, June 28, 1999, 2; interview with Dennis Lane, Toronto, August 26, 2016; Cole, *Osler, Hoskin & Harcourt,* 125; Anderson, *Judging Bertha Wilson,* 70–71.

35 Interview with Ron Ellis, Toronto, October 12, 2016.

36 Anderson, *Judging Bertha Wilson,* 58.

CHAPTER 8 Practising as a woman

1 In 1972, L'Heureux-Dubé's last year of practice, women represented 4.49 per cent of the lawyers in Quebec City; province-wide, women had grown to represent 6.7 per cent. *Canadian Law List, 1952* (Toronto: Cartwright & Sons, n.d.); *Tableau de l'ordre des avocats de la province de Québec, 1972–73* (Montréal: Barreau du Québec, 1972). When Wilson left in 1975, women called to the Ontario bar represented 10.4 per cent. Constance Backhouse, "A revolution in numbers" in Constance Backhouse and W. Wesley Pue, eds., *The Promise and Perils of Law* (Toronto: Irwin Law, 2009), 245, 289.

2 Interview with Roger Garneau, Quebec City, April 28, 2009.

3 Curtis Cole, *Osler, Hoskin & Harcourt* (Whitby: McGraw-Hill Ryerson, 1995), 125.

4 Bertha Wilson chapter in John Arnup, "Swearing out: An inside look, the Court of Appeal and some of its judges," Law Society of Upper Canada Archives, Toronto, #2014009-001, 179.

5 Patricia T. Rooke and R.L. Schnell, *No Bleeding Heart: Charlotte Whitton, A Feminist on the Right* (Vancouver: University of British Columbia Press, 1987), 2.

6 Claire L'Heureux-Dubé, "Femmes et droit : le regard d'une pionnière, une vision du passé et de l'avenir" in Hélène Dumont, ed., *Femmes et Droit : 50 ans de vie commune...et tout un avenir* (Montréal: Les Éditions Thémis, 1991), 314.

7 Peter Mark Roget. *Thesaurus of English Words and Phrases* (Toronto: Longmans, Green & Co., 1947), 120, 328, 440, 702.

8   Interview with Thérèse Dionne Lecomte, Rimouski, July 24, 2008; interview with Michèle Cloutier Mainguy, Quebec City, May 2, 2008.

9   Interview with Shiranee Tilakawardane, London UK, May 3, 2012, in reference to L'Heureux-Dubé's ability to charm judges internationally.

10   Interview with Roger Garneau, Quebec City, April 28, 2009.

11   Interview with Claire L'Heureux-Dubé, Quebec City, April 27–28, 2009.

12   Roget, *Thesaurus* (1947) lists "tiger" as synonymous with these, 328.

13   Bertha Wilson, "Tribute to Allan Leslie Beattie" and "Tribute to Mr. Justice John D. Arnup" in *Speeches Delivered by the Honourable Bertha Wilson 1976–1991* (Ottawa: Supreme Court of Canada, 1992).

14   Ellen Anderson, *Judging Bertha Wilson: Law as Large as Life* (Toronto: University of Toronto Press, 2001), 58, citing Stuart Thom.

15   Interview with Maurice Coombs, Toronto, July 22, 2016; interview with Moira McConnell, Montreal, November 13, 2017.

16   Interview with Timothy Kennish, Toronto, July 21, 2016.

17   Interview with Hester Lessard, Victoria, November 4, 2016.

18   Interview with David Stratas, Ottawa, August 31, 2016; interview with Kent Roach, Cambridge UK, July 5, 2017.

19   Interview with Ron Ellis, Toronto, October 12, 2016.

20   Interview with Jack Ground, Toronto, October 12, 2016.

21   Anderson, *Judging Bertha Wilson*, 57–72. Timothy Kennish added, "She was ambitious in what she chose to do, ambitious to do well in the area. She wasn't ambitious for the type of success that would have been enjoyed by other men in the roles that they had." Interview with Timothy Kennish, Toronto, July 21, 2016.

22   "It was never 'come back and see me tomorrow.' If you were in her office, you got her attention." Interview with Dennis Lane, Toronto, August 26, 2016.

23   Interview with Maurice Coombs, Toronto, July 22, 2016.

24   Angela Fernandez and Beatrice Tice, "Bertha Wilson's practice years (1958–1975)" in Kim Brooks, ed., *Justice Bertha Wilson: One Woman's Difference* (Vancouver: University of British Columbia Press, 2009), 15, 19.

25   Interview with Claire L'Heureux-Dubé, Quebec City, April 27–28, 2009.

26   "Wilson to lead status of women probe," *London Free Press* (August 20, 1991).

27   Wilson was made a partner on January 1, 1968. Some of her colleagues made partner in five years or less; the norm was six years. Wilson recalled that the explanation she was given was "that they didn't think I was going to stay…that my husband was going to move." Other rationalizations were also offered: the kind of work she was doing was different from that of the traditional career path and the three-year cycle of decision-making caused unavoidable delay depending on what year the individual came into the firm. Wilson laughed at the absurdity of some of the explanations while accepting others, but she was also "disappointed." Transcript of interview between Cole and Wilson, 11; Anderson, *Judging Bertha Wilson*, 58; interview with Edward Saunders, Toronto, July 22, 2016; interview with Timothy Kennish, Toronto, July 21, 2016. Colleague Jack Ground thought

that there might have been "some residual resistance to the notion of a female partner." Interview with Jack Ground, Toronto, 2016. Ellis speculated that Mockridge was the major point of resistance. Interview with Ron Ellis, Toronto, October 12, 2016.

28 Interview with Maurice Coombs, Toronto, July 22, 2016. Coombs stressed that this was undoubtedly meant affectionately.

29 Anderson, *Judging Bertha Wilson*, 62.

30 The comment was made in 1966. Cameron Harvey, "Women in law in Canada," *Manitoba Law Journal* 4 (1970) 9, 22.

31 Harvey, "Women in law in Canada," 14.

32 Interview with Claire L'Heureux-Dubé, Quebec City, April 27–28, 2009; interview with Claire L'Heureux-Dubé, Clearwater Florida, May 10–14, 2009.

33 Wilson's view was that she "didn't have any problems really as a woman practising there." Alicia Forgie became a lawyer with Osler in 1966 and Heather Frawley in 1970. By 1981, there were sixteen women lawyers (16.5 per cent) but only five (8.6 per cent) were partners. Wilson recalled that she thoroughly enjoyed raising the maternity policy at the partnership meeting: "It was great fun, from my point of view, hearing the male reactions to some of these questions." Transcript of interview between Cole and Wilson, 4, 12; Cole, *Osler, Hoskin & Harcourt*, 125, 143, 154, 339; interview with Jack Ground, Toronto, 2016; Anderson, *Judging Bertha Wilson*, 71.

34 Interview with Bill Bryden, Guelph, August 29, 2016; interview with Timothy Kennish, Toronto, July 21, 2016; interview with Dennis Lane, Toronto, August 26, 2016.

35 Interview with Curtis Cole, Toronto, October 13, 2016.

36 Interview with Claire L'Heureux-Dubé, Clearwater Florida, May 10–14, 2009.

CHAPTER 9 First judicial appointments: "No woman can do my job!"

1 "I later learned that these concerns were succinctly expressed by one prospective colleague as 'no woman can do my job!'" Bertha Wilson chapter in John Arnup, "Swearing out: An inside look, the Court of Appeal and some of its judges," Law Society of Upper Canada Archives, Toronto #2014009-001, 179.

2 Réjane Laberge-Colas, the first female judge of the Quebec Superior Court (in Montreal), was appointed by Justice Minister John Turner and Prime Minister Trudeau in February 1969. "Réjane Laberge-Colas (1923–2009). « Décès d'une pionnière de la magistrature » *Le Devoir* (August 11, 2009). Mabel Margaret Van Camp, the second, was appointed by Turner and Trudeau to the Supreme Court of Ontario in 1971. Obituary, William Illsey Atkinson, "I am the damn judge," *The Globe and Mail* (August 9, 2012), R5.

3 Gail Cuthbert Brandt et al., *Canadian Women: A History* 3rd edition (Toronto: Nelson, 2011).

4 Cuthbert Brandt et al., *Canadian Women*, 527; Clio Collective, *Quebec Women: A History* (Toronto: Women's Press, 1987), 358; Micheline Dumont, *Le féminisme québécois raconté à Camille* (Montréal: les éditions du remue-ménage, 2009),

106–7; Betty Friedan, *The Feminine Mystique* (New York: W.W. Norton, 1963); Simone de Beauvoir, *Le deuxième sexe* (Paris: Édition Gallimard, 1949); Marguerite Andersen, *Feminist Journeys/Voies féministes* (Ottawa: Feminist History Society, 2010).

5   Canadian Bar Association, *Touchstones for Change: Equality, Diversity and Accountability. The Report on Gender Equality in the Legal Profession* (Ottawa: Canadian Bar Association, 1993), 25.

6   Lawyers were involved in this campaign. Margaret Hyndman, called to the Ontario bar in 1926, was active with Business and Professional Women's clubs and the Committee on Equality for Women. Cuthbert Brandt et al., *Canadian Women*, 393, 526; "Margaret Hyndman" https://www.lsuc.on.ca/uploadedFiles/PDC/CR_and_A/PF86.pdf. Doris Ogilvie, a 1960 law graduate from the University of New Brunswick (appointed a deputy judge of the juvenile and provincial courts in 1965) would sit as a commissioner of the Royal Commission. http://www.inmemoriam.ca/voir-annonce-289419-doris-ogilvie.html.

7   Letter of Laura Sabia, April 18, 1966, quoted in Cerise Morris, "No more than simple justice: The Royal Commission on the Status of Women and social change in Canada," unpublished MA thesis (January 1982), McGill University Department of Sociology, 114.

8   *Report of the Royal Commission on the Status of Women in Canada* (Ottawa: Information Canada, 1970) noted (342) that there were 889 judges and magistrates in Canada, but only fourteen were women and only one, Réjane Laberge-Colas, was a member of a superior court.

9   Dumont, *Le féminisme québécois raconté à Camille*, 126–27.

10 Anthony Westell, "Report is more explosive," *Toronto Star* (December 8, 1970).

11 Marc Lalonde, Trudeau's principal secretary from 1968 to 1972, emphasized that "Trudeau was really supportive and we wanted to proceed with the [Royal Commission] recommendations." Interview with Marc Lalonde, Île Perrot, Quebec, August 16, 2012.

12 The CBA committee completed a confidential consultation and pronounced individuals to be "well qualified," "qualified," or "not qualified." The minister was not required to accept the recommendation, but it often carried the day. Ed Ratushny, "Judicial appointments: The Lang legacy" (1977–78) 1, *Advocates' Quarterly* 2, 6–11.

13 Lang served as minister of justice from 1972 to 1975, and Basford from 1975 to 1978.

14 Interview with Edward Ratushny, Ottawa, July 28, 2016. Ratushny did not begin to work for Lang until after L'Heureux-Dubé's appointment, although the changes in the consultation process were already under way.

15 During the 1970s, there was significant growth in the size of the judiciary, resulting from improved retirement options and an expansion of the courts. The number of new slots furnished opportunities for more diverse choices. Ratushny, "Judicial appointments," 4–7, 16.

16 Geoffrey Stevens, "What makes a good judge?" *The Globe and Mail* (March 8, 1974).

17 Interview with Ed Ratushny, Ottawa, July 28, 2016.

18 Ratushny, "Judicial appointments," 14–15.

19 Backhouse, *Claire L'Heureux-Dubé*, Chapter 17; interview with Monique Bégin, Ottawa, September 4, 2011.

20 Lily Tasso, "La famille avant la politique chez Madame Claire L'Heureux-Dubé" (October 5, 1972), clipping in scrapbook kept by Paul L'Heureux.

21 Backhouse, *Claire L'Heureux-Dubé*, chapters 14–17.

22 Interview with Albanie Morin (daughter of the deceased Albanie Paré Morin), Montreal, August 1, 2008; Backhouse, *Claire L'Heureux-Dubé*, Chapter 17.

23 Interview with Otto Lang, Winnipeg, September 4, 2009.

24 "First in Canada: Woman named to Appeal Court," *The Globe and Mail* (December 20, 1975), 11; Bertha Wilson curriculum vitae, copy on file with the author.

25 Bertha Wilson curriculum vitae; Anderson, *Judging Bertha Wilson*, 74–75. After her Supreme Court of Canada appointment, Wilson would later serve on the Judicial Committee of the United Church of Canada from 1986 to 1994, along with a number of other judges. Correspondence from Beth Symes, April 2018.

26 "96 lawyers named Queen's Counsel include three women," *The Globe and Mail* (January 1, 1974), 33.

27 Interview with Ed Ratushny, Ottawa, July 28, 2016.

28 Interview with Edward Saunders, Toronto, July 22, 2016; interview with Ron Ellis, Toronto, October 12, 2016; transcript of interview between Cole and Wilson, December 18, 1989, Osler Archives, Library Acquisitions and Resource Service, Toronto, 24.

29 Wilson chapter in Arnup, "Swearing out," 180; interview with Edward Saunders, Toronto, July 22, 2016; Anderson, *Judging Bertha Wilson*, 65–69.

30 Interview with Ed Ratushny, Ottawa, July 28, 2016.

31 Interview with Edward Saunders, Toronto, July 22, 2016; interview with John Brooke, Toronto, October 11, 2016; interview with Horace Krever, Toronto, July 20, 2016; interview with Jack Ground, Toronto, October 12, 2016; interview with John Morden, Toronto, July 20, 2016; interview with Tim Kennish, Toronto, July 21, 2016.

32 Interview with Thomas Zuber, Windsor, August 30, 2016.

33 Interviews with Claire L'Heureux-Dubé, Ottawa, March 5, 2009; September 21, 2009; Quebec City, August 30, 2012.

34 Backhouse, *Claire L'Heureux-Dubé*, Chapter 17.

35 Interview with André Desgagné, Quebec City, May 10, 2010.

36 Interview with Jacques Philippon, Quebec City, April 28, 2009.

37 Interview with Nicole L'Heureux, Clearwater, Florida, May 11–12, 2009.

38 Transcript of interview between Cole and Wilson, 24; notes from Bertha Wilson speech, Osler Partners' Tribute Dinner, January 12, 1976, Library and Archives Canada R15636, vol. 49, file 21.

39 Anderson, *Judging Bertha Wilson,* 84.

40 Interview with Jack Ground, Toronto, October 12, 2016; interview with Maurice Coombs, Toronto, July 22, 2016.

41 Nicole Beaulieu, "Première femme nommée juge à la Cour supérieure de Québec," *Action Québec* (March 10, 1973).

42 "First in Canada"; "Woman named to court of appeal," *Toronto Star* (December 19, 1975).

43 Interview with Dennis Lane, Haliburton, August 26, 2016.

44 Sandra Gwyn, "Sense and sensibility," *Saturday Night* (July 1985), 13, 17.

45 Recounted in interview with Dennis Lane, Haliburton, August 26, 2016.

46 Interview with Ed Ratushny, Ottawa, July 28, 2016.

47 Interview with Dennis Lane, Haliburton, August 26, 2016.

48 Interview with Ron Ellis, Toronto, October 12, 2016.

49 Interview with John Brooke, Toronto, October 11, 2016.

CHAPTER 10 Claire L'Heureux-Dubé and the Quebec Superior Court

1 Ignace-J. Deslauriers, *La Cour supérieure du Québec et ses juges 1849. 1er janvier 1980* (Québec: Bibliothèque Nationale du Québec, 1980), 10–56.

2 Allocution de L'Honorable Frédéric Dorion, Juge en Chef de la Cour Supérieure, à la prestation de serment de Me Claire L'Heureux-Dubé comme juge de la Cour Supérieure, le 9 Mars 1973, à Québec.

3 Interview with Pierre-Gabriel Jobin, Montreal, April 23, 2010; "Le juge Frédéric Dorion s'élève contre l'avortement," *L'Action Québec* (August 2, 1973); Lorne Slotnick, "Barbie aide was the darling of Quebec's conservatives," *The Globe and Mail* (February 11, 1983); Constance Backhouse, *Claire L'Heureux-Dubé: A Life* (Vancouver: University of British Columbia Press, 2017), Chapter 18.

4 L'Heureux-Dubé observed that the chief justice relaxed his critical views somewhat as her term wore on.

5 Nicolas Tremblay, "Parfum de sagesse," *Entre prendre* 10; *Femme : 100 Québécoises au sommet d'action* (1999), 43.

6 Interview with Claire L'Heureux-Dubé, Ottawa, September 13, 2010.

7 Interview with Claire L'Heureux-Dubé, Ottawa, September 21, 2009.

8 Interview with Claire L'Heureux-Dubé, Quebec City, August 30, 2012.

9 Interview with Claire L'Heureux-Dubé, Quebec City, August 30, 2012.

10 Interview with Claire L'Heureux-Dubé, Quebec City, August 30, 2012.

11 Backhouse, *Claire L'Heureux-Dubé,* Chapters 18 and 20. The 457 unreported trial decisions that survive from the years 1976–1979 are held in the Bibliothèque et Archives nationales du Québec.

[12] Claire L'Heureux-Dubé, "Femmes et droit: le regard d'une pionnière, une vision du passé et de l'avenir" in Hélène Dumont, ed., *Femmes et Droit : 50 ans de vie commune...et tout un avenir* (Montréal: Les Éditions Thémis, 1993), 314; interview with Claire L'Heureux-Dubé, Quebec City, August 30, 2012.

[13] Interview with Louise Dubé, Boston, May 22, 2012.

[14] J.-Claude Rivard, "Pour Claire L'Heureux-Dubé être juge, c'est exercer le plus beau métier du monde," Québec *Le Soleil* (October 20, 1979), A-7.

[15] Interview with Claire L'Heureux-Dubé, Quebec City, August 30, 2012.

[16] Interview with Claire L'Heureux-Dubé, Quebec City, August 30, 2012.

[17] Interview with Claire L'Heureux-Dubé, Clearwater Florida, May 10–14, 2009.

[18] Interview with Claire L'Heureux-Dubé, Quebec City, August 30, 2012.

[19] Backhouse, *Claire L'Heureux-Dubé*, Chapter 20.

[20] Interview with Claire L'Heureux-Dubé, Quebec City, August 30 2012.

[21] "Claire L'Heureux-Dubé: Une vision humaine de la justice," *Rimouski Progrès-Echo* (March 24, 1976), A-15.

[22] Backhouse, *Claire L'Heureux-Dubé*, Chapter 20.

[23] "Claire L'Heureux-Dubé: Une vision humaine de la justice."

[24] Backhouse, *Claire L'Heureux-Dubé*, Chapter 20.

CHAPTER 11 Claire L'Heureux-Dubé: Family tragedy and the Quebec Court of Appeal

[1] Interview with Claire L'Heureux-Dubé, Quebec City, July 4–5, 2013.

[2] Mary Kinnear, "That there woman lawyer: Women lawyers in Manitoba 1915–1970" *Canadian Journal of Women and the Law* 5 (1992), 418.

[3] Cécile Brosseau, "Claire L'Heureux-Dube, la femme des défis," *La Presse* (February 12, 1975); Constance Backhouse, *Claire L'Heureux-Dubé: A Life* (Vancouver: University of British Columbia Press, 2017), Chapter 14.

[4] Interview with Claire L'Heureux-Dubé, Clearwater Florida, May 10–14, 2009; Backhouse, *Claire L'Heureux-Dubé*, Chapters 14 and 21.

[5] Interviews with Claire L'Heureux-Dubé, Quebec City, July 4–5, 2013 and Ottawa, March 5, 2009; interview with Gisèle Blondeau-Labrie, Quebec City, May 1, 2008; Backhouse, *Claire L'Heureux-Dubé*, Chapters 14 and 21.

[6] Backhouse, *Claire L'Heureux-Dubé*, Chapter 21.

[7] Interview with Louise L'Heureux-Giliberti, Chicago, April 21, 2009.

[8] Backhouse, *Claire L'Heureux-Dubé*, Chapter 21.

[9] Interview with Claire L'Heureux-Dubé, Clearwater Florida, November 25–27, 2014.

[10] Comments by Claire L'Heureux-Dubé during interview with her brother-in-law Georges-Henri Dubé, Rimouski, July 24, 2008.

[11] Interview with Georges-Henri Dubé, Rimouski, July 24, 2008.

[12] Interview with Claire L'Heureux-Dubé, Ottawa, March 5, 2009.

[13] Interview with Louise Dubé, Boston, May 22, 2012.

14   "Juge à la Cour d'appel," Québec *Le Soleil* (October 18, 1979), A14; André Cedilot, "Première femme juge à la Cour d'appel," *La Presse* (November 3, 1979), C3.

15   Backhouse, *Claire L'Heureux-Dubé,* Chapter 22.

16   Backhouse, *Claire L'Heureux-Dubé,* Chapter 22.

17   Cedilot, "Première femme juge à la Cour d'appel"; Claude Roussin, "Hommage à Claire L'Heureux-Dubé," *Aristide* 6:3 (November 1979), 4; Claude de Cotret, "Une première: un juge féminin à la Cour d'appel," Montréal *Le Journal* (November 3, 1979); "First woman appointed to appeal court," Montreal *Gazette* (November 3, 1979).

18   Roussin, "Hommage à Claire L'Heureux-Dubé," 4.

19   Interview with Raymond Lessard, Quebec City, May 11, 2010.

20   Cedilot, "Première femme juge à la Cour d'appel."

21   Interview with Claire L'Heureux-Dubé, Quebec City, August 30, 2012.

22   Owen had been appointed directly to the Court of Appeal from his Montreal law practice in 1955 and held one of the positions ear-marked for Anglophone judges. Interviews with Claire L'Heureux-Dubé, Ottawa, September 13, 2010; Quebec City, July 4–5, 2013; Ignace-J. Deslauriers, *La Cour d'Appel du Québec et ses juges, 1849 à 1980* (Québec: Comité Général des juges de la Cour Supérieure de la Province de Québec, 1980), 17.

23   Interviews with Claire L'Heureux-Dubé, Ottawa, September 13, 2010; Quebec City, July 4–5, 2013. The story later circulated amongst other judges. Interview with Melvin Rothman, Montreal, August 12, 2008.

24   Interview with Claire L'Heureux-Dubé, Quebec City, July 4–5, 2013.

25   Interview with Claire L'Heureux-Dubé, Quebec City, July 4–5, 2013. Called to the bar in 1955, Kaufman practiced with Cohen, Leithman, and Kaufman, a firm that later became Kaufman, Yarosky, and Fish. He was named directly to the Court of Appeal in 1973. Deslauriers, *La Cour d'Appel du Québec,* 24.

26   Interview with Claire L'Heureux-Dubé, Quebec City, July 4–5, 2013.

27   Interview with her former law clerk Marie-Claude Belleau, Ottawa, December 11, 2013.

28   Interview with Melvin Rothman, Montreal, August 12, 2008.

29   Interview with Rosalie Abella, Ottawa, November 9, 2007.

30   Interview with Roger Chouinard, Quebec City, May 11, 2010.

31   Interview with Roger Chouinard, Quebec City, May 11, 2010.

32   Backhouse, *Claire L'Heureux-Dubé,* Chapter 23.

33   Backhouse, *Claire L'Heureux-Dubé,* Chapter 23.

34   Backhouse, *Claire L'Heureux-Dubé,* Chapter 23.

35   Richard A. Posner, "Judicial opinions and appellate advocacy in federal courts: One judge's views," *Duquesne Law Review* 51 (2013), 3, 7.

36   Interviews with Claire L'Heureux-Dubé, Quebec City, August 30, 2012; July 4–5, 2013.

CHAPTER 12 Bertha Wilson and the Ontario Court of Appeal

[1] Gale swearing-in speech, January 5, 1976, Law Society of Upper Canada Archives (Toronto), #2012018-084.

[2] Gale swearing-in speech.

[3] Sandra Chapnik and Janet Boland, address for Mabel Van Camp's retirement dinner, May 5, 1995, Law Society of Upper Canada Archives, #2000046; Van Camp obituary, William Atkinson, "I am the damn judge," *The Globe and Mail* (August 9, 2012), R5; interview with Horace Krever, Toronto, July 20, 2016.

[4] Interview with Horace Krever, Toronto, July 20, 2016.

[5] Ellen Anderson, *Judging Bertha Wilson: Law as Large as Life* (Toronto: University of Toronto Press, 2001), 85.

[6] Mabel Van Camp is the source for this quote. Prior to Wilson's appointment, there were just two other women at the trial division of the Ontario Superior Court: Van Camp and Janet Boland. Van Camp transcript, Osgoode Society for Canadian Legal History (Toronto), 243–45; interview with Boland by Allison Kirk-Montgomery, Law Society of Upper Canada, November 28, 2012, http://lsuc.on.ca/uploadedFiles/PDC/Archives/Diversifying_the_Bar/Interview%20with%20Hon.%20Janet%20Boland(1).pdf.

[7] Anderson, *Judging Bertha Wilson*, 87.

[8] "Wilson chapter" in John Arnup, "Swearing out: An inside look at the Court of Appeal and some of its judges," Law Society of Upper Canada Archives #2014009-001, 178, 179.

[9] "Wilson chapter," 179; Anderson, *Judging Bertha Wilson*, 88.

[10] Interview with John Brooke, Toronto, October 11, 2016.

[11] Interview with John Brooke, Toronto, October 11, 2016.

[12] "The Court of Appeal Part I and II" *Journal* (Toronto: Advocates' Society, Spring and Summer 2001) on reputations.

[13] Interview with John Brooke, Toronto, October 11, 2016.

[14] Interview with Horace Krever, Toronto, July 20, 2016.

[15] Interview with Thomas Zuber, Windsor, August 30, 2016.

[16] Interview with John Brooke, Toronto, October 11, 2016.

[17] Interview with Horace Krever, Toronto, July 20, 2016.

[18] Anderson, *Judging Bertha Wilson*, 94–95.

[19] "Wilson chapter," 181–82.

[20] Interview with Edward Saunders, Toronto, July 22, 2016; interview with Horace Krever, Toronto, July 20, 2016; interview with John Morden, Toronto, July 20, 2016.

[21] "Reminiscences of John Arnup," *Journal* (Toronto: Advocates' Society, Spring 2001), 12.

[22] Anderson, *Judging Bertha Wilson*, 88.

23 Anderson, *Judging Bertha Wilson*, 88–89.

24 "Wilson chapter," 181.

25 *R. v. Olbey* (1978), 37 CCC (2d) 390, appealed to the Supreme Court of Canada, which upheld Martin's decision (Bora Laskin dissenting): [1980] 1 SCR 1008.

26 *Becker v. Pettkus* (1978), 20 OR 105 (Ont. CA).

27 *Murdoch v. Murdoch* (1973), 41 DLR (3d) 367 (SCC).

28 "Common-law wife owns half of couple's business, appeal judges rule," *The Globe and Mail* (June 21, 1978), 5.

29 *Pettkus v. Becker*, [1980] 2 SCR 834.

30 *Board of Governors of Seneca College v. Bhadauria* (1979), 105 DLR (3d) 707 (Ont. CA); Kate Sutherland, "Precedent, principle, and pragmatism: Justice Wilson and the expansion of Canadian tort law" in Jamie Cameron, ed., *Reflections on the Legacy of Justice Bertha Wilson* (Markham, ON: LexisNexis, 2008), 131–133.

31 *Bhadauria*, 714.

32 Sutherland, "Precedent, principle, and pragmatism," 135; Elizabeth Adjin-Tettey, "Picking up where Justice Wilson left off: The tort of discrimination revisited" in Kim Brooks, ed., *Justice Bertha Wilson: One Woman's Difference* (Vancouver: University of British Columbia Press, 2009), 113.

33 *Seneca College v. Bhadauria*, [1981] 2 SCR 181, held that the statute codified a complete legal regime for the enforcement of human rights, precluding the expansion of tort law.

34 Anderson, *Judging Bertha Wilson*, 89–91.

35 Interview with Thomas Zuber, Windsor, August 30, 2016.

36 Interview with John Brooke, Toronto, October 11, 2016.

CHAPTER 13 Appointments to the Supreme Court of Canada,
1982 and 1987

1 Joan Biskupic, *Sandra Day O'Connor: How the First Woman on the Supreme Court Became Its Most Influential Justice* (New York: Harper Collins, 2005); Ellen Anderson, *Judging Bertha Wilson: Law as Large as Life* (Toronto: University of Toronto Press, 2001), 125.

2 In the 1928 ruling known as the Persons Case, the British Privy Council held that women were "persons" for the purpose of appointment to the Canadian Senate. "Persons Day" is celebrated annually in Canada. The National Action Committee on the Status of Women was founded in 1971 to lobby for the Canada-wide implementation of the Royal Commission recommendations.

3 Penney Kome, *The Taking of Twenty-Eight: Women Challenge the Constitution* (Toronto: Women's Press, 1983).

4 James G. Snell and Frederick Vaughan, *The Supreme Court of Canada: History of the Institution* (Toronto: Osgoode Society, 1985), 251.

5 The *Supreme Court Act, 1985,* R.S.C. 1985, c. S-26, s. 5, required three Quebec

judges. The other geographic divisions were more a matter of custom than law and were occasionally honoured more fluidly. In 1979, Ontario stood aside for a third Western judge (William Rogers McIntyre) in recognition that Ronald Martland (Alberta) would soon retire and Ontario would regain its third slot. Martland retired in February 1982. Interview with Edward Ratushny, Ottawa, July 28, 2016; Snell and Vaughan, *Supreme Court of Canada*, 259–61.

6   Other Ontario judges mentioned were Arthur Martin, Sydney Robins, Maurice Lecourcier, Donald Thorson, and Thomas Zuber. Robert Sheppard, "Next Supreme Court justice may be a woman, jurists feel," *The Globe and Mail* (January 13, 1982), 1–2.

7   Robert J. Sharpe and Kent Roach, *Brian Dickson: A Judge's Journey* (Toronto: University of Toronto Press, 2003), 186; interview with Edward Ratushny, Ottawa, July 28, 2016.

8   "The Honourable Gerald Eric Le Dain" official Supreme Court biography, http://www.scc-csc.ca/judges-juges/bio-eng.aspx?id=gerald-eric-le-dain.

9   Christopher Moore, *The Court of Appeal for Ontario* (Toronto: University of Toronto Press, 2014), 129; Sharpe and Roach, *Brian Dickson,* 186; interview with Horace Krever, Toronto, July 20, 2016.

10   Wilson was the only woman on the Ontario Court of Appeal. The two other senior female judges in Ontario, Janet Boland and Mabel Van Camp, sat on the Supreme Court trial division. Sheppard, "Next Supreme Court justice."

11   *Supreme Court Act*, RSC 1985, c. S-46, s. 4(2); Peter Russell, "Selecting Supreme Court judges" lecture, University of New Brunswick Faculty of Law, Fredericton, October 20, 2016.

12   Anderson, *Judging Bertha Wilson,* 124–25; interview with Allen Linden, Toronto, July 21, 2016. Linden recalled that the discussion had taken place at the Toronto film festival, when he was with his wife, Marjorie Anthony Linden (the first female vice-president of the Canadian television industry), and Trudeau was with Sherry Lansing (the first woman to head a Hollywood studio—Paramount). Trudeau also asked the two women what they thought. Linden was surprised when both women "were adamant that the fact she was a woman wasn't important. They advanced the view that you shouldn't appoint her just because she's a woman."

13   Christine Boyle, "The role of the judiciary in the work of Madam Justice Wilson" *Dalhousie Law Journal* 15 (1982), 241, 244.

14   Eddie Goldenberg, *The Way It Works: Inside Ottawa* (Toronto: McClelland and Stewart, 2006), 89. Goldenberg also cited Chief Justice Laskin for making such arguments "very vociferously" to Trudeau.

15   Ed Ratushny to the Right Honourable Pierre Elliott Trudeau, February 26, 1982.

16   Interview with Edward Ratushny, Ottawa, July 28, 2016.

17   Unsourced, undated clipping in Ratushny's personal files.

18   Sandra Gwyn, "Sense and sensibility," *Saturday Night* (July 1985), 13–19, 18.

19   Interview with Judy Erola, Sudbury, November 8, 2016; interview with Monique Bégin, Ottawa, November 3, 2016.

20   Cuthbert Brandt et al., *Canadian Women,* 566–70.

21 Interview with Jean Chrétien, Ottawa, December 5, 2016. A different version appeared in Gwyn, "Sense and sensibility," 18, suggesting that "Chrétien lobbied hard for a close friend and fellow Liberal, the Toronto lawyer Pierre Genest."

22 Anderson, *Judging Bertha Wilson*, 125.

23 Others under consideration apparently included Louis LeBel, Paul-Arthur Gendreau, Claude Bisson, Marc Beauregard, Maurice Jacques, Alan Gold, Jules Deschênes, James Hugessen, Georges Pouliot, and Lucien Bouchard. David Vienneau. "Appointment likely as Supreme Court loses another justice," *Toronto Star* (April 15, 1987), A10; David Vienneau, "Appointment to high court critical," *Toronto Star* (March 29, 1987), B5; CP "Who'll fill Chouinard's seat on top court?" *Montreal Gazette* (February 9, 1987), A5; Kirk Makin, "New judge called likely chief justice," *The Globe and* Mail (February 10, 1987), A15.

24 Drew Hasselback, "Yves Fortier to leave Norton Rose," *Financial Post* (October 24, 2011); Anthony Wilson-Smith, "A new face on the bench," *Maclean's* (April 27, 1987), 11; Spyros Bourboulis, "The diplomat," Canadian Bar Association *National Magazine* (January-February 2014), 12–19.

25 CP "Who'll fill Chouinard's seat."

26 Interview with Brian Mulroney, Montreal, August 22, 2013.

27 Vienneau, "Appointment to high court critical"; David Vienneau, "PM ponders crucial appointment of justice to top court," *Toronto Star* (February 23, 1987), A8.

28 Interview with Brian Mulroney, Montreal, August 22, 2013.

29 Interview with Brian Mulroney, Montreal, August 22, 2013.

30 Interview with Brian Mulroney, Montreal, August 22, 2013.

31 The Hon. Mr. Justice Robert J. Sharpe, "Brian Dickson: Portrait of a judge" *Advocates' Society Journal* 17:3 (Summer 1998), 3.

32 Louise Langevin, "Hon. L'Heureux-Dubé, Claire: Entrevue réalisée avec l'Hon. L'Heureux-Dubé," March 26, 2007, l'Université Laval, quoting L'Heureux-Dubé: *"nommer une femme pour nommer une femme n'est pas mon genre."*

33 Interview with Brian Mulroney, Montreal, August 22, 2013.

34 Jeff Sallot, "Second woman appointed to top court," *The Globe and Mail* (April 16, 1987), A1.

35 Interview with Claire L'Heureux-Dubé, Quebec City, August 30, 2012; interview with Claire L'Heureux-Dubé, Quebec City, April 29–30, 2008.

36 Anthony Wilson-Smith, "A new face on the bench," *Maclean's* (April 27, 1987), 11.

37 Interview with Claire L'Heureux-Dubé, Quebec City, April 29–30, 2008.

38 The official date of the appointment was April 15, 1987. Louise Mailhot was elevated from the Superior Court to take L'Heureux-Dubé's place as the only woman on the Quebec Court of Appeal. Christine Tourigny, L'Heureux-Dubé's former law partner, was named to the Superior Court. Louise Mailhot, *Les premières! L'histoire de l'accès des femmes à la pratique du droit et à la magistrature* (Cowansville: Éditions Yvon Blais, 2013), 199, 205.

39 Interview with Claire L'Heureux-Dubé, Ottawa, September 13, 2010, recounting Justice Réjane Laberge-Colas's disclosure of the comment.

CHAPTER 14 Contrasting family lives

1   Sandra Gwyn, "Sense and sensibility," photo caption, *Saturday Night* (July 1985), 13–19, 15.

2   Ellen Anderson, *Judging Bertha Wilson: Law as Large as Life* (Toronto: University of Toronto Press, 2001), 52, 75–79.

3   Anderson, *Judging Bertha Wilson*, 77–79; conversation with Mordecai Bubis, Benjamin Books, Ottawa, August 2017, regarding the purchase of part of the Wilsons' library.

4   Gwyn, "Sense and sensibility," 16.

5   Chris Wernham, quoted in Anderson, *Judging Bertha Wilson*, 77–79.

6   Anderson, *Judging Bertha Wilson*, 126. On arthritis, interview with Allen Linden, Toronto, July 21, 2016; interview with David Stratus, Ottawa, August 31, 2016; interview with Robert Yalden, Montreal, August 23, 2016; interview with Beverley McLachlin, Ottawa, October 6, 2017.

7   Gwyn, "Sense and sensibility," 16; Anderson, *Judging Bertha Wilson*, 77–79.

8   The booklet, alphabetized under a black shiny cover, is held in the Osler Archives, 1 First Canadian Place, 63rd Floor, Box 50, Toronto.

9   Anderson, *Judging Bertha Wilson*, 131.

10   Interview with Jim Phillips, Toronto, July 21, 2016.

11   Anderson, *Judging Bertha Wilson*, 401 footnote 1.

12   Gwyn, "Sense and sensibility," 16; "Samuel Pickwick," https://en.wikipedia.org/wiki/Samuel_Pickwick.

13   Interview with Allen Linden, Toronto, July 21, 2016.

14   Interview with Bill Bryden, Guelph, August 29, 2016.

15   Interview with James MacPherson, Toronto, September 6, 2016.

16   Interview with Dennis Lane, Haliburton, August 26, 2016.

17   Interview with Thomas Zuber, Windsor, August 30, 2016.

18   Interview with Thomas Zuber, Windsor, August 30, 2016.

19   "As a member of the 'Gang of 10' she was told: 'Take up crocheting,'" *Toronto Star* (March 5, 1982), A4.

20   Anderson, *Judging Bertha Wilson*, 77–79.

21   Interview with James MacPherson, Toronto, September 6, 2016.

22   Interview with Audrey Macklin, Toronto, October 14, 2016; interview with Donald McRae, Ottawa, October 25, 2016; interview with John Morden, Toronto, July 20, 2016.

23   Interview with Jeannie Thomas, Ottawa, October 31, 2016.

24   Interview with Audrey Macklin, Toronto, October 14, 2016.

25   Christie Blatchford, "Car accident set her on way to seat on top court," *Toronto Star* (March 5, 1982), A1, A12.

26   John's obituary, written by Bertha Wilson's biographer Ellen Anderson (described as "John's friend"), was published in *The Globe and Mail* (September 26, 2008), L6.

27   Sandra Gwyn, "Sense and sensibility," *Saturday Night* (July 1985), 14, 16.

28   Interview with Robert Sharpe, Toronto, July 25, 2016.

29   Interview with Rosalie Abella, Toronto, July 8, 2016.

30   Constance Backhouse, *Claire L'Heureux-Dubé: A Life* (Vancouver: University of British Columbia Press, 2017), Chapter 24.

31   Backhouse, *Claire L'Heureux-Dubé,* Chapters 24 and 33.

32   Interview with Claire L'Heureux-Dubé, Clearwater Florida, May 10–14, 2009.

33   Backhouse, *Claire L'Heureux-Dubé,* Chapters 24 and 33; interview with Claire L'Heureux-Dubé, Clearwater Florida, May 10–14, 2009.

34   Interview with Louise L'Heureux-Giliberti, Chicago, April 21, 2009.

35   Interview with Louise Dubé, Boston, May 22, 2012.

36   Interview with Nicole L'Heureux, Clearwater Florida, May 11–12, 2009.

37   Several judges described these; none wished to be personally quoted.

38   Interview with Roger Garneau, Quebec City, April 28, 2009.

39   Interview with Claire L'Heureux-Dubé, Clearwater Florida, November 25–27, 2014.

40   Interview with Nicole L'Heureux, Clearwater Florida, May 11–12, 2009.

41   Janice Tibbetts, "Supreme Court's great dissenter," *National Post* (February 27, 1999), A03.

42   "Particulars," *Lawyers Weekly* 11:31(December 13, 1991); "Pretrial date set for son of judge," *Ottawa Citizen* (January 12, 1992), A8; editor's note, Letters to Editor section, "Committal for trial of justice's son is gossip, not news, reader feels," *The Lawyers Weekly* 11:35 (January 24, 1992); "Justice: Son on probation for threat to mother," *Ottawa Citizen* (October 27, 1992), H6.

43   Interview with Roger Garneau, Quebec City, April 28, 2009; interview with Claire L'Heureux-Dubé, Clearwater Florida, November 25–27, 2014.

44   Interview with Gisèle Blondeau-Labrie, Quebec City, May 1, 2008; interview with Claire L'Heureux-Dubé, Clearwater Florida, November 25–27, 2014.

45   Interview with Simone Tardif, Montreal, August 4, 2008.

46   Interview with André Legault, Ottawa, December 10, 2007.

47   Interview with Louise L'Heureux-Giliberti, Chicago, April 21, 2009.

48   Interview with Gérard La Forest, Ottawa, June 30, 2014.

49   Interview with Jack Major, Calgary, November 13, 2013.

50   Interview with Claire L'Heureux-Dubé, Ottawa, March 5, 2009.

51   Interview with Claire L'Heureux-Dubé, Ottawa, March 5, 2009.

CHAPTER 15 Chilly reception at the Supreme Court of Canada

1 Vianney Carriere, "Woman judge still avoiding press," *The Globe and Mail* (March 9, 1982), 5.

2 Louise Brown, "A toast to Bertha! Our new Supreme Court Justice," *Toronto Star* (March 5, 1982); Laura Sabia, "Hurray for Bertha!" *Toronto Star* (March 12, 1982); CP "Woman gets high court's vacant seat," *Winnipeg Free Press* (March 5, 1982), 1–2; "Supreme Court's first woman may give it a more liberal look," *Montreal Gazette* (March 20, 1982), B4.

3 David Vienneau, "First woman judge for Supreme Court?" *Toronto Star* (February 10, 1982), A28, quoting Paul Weiler and Walter Tarnopolsky.

4 Vienneau, "First woman," quoting Peter Russell.

5 Kirk Makin, "Long hours, teamwork a habit for new Supreme Court judge," *The Globe and Mail* (April 23, 1987), A1.

6 "Metro woman named to Supreme Court, sources say" *Toronto Star* (March 4, 1982), A16; David Vienneau, "Wilson's appointment hailed as victory for women," *Toronto Star* (March 5, 1982), A12.

7 "Metro woman named."

8 David Vienneau, "New judge 'very able': Chretien," *Toronto Star* (March 5, 1982), A4.

9 David Vienneau, "Appointment to high court critical," *Toronto Star* (March 29, 1987), B5. Vienneau repeated that the same had been said of Wilson.

10 Anthony Wilson-Smith, "A new face on the bench," *Maclean's* (April 27, 1987), 11.

11 Interview with Pierre-Gabriel Jobin, Montreal, April 23, 2010.

12 Ellen Anderson, *Judging Bertha Wilson: Law as Large as Life* (Toronto: University of Toronto Press, 2001), 154.

13 Interview with Claire L'Heureux-Dubé, Ottawa, June 30, 2014; Robert J. Sharpe and Kent Roach, *Brian Dickson: A Judge's Journey* (Toronto: University of Toronto Press, 2003), 62.

14 Anderson, *Judging Bertha Wilson,* 152–54; interview with Marie-Claire Belleau, Ottawa, December 11, 2013.

15 Kirk Makin and Graeme Smith, "Gatecrashing the Old Boys' Club," *The Globe and Mail* (May 2, 2002), A8; interview with Rosalie Abella, Toronto, July 8, 2016; interview with Rosemary Cairns Way, Ottawa, March 30, 2017; interviews with Claire L'Heureux-Dubé, Clearwater Florida, May 10–14, 2009.

16 Sharpe and Roach, *Brian Dickson,* 406, 465; interview with David Stratas, Ottawa, August 31, 2016; interview with James MacPherson, Toronto, September 6, 2016; Cristin Schmitz, "Our one-on-one with Justice Claire L'Heureux-Dubé," *The Lawyers Weekly* (May 17, 2002), 18, 23.

17 Much later, Lamer explained that he felt it was inappropriate to show "traditional gallantry" by standing to honour Wilson as a woman. Anderson, *Judging Bertha Wilson,* 150, 414.

18 Interviews with Claire L'Heureux-Dubé, Ottawa, June 30, 2010; Quebec City, April 27–29, 2009; comments from law clerks who wished not to be identified.

19 Anderson, *Judging Bertha Wilson,* Chapters 11 and 13.

20 Constance Backhouse, *Claire L'Heureux-Dubé: A Life* (Vancouver: University of British Columbia Press, 2017), Chapters 27 and 28.

21 Interview with Hester Lessard, Victoria, November 4, 2016.

22 Interview with Audrey Macklin, Toronto, October 14, 2016; interview with Marie-Claire Belleau, Quebec City, July 13, 2016.

23 Anderson, *Judging Bertha Wilson,* 153.

24 Kirk Makin, "Lobbying hurt court, book says," *The Globe and Mail* (March 11, 1992), A9.

25 At a dinner celebrating her top court appointment, a musical trio played a "medley of Scottish airs" and the speaker who introduced Wilson asked, "Does she really cook haggis in the morning for breakfast or go jogging in the heather?" Speech of Chief Justice Howland to honour Bertha Wilson and Edson Haines, Toronto, May 14, 1982, Law Society of Upper Canada Archives, 994001-2-3.

26 Wilson explained her accent as one among many various dialects, "special words," and "peculiar vowel sounds" of Scotland. Bertha Wilson, "The Scottish Enlightenment," 1987 Shumiatcher Lecture on Literature and the Law, Saskatoon, offprint.

27 Interview with Audrey Macklin, Toronto, October 14, 2016.

28 Interview with Rosemary Cairns Way, Ottawa, March 30, 2017.

29 Interview with Claire L'Heureux-Dubé, Clearwater Florida, May 10–14, 2009; Stephen Bindman, "Judging in a man's world," *Ottawa Citizen* (April 13, 1992), A3.

30 Interview with Marie-Claire Belleau, Quebec City, April 30, 2008.

31 Interview with Peter Sankoff, Ottawa, June 27, 2014.

32 Interview with Teresa Scassa, Ottawa, May 16, 2014.

33 Interview with Danièle Tremblay-Lamer, Ottawa, March 12, 2015; interview with Marie-Claire Belleau, Ottawa, December 11, 2013.

34 Interview with Teresa Scassa, Ottawa, May 16, 2014.

35 Interview with James MacPherson, Toronto, September 6, 2016.

36 Anderson, *Judging Bertha Wilson,* 159–161.

37 Interview with David Stratas, Ottawa, August 31, 2016.

38 Interview with Gérard La Forest, Ottawa, June 30, 2014.

39 Makin, "Long hours, teamwork a habit."

40 Interview with James MacPherson, Toronto, September 6, 2016; interview with Robert Sharpe, Toronto, July 25, 2016; interview with Stephen Goudge, Toronto, July 20, 2016; interview with Sean Fine, Toronto, April 8, 2015.

41 Interview with Marie-Claire Belleau, Ottawa, April 30, 2008; interview with Kent Roach, Cambridge UK, July 25, 2017.

42   Interview with David Stratas, Ottawa, August 31, 2016.

43   Interview with Hester Lessard, Victoria, November 4, 2016.

44   Interview with David Stratas, Ottawa, August 31, 2016.

45   Backhouse, *Claire L'Heureux-Dubé*, Chapter 27.

46   Interview with Claire L'Heureux-Dubé, Ottawa, June 30, 2014.

47   Interview with David Stratas, Ottawa, August 31, 2016.

48   Interview with Marie-Claire Belleau, Quebec City, April 30, 2008; Charlotte Gray, *The Promise of Canada* (New York: Simon & Schuster Canada, 2016), 233–67.

49   Interview with Claire L'Heureux-Dubé, Quebec City, July 12, 2016.

50   Interview with James MacPherson, Toronto, September 6, 2016.

51   Susan Lightstone, "Bertha Wilson, a personal view of women and the law," *National* (August–September 1993), 14.

52   Interview with Moira McConnell, Montreal, November 13, 2017.

53   Makin, "Lobbying hurt court"; Anderson, *Judging Bertha Wilson,* 164–65.

54   Interview with Claire L'Heureux-Dubé, Clearwater Florida, May 10–14, 2009; Bindman, "Judging in a Man's World"; Schmitz, "Our one-on-one."

CHAPTER 16 Bertha Wilson's Supreme Court decisions

1   Marie-Claire Belleau, Rebecca Johnson, and Christina Vinters, "I agree/disagree for the following reasons: Convergence, divergence, and Justice Wilson's 'modest degree of creativity'" in Kim Brooks, ed., *Justice Bertha Wilson: One Woman's Difference* (Vancouver: University of British Columbia Press, 2009), 229–45.

2   Ellen Anderson, *Judging Bertha Wilson: Law as Large as Life* (Toronto: University of Toronto Press, 2001), 149–279; Brooks, ed., *Justice Bertha Wilson;* Jamie Cameron, ed., *Reflections on the Legacy of Justice Bertha Wilson* (Markham, ON: LexisNexis, 2008); "Symposium to honour the contributions of Madame Justice Bertha Wilson" *Dalhousie Law Journal* 15 (1992), full volume.

3   *Pelech v. Pelech,* [1987] 1 SCR 801.

4   Mr. Pelech had custody of the children, so there was no child support to pay. The court rejected Mrs. Pelech's claim that her ex-husband's cruelty had caused the deterioration in her health.

5   *Pelech,* paras. 80–88.

6   *Pelech,* para. 80.

7   Brooks, ed., *Justice Bertha Wilson:* Beverley Baines, "But was she a feminist judge?" 216–18; Mary Jane Mossman, "Bertha Wilson," 306–10; Colleen Sheppard, "Feminist pragmatism," 89–90; Robert Leckey, "What is left of *Pelech?*" 103–29.

8   *R. v. Lavallee,* [1990] 1 SCR 852.

9   Interview with Greg Brodsky (defence counsel), Winnipeg, November 18, 2017; Anderson, *Judging Bertha Wilson,* 219.

10   *Criminal Code*, RSC 1985, c.C-46, s.34.

11   *Lavallee*, 874, 889.

12   Anderson, *Judging Bertha Wilson*, 219–21.

13   Anderson, *Judging Bertha Wilson*, 221.

14   Wilson's majority decision was signed by Dickson, Lamer, and Gonthier, along
      with L'Heureux-Dubé and McLachlin (who was appointed in 1989); Sopinka
      concurred.

15   Brian Dickson, "Madame Justice Wilson: Trailblazer for justice," *Dalhousie Law
      Journal* 15 (1992), 1, 5.

16   Elizabeth Payne, "Licence to kill?" *Ottawa Citizen* (May 12, 1990), B5; editorial,
      "Court's ruling breaks new ground," *Montreal Gazette* (May 5, 1990), B2; editorial,
      "Life of terror," *Vancouver Province* (May 6, 1990), 32; Benjamin L. Berger, "A due
      measure of fear in criminal judgment," *The Supreme Court Law Review*, Osgoode's
      Annual Constitutional Cases Conference 41 (2008) also noted the need for
      caution over the potential stereotyping of battered women as pathological.

17   *[Prostitution] Reference re ss.193 and 195.1(1)(c) of the Criminal Code (Man.)*
      [1990] 1 SCR 1123.

18   Challenges to the offences of "keeping" and "frequenting" a "common bawdy
      house" were dismissed.

19   Janine Benedet, "Paradigms of prostitution" in Brooks, *Justice Bertha Wilson*,
      131–52; Catharine A. MacKinnon, "Trafficking, prostitution, and inequality" in
      Butterfly Politics (Cambridge: Harvard University Press, 2017), 162.

20   *Prostitution Reference*, 1221–23.

21   *Canada (Attorney General) v. Bedford*, [2013] 3 SCR 1101.

22   *R. v. Morgentaler*, [1988] 1 SCR 30; William Walker, "Ruling leaves door open"
      Toronto Star (January 29, 1988), A1.

23   *Criminal Code*, R.S.C. 1970, c.C-34, s.251.

24   Morgentaler's claims regarding other *Charter* sections were dismissed, except for
      s.2(a) freedom of conscience, which Wilson accepted.

25   Kirk Makin, "Crown rejects abortion law compromise as hearing ends," *The Globe
      and Mail* (October 11, 1986) as quoted in Robert J. Sharpe and Kent Roach, *Brian
      Dickson: A Judge's Journey* (Toronto: University of Toronto Press, 2003), 18.

26   Sharpe and Roach, *Brian Dickson*, 18–23.

27   L'Heureux-Dubé's appointment came too late for her to participate.

28   Dickson and Lamer wrote one opinion, Beetz and Estey another; McIntyre and La
      Forest dissented.

29   *Morgentaler*, 171–74.

30   *Morgentaler*, 183.

31   Anderson, *Judging Bertha Wilson*, 231.

32   Letters to the editor, *The Lawyers Weekly* 17:44 (April 3, 1988).

33   *The Globe and Mail* (February 15, 1988), A6.

34 Anderson, *Judging Bertha Wilson*, 228–30; interview with Rosemary Cairns Way, Ottawa, March 30, 2017.

35 Note from Bertha Wilson to Moira McConnell, February 9, 1988.

CHAPTER 17 Claire L'Heureux-Dubé's Supreme Court decisions

1 Interviews with Claire L'Heureux-Dubé, Ottawa, June 30, 2014; Clearwater Florida, November 25–27, 2014.

2 Elizabeth Sheehy, ed., *Adding Feminism to Law: The Contributions of Justice Claire L'Heureux-Dubé* (Toronto: Irwin Law, 2004); Marie-Claire Belleau and François Lacasse, eds., *Claire L'Heureux-Dubé à la Cour Suprême du Canada 1987–2002* (Montréal: Wilson & Lafleur, 2004); *Canadian Journal of Women and the Law* 15:1 (2003), full volume.

3 *Moge v. Moge*, [1992] 3 SCR 813.

4 L'Heureux-Dubé did not expressly overrule *Pelech*, distinguishing it as applicable only to support agreements negotiated by both parties, but the thrust was to rewrite the rules of spousal support.

5 All of the male colleagues who sat with L'Heureux-Dubé on the case signed onto her *Moge* ruling. McLachlin, the third woman appointed to the top court, wrote a brief concurring judgment. Constance Backhouse, *Claire L'Heureux-Dubé: A Life* (Vancouver: University of British Columbia Press, 2017), Chapter 30.

6 For details on the varying lower court rulings, see Backhouse, *Claire L'Heureux-Dubé*, Chapter 30.

7 John Douglas, "Supreme Court to decide if 19 years long enough for alimony payments," *Winnipeg Free Press* (April 2, 1992), A1.

8 Backhouse, *Claire L'Heureux-Dubé*, Chapter 30.

9 *Moge*, 853, 861–64.

10 *Moge*, 865; National Council of Welfare, *Women and Poverty Revisited* (Ottawa: Minister of Supply and Services Canada, 1990), 73–74.

11 Interview with Julien Payne, Ottawa, July 7, 2009.

12 *Canada (Attorney-General) v. Mossop*, [1993] 1 SCR 554.

13 Interview with Rebecca Johnson, Victoria, August 22, 2013.

14 Backhouse, *Claire L'Heureux-Dubé*, Chapter 31.

15 Interview with Ken Popert, Toronto, August 7, 2014.

16 *Mossop*, 580.

17 *Mossop*, 627, 631, 634, 645.

18 Interview with Brian Mossop, Toronto, July 31, 2014; interview with Ken Popert, Toronto, August 7, 2014.

19 Interview with Brian Mossop, Toronto, July 31, 2014.

20 Cristin Schmitz, "Our one-on-one with Justice Claire L'Heureux-Dubé," *The Lawyers Weekly* 22:3 (May 17, 2002).

21 *R. v. Seaboyer,* [1991] 2 SCR 577.

22 Constance Backhouse, *Carnal Crimes: Sexual Assault Law in Canada, 1900–1975* (Toronto: Irwin Law, 2008).

23 *Criminal Code,* RSC 1985, c.C-46, ss.276, 277.

24 *Seaboyer,* 665. Her dissent was signed by Charles Gonthier.

25 *Seaboyer,* 660, 666, 648–49.

26 *Seaboyer,* 683–85, 690.

27 Sean Fine, "The most important woman in Canada," *Saturday Night* (December 1995), 46.

28 Note from Bertha Wilson in Claire L'Heureux-Dubé's private personal papers.

29 *R. v. Ewanchuk,* [1999] 1 SCR 330.

30 Backhouse, *Claire L'Heureux-Dubé,* Chapter 1.

31 *R. v. Ewanchuk,* [1998] 6 WWR 8 (Alta. CA).

32 *Ewanchuk,* 369–79.

33 Sheehy, ed., *Adding Feminism to Law.*

34 Alanna Mitchell, Jill Mahoney, and Sean Fine, "Legal experts outraged by personal attack on Supreme Court judge," *The Globe and Mail* (February 27, 1999), A1.

35 Justice J.W. McClung, "Right of reply," *National Post* (February 26, 1999), A19.

36 Interview with Jack Major, Calgary, November 13, 2013.

37 Interview with Jack Major, Calgary, November 13, 2013.

38 Edward L. Greenspan, "Judges have no right to be bullies," *National Post* (March 2, 1999), A18.

39 Rick Salutin, "Feminism, humanism and the battle of the judges," *The Globe and Mail* (March 4, 1999), D1.

40 Backhouse, *Claire L'Heureux-Dubé,* Chapter 36.

CHAPTER 18 The conundrum of feminism and the complexities of race

1 Ellen Anderson, *Judging Bertha Wilson: Law as Large as Life* (Toronto: University of Toronto Press, 2001), xiv, 135–36, 197.

2 Sandra Gwyn, "Sense and sensibility," *Saturday Night* (July 1985) 13, 19. Gwyn reported that Wilson considered herself "a moderate feminist," but Gwyn's was a minority opinion.

3 Interview with Claire L'Heureux-Dubé, Clearwater Florida, May 10–14, 2009; interview with Claire L'Heureux-Dubé, Clearwater Beach Florida, November 25–27, 2014.

4   "Law ladies just love housework," *Toronto Telegram*, undated clipping, Library and Archives Canada R15636, vol. 49, file 15.

5   Constance Backhouse, *Claire L'Heureux-Dubé: A Life* (Vancouver: University of British Columbia Press, 2017), Chapter 14.

6   Nicole Beaulieu, "Première femme nommée juge à la Cour supérieure de Québec," *Action Québec* (March 10, 1973).

7   Linda Hirshman, *Sisters in Law: How Sandra Day O'Connor and Ruth Bader Ginsburg Went to the Supreme Court and Changed the World* (New York: HarperCollins, 2015), introduction. In contrast, see Afua Hirsch, "Lady justice: Is the judiciary ready for Brenda Hale?" *Prospect* (November 14, 2017).

8   Interview with Maureen McTeer, Ottawa, June 7, 2013.

9   L'Heureux-Dubé objected to the tactics of feminists who demonstrated outside a Quebec tavern demanding equal access; Backhouse, *Claire L'Heureux-Dubé*, 543. Wilson objected to feminism's overemphasis on middle-class women's rights; Gwyn, "Sense and sensibility," 19.

10   Gwyn, "Sense and sensibility," 19.

11   Shawn Ohler, "Women's group turns tables on L'Heureux-Dubé," *National Post* (March 4, 1999), A5.

12   Anderson, *Judging Bertha Wilson*, xv–xvi; speech published as "Law in society: The principle of sexual equality," *Manitoba Law Journal* 13:2 (1983), 225.

13   Speech published in *Osgoode Hall Law Journal* 28 (1990), 507.

14   Stephen Bindman, "REAL Women file protest against high court judge," *Ottawa Citizen* (February 14, 1990); Kirk Makin, "Inject female values into judiciary, Supreme Court judge urges," *The Globe and Mail* (February 10, 1990), A4; Brian Bucknall, "Letter to the editor," *Toronto Star* (February 24, 1990); interview with James MacPherson, Toronto, September 6, 2016.

15   REAL Women complaint to CJC, February 13, 1990, File RD-89-68.

16   Editorial, *Toronto Star* (April 25, 1989), A18.

17   In the 1928 ruling known as the Persons Case, the British Privy Council held that women were "persons" for the purpose of appointment to the Canadian Senate.

18   CJC File RD-89-27 (October 10, 1989); File RD-89-68 (February 21, 1990); File 98-129 (March 31, 1999); Anderson, *Judging Bertha Wilson*, xv–xvi; Stephen Bindman, "Complaint against woman judge is dismissed," *Montreal Gazette* (March 30, 1990), B1; Christin Schmitz, "CJC dismisses bias complaint against Dubé," *The Lawyers Weekly* 19:13 (August 3, 1999), 3.

19   Constance Backhouse, *Colour-Coded: A Legal History of Racism in Canada, 1900–1950* (Toronto: University of Toronto Press, 1999); James W. St. G. Walker, *'Race,' Rights and the Law in the Supreme Court of Canada* (Waterloo: Wilfrid Laurier University Press, 1997).

20   Interview with Audrey Macklin, Toronto, October 14, 2016; interview with Greg Brodsky, Winnipeg, November 18, 2017.

21   *Racine v. Woods*, [1983] 2 SCR 173.

22   *Racine*, 187–88.

23   *Racine,* 176–79, 188.

24   Gillian Calder, "Finally I know where I am going to be from" in Kim Brooks, ed., *Justice Bertha Wilson* (Vancouver: University of British Columbia Press, 2009), 173; Suzanne Fournier and Ernie Crey, *Stolen From Our Embrace* (Vancouver: Douglas and McIntyre, 1997); *Report of the Royal Commission on Aboriginal Peoples* (Ottawa: Queen's Printer, 1997) vol. 3; Ian Austen, "Canada to pay millions in Indigenous lawsuit over forced adoptions," *New York Times* (October 6, 2017).

25   Backhouse, *Claire L'Heureux-Dubé,* Chapter 19.

26   National Film Board of Canada 2015 film *Ninth Floor* documented the 1969 complaints of racism, allegations of misdoing by undercover police, unruly crowds of whites chanting messages of hate, and riots between police, the public, and racialized students.

27   *Baker v. Canada,* [1999] 2 SCR 817.

28   *Baker,* 827–28.

29   *Baker,* 837, 843, 855.

30   *Baker,* 864–65.

31   Sharryn Aiken and Sheena Scott, "Baker v. Canada (Minister of Citizenship and Immigration) and the Rights of Children" *Journal of Law and Social Policy* 15 (2000), 211, 221.

32   Interview with Roger Rowe, Toronto, November 1, 2014.

33   Simone A. Browne, "Of 'passport babies' and 'border control': The case of Mavis Baker" *Atlantis* 26:2 (Spring 2002), 97.

CHAPTER 19 Retirement and after

1   Kirk Makin, "Top court's first woman judge retires," *The Globe and Mail* (November 21, 1990), A1.

2   Philip Slayton, *Mighty Judgment: How the Supreme Court of Canada Runs Your Life* (Toronto: Penguin, 2011), 215–16; interview with Claire L'Heureux-Dubé, November 25–27, 2014.

3   Ellen Anderson, *Judging Bertha Wilson: Law as Large as Life* (Toronto: University of Toronto Press, 2001), 325–31, 414; interview with Beverley McLachlin, Ottawa, October 6, 2017.

4   Makin, "Top court's first woman judge retires."

5   Interview with Moira McConnell, Montreal, November 13, 2017.

6   Sean Fine, "The most important woman in Canada," *Saturday Night* (December 1995), 46.

7   Luiza Chwialkowska, "Retiring judge," *National Post* (July 2, 2002), A6.

8   Constance Backhouse, *Claire L'Heureux-Dubé: A Life* (Vancouver: University of British Columbia Press, 2017), Chapter 38.

9   "Remarks of Beverley McLachlin, the retirement ceremony of L'Heureux-Dubé," June 10, 2002; interview with Beverley McLachlin, Ottawa, October 6, 2017.

10 Interview with James MacPherson, Toronto, September 6, 2016; interview with David Stratas, Ottawa, August 31, 2016.

11 Anderson, *Judging Bertha Wilson*, Chapter 14.

12 *Report of the Royal Commission on Aboriginal People* (Ottawa, 1997) vols. 1–5; Anderson, *Judging Bertha Wilson*, 357–58.

13 Anderson, *Judging Bertha Wilson*, 354.

14 Interview with Ontario Superior Court Justice Margaret Eberhard, Toronto, June 7, 2017.

15 Interview with Ontario Superior Court Justice Margaret Eberhard, Toronto, June 7, 2017.

16 *Report of the Royal Commission on Aboriginal People,* vols. 1–5.

17 *Report of the Royal Commission on Aboriginal People, Gathering Strength* vol. 3, 21–26.

18 Anderson, *Judging Bertha Wilson*, 190.

19 Interview with Audrey Macklin, Toronto, October 14, 2016.

20 Interview with Rosemary Cairns Way, Ottawa, March 30, 2017.

21 Assembly of First Nations, *Royal Commission on Aboriginal People, 10 Years: A Report Card* (Ottawa: Assembly of First Nations, 2007).

22 Melina Buckley, "Ideas and transformation" in Kim Brooks, ed., *Justice Bertha Wilson* (Vancouver: University of British Columbia Press, 2009), 262, 266–67, 275.

23 *Touchstones for Change: Equality, Diversity and Accountability* (Ottawa: Canadian Bar Association, 1993).

24 David Shoalts, "Women lawyers face dual struggle," *The Globe and Mail* (August 20, 1991), A4; *Touchstones*, 4. Wilson insisted that, least two of the six task force members must be male, but no one sought racialized members until 1992 when, due to complaints about the all-white body, Sharon McIvor and Justice Corrine Sparks from the Indigenous and African-Canadian communities respectively were added. Anderson, *Judging Bertha Wilson*, 342.

25 Rosemary Cairns Way and T. Brettel Dawson, "Taking a stand on equality" in Brooks, ed., *Justice Bertha Wilson*, 278, 283, documenting federally appointed judges.

26 *Touchstones*, Chapter 10.

27 Anderson, *Judging Bertha Wilson*, 348–51; Buckley, "Ideas and transformations," 274.

28 *Touchstones*, 285; Backhouse, *Claire L'Heureux-Dubé*, 514.

29 Interview with Jeannie Thomas, Ottawa, October 31, 2016.

30 Backhouse, *Claire L'Heureux-Dubé*, 514–16.

31 Anderson, *Judging Bertha Wilson*, 348–51.

32 Interview with Catherine Fraser, Edmonton, November 13, 2013; Backhouse, *Claire L'Heureux-Dubé*, Chapter 37.

33 Correspondence from Baroness Kennedy, August 1, 2015.

34 Phone interview with Naina Kapur from Ottawa, April 20, 2010.

35 Interview with Arlene Pacht, founder of the IAWJ, London UK, May 3, 2012; "The Honourable Claire L'Heureux-Dubé—a living legend," *IAWJ News* (May 2, 2012).

36 Backhouse, *Claire L'Heureux-Dubé*, 519, 542–45.

37 Interview with Rosalie Abella, Toronto, July 8, 2016.

38 Interview with Audrey Macklin, Toronto, October 14, 2016; interview with Moira McConnell, Montreal, November 13, 2017.

39 Phone interview with Naina Kapur from Ottawa, April 20, 2010; Backhouse, *Claire L'Heureux-Dubé*, 517–19.

40 Backhouse, *Claire L'Heureux-Dubé*, 531–39.

41 Correspondence from Claire L'Heureux-Dubé to Constance Backhouse, August 5, 2016.

42 Backhouse, *Claire L'Heureux-Dubé*, 531–39.

43 Ingrid Peritz, "Ex-Supreme Court justice said to be a Quebec charter backer," *The Globe and Mail* (September 23, 2013); Allan Woods, "Ex-Supreme Court judge expected to back Quebec Charter values," *Toronto Star* (September 23, 2013).

44 Mémoire présenté à la Commission des institutions, Assemblée nationale du Québec, Projet de loi n. 60, par Les Juristes pour la laïcité et la neutralité religieuse de l'État, 18 décembre 2013, 1–2; Sean Fine, "Ex- Supreme Court judge backs charter" *The Globe and Mail* (February 14, 2014), A4.

45 Haroon Siddiqui, "Quebec Charter's authoritarian streak: Siddiqui" *Toronto Star* (September 23, 2013); Backhouse, *Claire L'Heureux-Dubé*, 531–39.

46 Backhouse, *Claire L'Heureux-Dubé*, 531–39.

CONCLUSION

1 The concept of the French and the British empires as two "founding nations" is problematized by the presence of untold generations of First Nations peoples long before the arrival of the Europeans on the land the settlers claimed as Canada.

2 Interview with Moira McConnell, Montreal, November 13, 2017.

Index

Italicized page numbers indicate illustrations. The initials CLD and BW stand for Claire L'Heureux-Dubé and Bertha Wilson, respectively.

Osler, Featherston, 87
Owen, George W.R., 130–31, *130*, 133, 156

Pabi, Bredu, *72*
Pelech v. Pelech, 180–82, 191
Pettkus, Becker v., *142*, 143
Pettkus, Lothar, 143
Philippon, Jacques, *155*
Pigeon, Louis-Philippe, 55
Popert, Ken, 194–95, *194*, *195*, 197
Pottier, Vincent, 67
poverty, 193, 214
property disputes, *142*, 143
prostitution, 185
Prostitution Reference, 185
Pugsley, Ron, 66
Pugsley, Ronald Newton, *72*

Quebec Bar, 59
Quebec Civil Code, 77, 79–80, 109
Quebec Court of Appeal, 130–31, *130*
Quebec Superior Courts, 11

R. v. Ewanchuk, 199–201, 208
R. v. Lavallee, 182–84
R. v. Morgentaler, 185–89
R. v. Olbey, 140–41
R. v. Seaboyer, 197–98
racial insensitivity, 213–18
Racine, Sandra and Allan, 213
Racine v. Woods, 213–14, 224
racism, 213–15, 217–18, 223–24, 232
rape, 197–201
rape shield law, 197–98
Ratushny, Edward, 107, 109–10, 114, 149–50
RCAP (Royal Commission on Aboriginal Peoples), 223–24
Read, Horace E., 61, *62*, 63, 64–65, 67, 69
REAL Women, 208–11, *210*, *212*
reproductive rights. *See* abortion
residential schools, 214
rights: constitutional, 185–89; domestic, 180–84; LGBT, 194–97
Rinfret, Édouard, 128, *130*
Rowe, Roger, 217

Royal Commission on Aboriginal Peoples, 223–24
Royal Commission on the Status of Women, 106, 109

Saturday Night magazine, 150, 158, 161, 163
Saunders, Edward, 110
Scassa, Teresa, 8
Scotland, women lawyers in, 42
Scott, F.R., *62*
Second Sex, The (Beauvoir), 105
self-defence, 182–84. *See also* battered women
Seneca College, 143, *144*
"separate spheres" ideology, 9, 41–42, 61, 63, 159, 161
sexism: CLD's lectures on, 228–30; coping with, 96–97, 100, 102, 103, 175–76; double standards, 140, 197–98; "implied consent", 199–201; issue of face-coverings, 231–32; in language, 116–17; in Quebec, 43; "separate spheres" ideology, 9, 41–42, 61, 63, 159, 161. *See also* feminism
sexism in legal field: denial of scholarships, 51, 57, 67, 69; disrespectful treatment, 100, 135, 137, 171; double standards, 96–97, 102; doubts about competence, 61, 63, 114, 115–16, 149, 173; forcing women into niches, 77, 79, 89, 95–96; task force on, 224–28
sexual assault, 197–201
sexual harassment, 57, 73, 215
Sir George Williams University, 215
"Sixties Scoop", 214
Smith Shield Moot Court, 69, *70*, *71*
Somerville, William, 110
spousal support, 79, 180–82, 191, 193–94
St. Machar's Cathedral, 18, *18*
status of women in Quebec, 43. *See also* feminism; sexism *headings*
suicide, 126, 201
support payments, 79, 180–82, 191, 193–94

Supreme Court of Canada: appointments to, 149; as check on parliament, 179; as geographically representative, 148; as male milieu, 147, 173; racial insensitivity of, 213–15, 217–18
Supreme Court (U.S.), 147
Swenarchuk, Michelle, *211*

Task Force on Gender Equality in the Legal Profession, 224–28
therapeutic abortion committees, 186
Thom, Stuart, *90*, 109–10
Thomas, Jeannie, *162, 227*
tort of discrimination, 145
Toward, Lilias, 65, 66, 67
Trudeau, Pierre Elliott, 77, 106, 107, 148–51
Turgeon, Henri, *56*

University of Aberdeen, *34*
University of Montreal law school, 69

Van Camp, Mabel Margaret, *10*, 137, 139
violence, marital, 79, 182–84

Ward, David, *72*
Wernham, Archibald (BW's father), 17, 18, 19
Wernham, Archie (BW's brother), 20, 21
Wernham, Bertha. *See* Wilson, Bertha
Wernham, Christina (BW's mother), 18, 19, 20, 47
Wernham, Jim (BW's brother), 21, 36, 47
"When does life begin?" cartoon, *188*
White, David Bertram, *72*
Whitton, Charlotte, 96
Wikler, Norma, *226, 228*
Wilson, Bertha: appearance, *89*, 97, 99, *99, 101, 190*; birth, 17; childhood, *20, 23, 32*; entry into work force, 39; family, 17–21, *21*; move to Canada, 36, 37, *38*, 39; move to Halifax, 39–40; personality, 100, 175–76;

Scottish/Canadian experience, 37, 39, 91, 173–74; work ethic, 88, 96, 175
—AWARDS AND HONOURS: Companion of the Order of Canada, 244, *246*; Dalhousie honorary doctorate, *190*; "Queen's Counsel" designation, 109; Smith Shield Moot Court award, 69, *70, 71*; "Women Are Persons" medallion, 209, *211*
—COMPARED TO CLD: childhood, 233; education, 233–35; entry into law, 235; as judge, 235–36, 237–39, 242–43; marriage, 234, 237; personality, 14, 100, 145, 175–76; retirement and after, 239; view of discrimination, 230–31
—EDUCATION: early schooling, 21, *22*, 23; University of Aberdeen, 23–24; law school, 49, 61, 63, 65–67; graduation with LL.B., *63, 67, 68*; scholarship denied, 67, 69; qualifying for NS bar, 69, 71; move to ON and re-qualifying for bar, 85–86
—AS LAWYER: at CBA meetings, *183*; elected to CBA national council, 109; interest in technology, 88–89; at Osler firm, 86, 88–93, 95–96, 102–3
—MARRIAGE: meeting future husband, 31; wedding, 33, *34, 35*; early years in Scotland, 35, *36*; childlessness of, 163, 209; later years in Canada, 157–59, *158, 160, 162*
—AT ONTARIO COURT OF APPEAL, *110*, 135–46, *136, 141*; appointment, *10*, 109–10, *111*, 112, 113; decisions, 140–41, *142*, 143–45; reception as woman, 113–14, 135–37
—POLITICS: party affiliation, 91; racial sensitivity, 213–14, 223–24, 230–31; view of feminism, 205, 230
—RETIREMENT AND AFTER, 197, 219, *221*; health, 219, 223, 242; work with RCAP, 223–24, *239*; work with CBA task force, 224–25, *224, 228*; death, 242
—AT SUPREME COURT, *12, 15, 170*,

Photo Credits

INTRODUCTION
page 8: Teresa Scassa
page 12: courtesy of Claire L'Heureux-Dubé
page 15: courtesy of Claire L'Heureux-Dubé
page 16: courtsey of Veronique Larose

CHAPTER 1
page 18: courtesy of Constance Backhouse, 2017
page 20: Library and Archives Canada R15636 vol. 49, file 13
page 21: Library and Archives Canada R15636 v. 48, file 9
page 22: Library and Archives Canada R15636, vol. 49, file 13
page 23: Library and Archives Canada R15636 vol. 49, file 13
page 25 (top): courtesy of Claire L'Heureux-Dubé
page 25 (bottom): courtesy of Claire L'Heureux-Dubé
page 26: courtesy of Claire L'Heureux-Dubé
page 27: courtesy of Les Ursulines de Rimouski
page 28: courtesy of Les Ursulines de Rimouski
page 30: courtesy of Claire L'Heureux-Dubé

CHAPTER 2
page 32: Library and Archives Canada R15636, vol. 48, file 9
page 34 (top): Library and Archives Canada R15636, vol. 49, file 4
page 34 (bottom left): courtesy of Maureen Lennon
page 34 (bottom right): courtesy of Constance Backhouse
page 35: Library and Archives Canada R15636, vol. 49, file 4
page 36: Library and Archives Canada R15636, vol. 49, file 13
page 38: courtesy of Maureen Lennon
page 39: Library and Archives Canada R15636, vol. 48, file 9

CHAPTER 3
page 42: Law Society of Ontario Archives, Archives Department collection, "Photograph of Clara Brett Martin", P291
page 44: courtesy of Claire L'Heureux-Dubé
page 45: courtesy of Claire L'Heureux-Dubé
page 46: courtesy of Claire L'Heureux-Dubé

CHAPTER 4
page 52: Les Archives de l'Université Laval
page 53: courtesy of Claire L'Heureux-Dubé
page 54: Les Archives de l'Université Laval, U519/3310,1,1
page 56: Les Archives de l'Université Laval, Fonds Association générale des étudiants de l'Université Laval, AGEL, cote n. P116/12/2 [J/51]
page 58: courtesy of Claire L'Heureux-Dubé
page 59: Les Archives de l'Université Laval, U539/47/4

CHAPTER 5
page 62 (top and bottom): *The Ansul*, Halifax, Dalhousie University, vol. 2 (December 1977), p. 59
page 63: courtesy of Dalhousie Law School
page 64: *The Ansul*, Halifax, Dalhousie University, vol. 2 (December 1977), p. 59
page 68: Law Society of Upper Canada
page 70 (top and bottom): Library and Archives Canada R15636 vol. 47, file 10
page 71: Library and Archives Canada R15636 vol. 47, file 10
page 72: Library and Archives Canada R15636 vol. 47, file 10

CHAPTER 6
page 75: courtesy of Joel and Perry Bard
page 76: courtesy of Claire L'Heureux-Dubé
page 78: Gaby Montreal
page 81: courtesy of Claire L'Heureux-Dubé
page 82: courtesy of Claire L'Heureux-Dubé
page 83 (top and bottom): courtesy of Claire L'Heureux-Dubé

CHAPTER 7
page 87: Osler Archives, Library Acquisitions and Resource Service, Toronto
page 89: Library and Archives Canada R15636, vol. 49, file 14
page 90: Osler Archives, Library Acquisitions and Resource Service, Toronto
page 92: Osler Archives, Library Acquisitions and Resource Service, Toronto

CHAPTER 8
page 98 (all photos): courtesy of Claire L'Heureux-Dubé
page 99: Library and Archives Canada R15636 vol. 1, file 3. Photos commissioned by Osler, Hoskin, and Harcourt, undated, possibly Howard Anderson Photography, Toronto, as mentioned in Ellen Anderson's *Judging Bertha Wilson.*
page 101: Osler Archives, Library Acquisitions and Resource Service, Toronto

CHAPTER 9
page 108 (top and bottom): courtesy of Claire L'Heureux-Dubé
page 110: courtesy of Thomas Zuber
page 111: Library and Archives Canada R15636 vol. 47, file 10

CHAPTER 10
page 116: Harvey, BANQ, P428, S3, SS1, D44, P107
page 117: courtesy of Claire L'Heureux-Dubé
page 119: courtesy of Claire L'Heureux-Dubé

CHAPTER 11
All photos courtesy of Claire L'Heureux-Dubé

CHAPTER 12
page 136: Colin McConnell/Getty Images
page 141: Law Society of Upper Canada Archives/Onnig J. Cavoukian,
Cavouk Portraits Toronto
page 142: Library and Archives Canada R15636 vol. 47, file 10
page 144: Library and Archives Canada R15636 vol. 47, file 10

CHAPTER 13
page 152: Law Society of Upper Canada Archives 2001088-2318;
copyright Michael Bedford
page 153: Yousuf Karsh
page 155: courtesy of Claire L'Heureux-Dubé
page 156: courtesy of Claire L'Heureux-Dubé

CHAPTER 14
page 158: *Saturday Night*, July 1985
page 160: courtesy of Jeannie Thomas
page 162: courtesy of Jeannie Thomas
page 164: courtesy of Claire L'Heureux-Dubé

CHAPTER 15
page 168: Library and Archives Canada R15636, vol. 49, file 15
page 170: courtesy of the Supreme Court of Canada
page 171: Michael Bedford
page 172 (top): courtesy of the Supreme Court of Canada/Paul Couvrette
page 172 (bottom): Michael Bedford
page 174: courtesy of the Supreme Court of Canada/Philippe Landreville

CHAPTER 16
page 180: courtesy of Dalhousie Law School
page 183: Law Society of Upper Canada Archives 200088-498_6
page 186: John Mahler/*Toronto Star*
page 188: © Bob Englehart/*The Hartfort Courant,* 1981
page 190 (top): *Dalhousie Law Journal*/Moira McConnell
page 190 (bottom): Library and Archives Canada R15636 vol. 47, file 10

CHAPTER 17
page 192: Registrar, Supreme Court of Canada
page 194: courtesy of Popert and Mossop
page 195: courtesy of Popert and Mossop
page 196: courtesy of Claire L'Heureux-Dubé
page 200: Paul Latour/*Ottawa Citizen*
page 202: *Edmonton Journal* (February 14, 1996), A1

CHAPTER 18
page 206: courtesy of Claire L'Heureux-Dubé
page 207 (left and right): courtesy of Claire L'Heureux-Dubé
page 209: Law Society of Upper Canada Archives 2001088-703_24
page 210: Library and Archives Canada R15636, vol. 14, file 15
page 211: courtesy of Michele Landsberg
page 212: *Montreal Gazette*, March 30, 1990. Library and Archives Canada R15636, vol. 49, file 15
page 216: Hans Deryk/*National Post*

CHAPTER 19
page 220 (top and bottom): courtesy of Jeannie Thomas
page 221: Peter Power, *Toronto Star* Licence, from *Toronto Star* Archives held at Toronto Reference Library
page 222: Pascal Elie (artist)
page 224: Law Society of Upper Canada Archives, 2001088-2205
page 226 (top and bottom): courtesy of Jeannie Thomas
page 227: courtesy of Jeannie Thomas
page 229: courtesy of Claire L'Heureux-Dubé
page 230: courtesy of Constance Backhouse

CONCLUSION
page 240: courtesy of Claire L'Heureux-Dubé
page 241 (top): courtesy of Constance Backhouse
page 241 (bottom): courtesy of Claire L'Heureux-Dubé
page 243: *Canadian Press,* 1989
page 245: courtesy of Claire L'Heureux-Dubé
page 246: with permission of the Secretary to the Governor General

About the Author

CONSTANCE BACKHOUSE is a Professor of Law at the University of Ottawa. She has published a number of prize-winning books: *Petticoats and Prejudice: Women and Law in Nineteenth-Century Canada*; *Colour-Coded: A Legal History of Racism in Canada, 1900-1950*; *The Heiress vs the Establishment: Mrs. Campbell's Campaign for Legal Justice*; and *Carnal Crimes: Sexual Assault Law in Canada, 1900-1975*. Her latest book, *Claire L'Heureux-Dubé: A Life*, was published in 2017. She was named to the Order of Canada in 2008.

THE FEMINIST HISTORY SOCIETY SERIES

The Feminist History Society is committed to creating a lasting record of the women's movement in Canada and Québec for the fifty years between 1960 and the year of the Society's founding, 2010. Feminism has a history that predates the 1960s and continues long after 2010.

The energy that women brought to their quest for equality in these decades is beyond dispute, and it is that energy that we capture in this series. Our movement is not over and new campaigns are upon us. But the FHS series presents an opportunity to take stock of the wide-ranging campaigns for equality that occurred in Canada between 1960 and 2010. There was much transformative social, economic, civil, political, and cultural change.

We maintain an open call for submissions (https://secondstorypress.ca/submissions/) across a full range of approaches to the period, including autobiographies, biographies, edited collections, pictorial histories, plays and novels. There will be many different authors as all individuals and organizations that were participants in the movement are encouraged to contribute. We make every effort to be inclusive of gender, race, class, geography, culture, dis/ability, language, sexual identity, and age.

Beth Atcheson, Constance Backhouse, Lorraine Greaves, Diana Majury, and Beth Symes form the working collective of the Feminist History Society. Margie Wolfe, Publisher, Second Story Feminist Press Inc. and her talented team of women, are presenting the Series.

https://secondstorypress.ca/feminist-history-society-series/